Since childhood, Søren Krause has been interested in the big question of life. It brought him in many directions, e.g., philosophy, religion, and spiritualism, and raised many existential questions.

The second track came through his work, where he has been responsible for large projects. He realised that one significant challenge was to overcome people's reservations about change. It intensified his interest in human resources, which has been his working area for about 20 years. On the way, he has joined more programs, e.g., certified coach, that deals with overcoming counterproductive beliefs to achieve one's aims.

Søren Krause

THE RAINBOW PORTAL OF BELIEFS

AUSTIN MACAULEY PUBLISHERS™

LONDON * CAMBRIDGE * NEW YORK * SHARJAH

A CIP catalogue record for this title is available from the British Library.

ISBN 9781398481015 (Paperback)
ISBN 9781398481022 (ePub e-book)

www.austinmacauley.com

First Published 2022
Austin Macauley Publishers Ltd®
1 Canada Square
Canary Wharf
London
E14 5AA

Table of Contents

Alfa

Growth of consciousness:
The soul takes control of the ego

Wide is the audience for who the gift of faith is prepared for.
Few are those who shall be preserved in its simple-minded bliss.
Fewer are those who seek the truth or even want to possess it.
But the ones who manage it will become happy, peaceful
and live in freedom and die with confidence.
The time shall come when the truth shall
be revealed to all those who seek it.
In the name of love
and wisdom,
Amen.

Source: Oracle, the spiritual guide of Senius

Foreword

Dear Reader,

It is with great pleasure I share my experiences from a journey that was a significant part of my life. The process has filled me with enthusiasm and joy, and at the same time, it tells me that I comply with the omnipotent Source, who is always there for all of us when we are ready to follow the path we have deliberately chosen while entering accommodating surroundings.

In the end, it may leave you with the impression that I am talking about a predetermined destiny, but that is by no means the case. On the contrary, it is your door to a paradise of opportunities where you can gain valuable experiences that comply with your deepest longing.

Through writing, my thoughts have become clearer, and to ensure that the messages I want to convey to you are as straightforward as possible, I have invited four of my dearest friends to act as opponents:

Jan Overgaard

Enrica Stucchi

Per Thomsen

Svend Arne Volden

In addition, Enrica Stucchi graced the front cover with her excellent drawing skills and contributed to the time-consuming proofreading process, which has made the text more readable. The remaining ones have also joined the quality assurance process.

I am extremely thankful to all of you for your valuable contributions.

I also want to express my sincere gratitude to my dearest family, my wife Anne Marie and our children Helena, Jesper and Sara, who have played an essential role in my development journey. Thank you Helena and Sara for taking part in different parts of the development of the manuscript.

Furthermore, I want to send my warm regards to my grandparents, parents, parents-in-law and siblings for playing a notable role in forming my life path.

I am extremely grateful for all the people I have met and who inspired me in many ways throughout my life, either personally, through books or in many other ways.

Last but not least, I am grateful for all the inspiration I have received through my connections in the spiritual world.

Introduction

Dear Reader,

Welcome to an extraordinary story that I hope will be an eye-opener and make your life more beautiful, filled with purpose, meaning, peace and happiness.

Let me start with a question:

What is the most decisive life issue you need to figure out?

I will leave my question open for a moment and give you a chance to consider your response.

My story begins while hiking 'El Camino' in spring 2019.

It is early morning and still dark outside. The room is a bit noisy as some of the other pilgrims are snoring. I silently pick up my belongings and walk unnoticed out of the room. After visiting the bathroom, I leave the hostel in Astorga.

On the outskirts of the village, there is a small café that is already opened. I am starving, probably because I hiked approximately 50 kilometres the previous day. I enter the café and order a substantial breakfast with a big tortilla as a starter. While I am eating, it starts to rain; I notice quite a few pilgrims passing by and adequately dressed for the weather.

As I leave the café, I still see dark clouds above me but almost no more rain. Onwards into my journey, between Murias de Rechivaldo and Santa Catalina de Somoza, an overwhelming scenery unravels in front of my eyes. The sun shines behind me, and my body casts a long shadow on the path in front of me.

At the end of the trail, I can discern an old church surrounded by dark clouds. Suddenly, a bright and beautiful rainbow appears, and it looks like the path I am walking on is leading straight into that colourful portal. A profound feeling of love hits me, and the falling raindrops feel like tears of joy.

I feel an instant longing—a familiar experience, an experience of feeling homesick when as a child. After a few minutes, I somehow feel that this longing will be accommodated. At this point, however, this feeling does not make any sense, but the scenery is impressed into my memory[1].

I then visit a nearby café to write down on my phone events what just happened. As I am finishing my notes, a pilgrim I met earlier on the route greets me. We share another breakfast. We then walk a little bit further till we reach her hostel that she had booked in advance.

As I continue walking alone reflecting on this recent experience, I realise that one of the significant characteristics of the rainbow is its magnificent colours—it is not just black and white. With a smile on my lips, I see that my life has developed the same way. The rainbow is a metaphor of beliefs inherited from history or the church, in this context, and the experiences I have gained throughout my life.

I also notice that some of my views have supported and guided me in achieving my aims, while others did not. I realise that I may have either taken them for granted or may have been unconscious about many of my beliefs. The unconscious ones caused me the most trouble.

As individuals, we all have different references; therefore, we have different beliefs, depending on our upbringing, culture, religion and so on. This also implies that some of our ideas are non-convertible. When you are a child, you merely imitate your parents' behaviour and close relations without questioning them, thus becoming the way you interpret the world.

The same applies to everyone else, with perhaps a different outcome; this leads to the co-existence of so many contradictory ideas, beliefs and

---

[1] An illustration of the scenery also decorates the cover of the book.

so on. These contradictory ideas have caused many conflicts, including wars, throughout history, because most often, we do not like what we do not understand.

When such ideas are seen from an outside observer's standpoint, it is sad and often misunderstood because nobody knows the reality objectively but only has a perception of it. If you are a religious person, I understand that this idea may be challenging to accept.

My view, however, is that whatever religion you belong to, you perceive its doctrines as unquestionable, and therefore seek evidence that can confirm with your faith. The same applies to everybody else and the faith they follow.

It is an example of a rainbow perspective. Different cultures have formed their story in compliance with their time of living, culture and so on. Tension arises when you make the immediate logical implication that your faith is the only truth and everyone else's convictions are wrong. As a result, religions become mutually exclusive.

On the contrary, religions share many similarities if you dare to interpret them with your heart in a contemporary context. You will realise that *God is love*, from which derives that everybody should love themselves and everyone else despite the differences.

At the beginning of the second millennium, the church's power was supreme until the Enlightenment challenged its view in the 18th century. The Enlightenment affirms the supremacy of reason. In the following century, Charles Darwin formulated the evolution theory, which was refined by natural science.

Some see this theory as the truth and consider themselves atheists or non-believers. However, this is also a belief. Its rationale is that if you cannot prove something scientifically, then it is false.

On the other hand, I have experienced that there is more to between Heaven and Earth than science can capture because its approach has constrained truth that can be experienced through your five senses only. According to this view, 'the survival of the fittest' drives evolution, and physical dominance becomes the reason why human beings are the most developed species. Power is needed to control the environment and other people.

Our patriarchal history shows that this *external power* builds on fear and impacts all aspects of our lives, e.g., conflicts between races, religions, superpowers, nations, communities, social classes and gender, including relationships with parents and siblings. Physical dominance drives the competition for *external power*, creating fear and feeling of insecurity among members.

The question is, *what is the critical spot to challenge this view?* To answer this question, you must be willing to challenge your former views and enter another perspective. Ask yourself, *Do I have the courage to leave my comfort zone and the personal background aspects I have inherited more or less unconsciously during my life and seek new perspectives where I feel less confident?*

Or as Søren Kierkegaard, a Danish philosopher, stated, "To dare is to lose foothold for a moment. Not to dare is to lose oneself".

Furthermore, if you study interactions between people to understand how perceptions are formed and integrated into a common understanding, you will find a more complex world than the one studied in natural science. In the latter, it is often possible to isolate the factor you want to analyse.

On the other hand, in social science, it is impossible to detach individual elements when dealing with a social phenomenon, because it results from multiple factors simultaneously at work, and it develops differently depending on the environment.

I recommend you to be open-minded and simultaneously be critical towards both your views and mine. What I mean by this is that whenever you disagree on, do allow yourself to challenge your perspective and ask questions, for example, *what is the reason for my point of view?*

Do spend some time to make a sanity check of its fundamentals. On the other hand, I do not expect you to share my opinion. As in any discussion, I find it more interesting to understand why we disagree because this is where the learning potential lies.

From our early primitive religions until now, we understand that we live in two worlds: a physical world and an invisible world, which I designate as the spiritual world. The latter sets the frames for the physical world. Furthermore, it can be concluded that any believer keeps their faith because they consider it as the truth or have inherited it without questioning.

You cannot prove it nor disprove it. The only way to get access to it is to believe and experience it. Therefore, I have to choose another path to present my point of view.

I will do my utmost to present a coherent argumentation to you. The methodology I will use is inspired by social science. I present a narration that has already been used in the past to convey our collective history. I draw on my own experiences and recognitions until now.

They are beyond natural science and cannot be proved but rest on the convictions I have developed through my life experiences. It is just like faith, hope, love, joy and peace: they belong to another kind of power that comes from within as qualities of the soul. This *internal power* is the opposite of *the external power* mentioned previously, which is driven by competition and the 'them versus us' illusion.

I guess it is now time for me to get back to my original question.

What is the most decisive life issue you need to figure out?

My answer is brief: *To know why you are here.*

My answer entails a few more considerations. First of all, we are here to obtain experiences, which is only possible by being physically present in this world. Secondly, we all have a universal call to serve mankind and make the world a better place. Our individual task is to find our specific call or our life's purpose.

In doing so, you create the best version of yourself, which, at the same time, is paramount for your environment. This new perspective on a more self-conscious individual supersedes what you can observe and experience through your five senses.

My purpose with this book is to share how you can find your specific call and nurture it, taking inspiration from my story. Besides, what you choose to do also shapes who you are.

In the process of consciously following our call, we bring joy into our lives through a higher level of understanding derived from an unselfish and altruistic perspective. This consciousness permeates all areas of our life, which is why we will be dealing with various aspects of our lives in this book.

Let me end this introduction with some practical remarks about the structure of the book.

We follow the life cycle of Senius, a fictive character, who inherited experiences from my life. To ensure that my message is precise and useful and hopefully be an inspiration to improve your life, I have made some strategic adjustments.

In 'Visiting the Melting Pot,' the journey starts in a spiritual world where Senius plans his next incarnation circumstances. In addition, a few other characters who have a significant impact on his life join the conversation.

In 'A New Transition,' Senius leaves the spiritual world. Here, you will learn how the transition takes place. During this process, the soul temporarily loses memory from its time in the spiritual world.

In 'The life of Senius in Brief,' Senius returns to the spiritual world, allowing us to follow the reflections he makes. He figures out the initial thoughts about his call in life and starts to understand how his surroundings have supported it.

In 'A Perspective in the Back Mirror,' we delve into the life of Senius, giving us further clues about his life and his call.

In 'On the Life Journey,' Senius is capable of describing the critical areas of his life using his call as the baseline.

Up to this point, the perspective described is based on Senius' perception of it. In 'The Community,' you will find the community's dynamics, and the contrast between egoism and holism becomes crucial.

In 'Foundations,' you are presented with different frameworks of understanding. Furthermore, Senius uses his call and the resources he possesses as critical elements to determine the experiences he wants to gain.

In 'Tools to Release Your Call,' you will find practical advice on how to help you release your call.

There are, however, stones you will find along the path, which you need to overcome and be aware of. The chapter 'Faces of Fear' is introduced to describe them in detail.

The chapter 'Yoga and Meditation' gives an account of tools that have been a unique challenge in the life of Senius, and at the same time, a major channel to enlightenment.

'The Process of Death' describes what happens when an incarnation comes to an end.

In 'Preparation to Birth,' you will find the preparations that take place before birth to give a complete account of the life cycle.

'The New World' gives a status of our individual contribution to the overall development.

'The Beginning of the Universe' gives a contemporary perspective on our history, taking into account what has been covered in the previous chapters.

In 'The Ultimate Dream,' a new future is presented where the gained experiences come into play. 'Synthesis' is the last chapter. It summarises what you have read so far, with new insights.

To give you a little rest for contemplation between the chapters, you will find a poem related to what you just read and/or pointing to the following chapter. I wish you an incredible and fruitful journey.

In Despair

A hunch has created me a vision
as an offset for my life mission.
But how can I become in control
without from the building to roll?

I know I have the mission as call,
But what is it I have to recall?
I need to build on my foundations
while collecting new observations.

In my heart, I have an unknown longing:
where to is the architect belonging?
I build the temple, stone by stone,
But how do I manage on my own?

I need guidance to find my way
So where is my guide, anyway?
How do I connect to my source?
That's how a team becomes my resource.

I miss a roadmap for my destination.
Or is the journey itself my realisation?
Without a map, I build in blindness.
Or will I remain in my wilderness?

Source: Senius

Visiting the Melting Pot

During one of my daily hikes, I realised that the rainbow portal has a far deeper purpose—a portal into another world. So as soon as I returned home to Denmark, I started writing what was on my mind.

I recalled my Camino experience. I see the portal very clearly in front of me. As I take my first step into the portal, I can feel a strong pull drawing me further and further into the portal.

My surroundings disappear. I feel I am in a tunnel with a bright light at the end. As I beam through, it becomes more radiant.

I am a little scared, but as I move ahead, I sense potent thoughts and feelings, filled with love and compassion. I feel as if somebody is expecting me and is reaching out for me.

I see the portal for the first time, yet this feeling though, is quite strange—it's the same feeling of being home. It feels like I have been here before.

When I arrive at the other end of the tunnel, I see a tall person wearing a long white robe radiating warm golden light. It is so surreal. And his appearance makes me feel calm. He brings me back to the present by saying: 'Welcome, your seeking soul. I have expected your arrival. Please follow me.'

As I follow, we float through an environment that I find hard to describe, but the energy the surroundings generated makes me peaceful and happy deep inside. The place still looks and feels very familiar, strangely! We exchange no words. Yet this person continues to guide me through—as my guide.

We arrive at an old library in the non-physical world. I see a fireplace, four chairs in front of it and a tiny table placed between them.

As I look around the library, I see two other people occupying their respective chairs, wearing a similar dress as my guide. I cannot identify them because of their hoods almost entirely covering their heads.

Using his comforting hand gesture, the guide asks me to sit down. He then takes the last vacant seat.

The guide says: 'Dear soul, be my guest. We rarely get the visit of an incarnated soul. I know you are curious to know who we are. I will let you know when the time is ripe.'

'Till then, you can call me whatever you like. Now let me introduce you to one of my students—the one who requested this session to take place.'

The second person removes the hood. I see a man with a warm, big smile. I am astonished! It is Senius!

Senius is one of my soulmates who I have not seen in a while.

I spontaneously react by saying: 'Hi, my dear old friend, how great to see you again!'

Senius responds: 'The pleasure is fully on my side as you are here partly on my initiative.'

Guide: 'I am glad that you recognise your soulmate. Senius had requested for you to be here as a referent so our conversation becomes publicly known to benefit the people in your physical world. As Senius rightly said, he is partly responsible for your presence here and partly because you are also seeking answers—it is a match of desires.'

The last person then removes the hood. It is a woman with deep and warm brown eyes and an arch smile. She is Rhodopis, an Egyptian Princess, who I met in a former incarnation.

I am wondering why she is here. I react by saying: 'Hi, Rhodopis, I am very pleased to meet you again in these extraordinary surroundings.'

Rhodopis: 'I am pleased to meet you too, my dear soulmate. Quite some time has passed since we last met.'

Guide: 'I sense you are wondering why Rhodopis is here?'

'Rhodopis, Senius' and your calls are interrelated and mutually dependent. You will figure it out when the time is ripe.

'As you may have already noticed, here all thoughts are visible and transmitted in the form of pictures. But in your state, you can only see images within your narrow frequency band.

'Nevertheless, you have felt a lot of accommodating feelings during your journey to this place. To avoid confusing you, I prepared this room as a shield of energy for outcoming thoughts.

'By the way, if you're wondering, my appearance only reflects your expectations considering your beliefs. My dressing is white as snow to match your illusion about innocence, and my appearance reflects the impression you have of a mature and wise advisor. However, let me tell you that the two attributes are contradictory, at least at your level of insight.'

Referent: 'Pardon me, but I want to know why the views are contradictory?'

Guide: 'A significant part of your experience comes from what works and what does not work for you. It is a trial-and-error process. During the process of harvesting your experiences, harming others is inevitable, and of course with varying degrees, and it is often unintentional.

'For example, values often differ between different social classes and generations, and as you grow older, you start to notice these differences between various cultures as well.

'The line between intentional and unintentional is a matter of consciousness. For example, in kindergarten, you fight over a specific toy, and if you do it solely to please your own needs, it may be unintentional. However, if you have done it several times before and take pleasure in seeing that the other child gets angry, sad or even fighting you back, you may be intentionally harming the other child.

'My point is that before you become wise, you harm a lot of people as a child and as an adult before acknowledging all these mechanisms and consciously choose to avoid them.'

Referent: 'I do not know your past, but I have imagined you and associated you with white—purity, integrity and goodness.'

Guide: 'I sense your reply is something you have inherited from your history. You let your God, his servants and your heroes wear white clothes. Besides, white represents the holiness of the spirit in western cultures.'

Referent: 'Why do you choose to adapt your appearance to my expectations?'

Guide: 'I do not want to distract you. I want you to be relaxed so we can focus on things that matter to you through the life of Senius.

'I know you are here to seek information so you can accelerate the development not just for yourself but for anybody else who shares the same need. I allow you to ask some initial questions before we enter the life of Senius. I know you have many questions, so please go ahead.'

Referent: 'Thank you. I am overwhelmed. On the one hand, I feel like I know that you are my guide and that I am quite familiar with this place. On the other hand, I find it difficult to draw all my impressions into a meaningful context. So, what am I missing?'

Senius: 'As I told you before, we rarely have visits from incarnated souls, and the vast majority of them in this place are here between two incarnations to consolidate their experiences with their former lives while preparing for the next. Even with your limited knowledge of things, you may define it as a melting pot of beliefs, intentions, experiences, reactions and recognitions.'

Referent: 'I can imagine that many believers will disagree with the possibility of reincarnation. Can you shed some light on this?'

Guide: 'Since you have a Christian background, I will refer to Christianity throughout our conversation. Please note that this is one of many religions, and it is definitely not my intention to preach for any of them. As long as they are built on unconditional love, they are all equivalent; *God is love.* As you mentioned before, this should also guide us to show love to ourselves and anybody else despite our different views.

'In those days, Christianity disseminated to other countries and merged with existing beliefs, thus creating local adaptations. With time, new interpretations emerged to fit into the ongoing development of their societies. In the early days of the church, it formed an ecumenical council to decide on various disputes such as what they considered to be the right teachings. In particular, reincarnation was a highly debated topic during such meetings, and they, unfortunately, decided to exclude it.

'In the ecumenical council, the general opinion was that the *Holy Spirit* was present at that moment and guided them to take the right decisions, making them ironclad.'

Referent: 'But I assume that the members' willingness to accept this was bound to their time of living. Isn't it?'

Guide: 'I agree. But as I said, they proclaimed to the public that the *Holy Spirit* was among them to secure the right decisions. Whether they believed it or it was just a tactical move, I will leave it to your judgment to decide. But the consequence was that nobody dared to question the judgments and decisions made by the council.

'Besides, if the ecumenical council had accepted reincarnation, it would have contradicted other parts of the Bible, and this could have undermined the council's documents and the people's faith. Remember, they stated that their truth is absolute and cannot be questioned. Furthermore, this could have weakened their control over the people, which should not be underestimated either.'

Referent: 'What is your standpoint on this important question?'

Guide: 'I did reveal my standpoint. As I told you, they, unfortunately, excluded reincarnation for good reasons because it did not fit into the general picture of Christianity, as well as other monotheistic religions. Their view of life is that you only have one lifetime and you have to live up to the prescripts of your religion.

'Your ability to abide by the rules determines your access to the Kingdom of God. It is only the deity who decides, punishes and forgives. The critical element is that the people are obedient to the Laws of God as the priesthood interprets them.

'But your reaction tells me that it is a good idea to come up with an introduction right away. The reason I have been reluctant to bring it up is that many associate reincarnations with specific religions. As a matter of fact, you can find bits and pieces of what we are discussing in any religion.

'This is still valid when seen in the light of their time of creation. The main problem, however, is that present religions fail to recognise that these beliefs were built on primitive religions. Evolution does not fit well with established religions because they believe that all that the prophets have declared is nothing but universal and everlasting truths.

'However, reincarnation goes further back in history, and in fact, is a principle of development. Human evolution has, in general, been an ongoing process which manifests in bringing birth to more and more developed individuals. Each reincarnation represents another step in evolution.

'When you incarnate, you live in a mortal body with a personality which is a pale reflection of your immortal soul; you incarnate to increase your wisdom through specific experiences.

'Deep inside you, you know that your soul is your true self, and your soul knows that all souls are part of the same Source. On the other hand, ego is only a device with a personality in a body, making it possible for you to manifest your call.

'When you die, you leave your mortal body behind and you return home to the spiritual realm. And after considering your experiences in your former lives and you define the experiences for the next one, you are ready to incarnate again. This process continues until you do not need to return anymore. I will shed some more light on this topic later.'

Senius: 'Were there any other main topics that were suppressed?'

Guide: 'Yes, indeed. An interesting example is the Gospel of Thomas. Many of its statements do not fit into the interpretation of the four accredited Gospels. The Gospel of Thomas states, among other things, that the one who knows everything but not himself, knows nothing.

'If you know yourself, you also know that you are the son or daughter of God. Jesus promulgates that people should release themselves from everyday life and seek the truth from within, and let their divine light shine.'

Senius: 'Well, it is understandable that it has been suppressed. On the other hand, this fits right into my way of thinking.'

Referent: 'Okay. Thank you. Now to an entirely different question: Why could I recognise Rhodopis and Senius but only have intuitive feelings about you?'

Guide: 'Rhodopis and Senius are within a similar frequency band to yours, and I am on a higher frequency level. This is why you could not fully recognise me, although you could sense me through your intuition. And yes, I am your guide.

'It is the same reason why you have these intuitive feelings for this place. Most importantly, though, you have been here before—plenty of times.

'As an incarnated person, you do not have access to this spiritual realm because it would spoil the whole idea of being embodied. Whenever an incarnation occurs, it starts with an empty board. The only reason you are granted access to this place is because we believe your experience will be beneficial for other people. And as a bonus, your thirst for answers will be quenched.'

Referent: 'Well, what you just said surely raises some questions, and I am a little confused about your usage of "we". It seems to me that you use it to describe yourself and maybe others too. It surprises me. Has it any parallel to Gen. 1:26?

'Then God said, "Let us make mankind in our image, in our likeness, so that they may rule over the fish in the sea and the birds in the sky, over the livestock and all the wild animals, and overall, the creatures that move along the ground".'

Guide: 'Dear seeking soul, I am not God, but I have lived many lives; lives of both men and women, although gender has no meaning here. Our masculine and feminine sides are, at least in our group, fully integrated into our souls. In the spiritual realm, the physical form of gender has no sense.

25

'We are above this perspective. My choice of attire and aspect is made merely to match your expectations and comfort you. But just as the room we are sitting in, my form is nothing but a manipulation of energy.

'In this realm, I am qualified and assigned as a guide for individual souls, a group where you belong too. The same goes for Rhodopis and Senius.

'Your question is an excellent example of how your background influences you. You use references from the Bible because of your Christian upbringing; I emphasise this just to let you know that your point of view is as biased as anybody else is, including Rhodopis and Senius,' whose background is similar to yours.

'I know I have not fully answered your question. The issue is that every time I give you an answer, it becomes a starting point for a never-ending chain of further questions. Therefore, I have a few recommendations for you:

1. Although it may be evident, I believe I still need to emphasise that God has written no statement in the Bible nor in any other holy book; human beings did, flavouring the texts with their own culture and time of living, such as their own context. Nevertheless, the Bible is a general reference for quite a few people. It has been incorporated in various forms in many nations' constitutions and is part of their value system.
2. Focus only on the topics relevant for your present call.
3. Let us deal with one issue at a time. We will come back to the other matters later, as I will be keeping track of them whenever they occur.

'I want to align your expectations a little bit more. You prefer being in control, and if you could, you would like to have a clear overview. However, as you have noticed, your life has not developed that way. It has been an iterative process with many detours, which were necessary for you.

'It appears as if you were trying to put together the pieces of a jigsaw puzzle and missed the final picture you are trying to build. It is part of your learning process that also gives you a better understanding of the detours of other people.'

Referent: 'Okay. Thank you. Allow me to name you in singular and male, as that is how I perceive you now. And until I know better, I will call you Oracle.'

Guide, now labelled Oracle: 'Fine with me, but not without humour!'

Referent: 'I will do my best to follow your guidelines. Concerning the detours you just mentioned, I understand that they have a purpose that develops empathy besides being part of my learning process. But couldn't it be less time-consuming?'

Oracle: 'I understand your frustration, but there are no shortcuts! A way to restrict the detours is to reflect on why they happen and learn the lesson from there; this way, at least you do not repeat them. It would save you a lot of time.

'However, do not expect to have tailwind all your entire life. Headwind, on the other hand, makes you stronger and teaches you to appreciate tailwind. So, whenever you feel any resistance, frame it as an opportunity rather than an obstacle.

'Another weather metaphor, sunshine every day makes a desert. Now and then you need rain to make the soil fertile.

'You probably may have noticed that other people do not have the same issues as you have, and there are many reasons for that. But two significant factors, in particular, determine the number and type of detours you will take. These two factors are interdependent.

'First, it depends on whom you are connected to, and second, your consciousness level. The higher your consciousness is, the fewer but more refined the detours are.'

Referent: 'I see. Now on a different topic. How is it possible for us to follow the life of Senius?'

Oracle: 'Do not concern yourself with this. You will learn it along the way, just as you are doing here and now with Senius, Rhodopis and me.

We will follow Senius during one life cycle, starting from preparing and choosing the incarnation circumstances before entering the physical world.

'You look surprised?'

Referent: 'I am merely chocked! I have believed that it was solely my parents' decision to make that choice?'

Oracle: 'There are no coincidences, in general. When you believe it is a coincidence, it may be because you have missed some insights.

'There is a match between what Senius desires to experience and the family he will be joining. I say "family" because there is a match between the wishes of Senius, his parents, possible siblings and other close relations to the family. Each person involved is there to serve the other members.

'Your question is very relevant though, and it may be a new insight for quite a few readers. In case you find it too hard to accept, I recommend you consider it as a hypothesis and re-examine it after reading the entire book.

'I can see on your face that you need a break. I think it is time to hand the lead over to Senius and let him introduce his life to us in brief.'

Referent: 'Yes, you are right, but what is the purpose of allowing Senius to present his life to us?'

Oracle: 'If you look at your close relations and how your life has developed so far, it can be your first stepping stone to figure out what your call in life is. Perhaps you can use this example as an inspiration to look into your own life.'

Oracle and Senius leave the room.

Referent looks at Rhodopis and asks: 'Rhodopis, do you know why you are here?'

Rhodopis: 'I do not have the full picture either, but my presence here is part of the preparation of my call for the next incarnation. I have a more resigned role compared to what I am used to.

'But I enjoyed meeting you and Senius because it brings back many happy memories. I think we need to be patient and allow ourselves to absorb what we experience during this extraordinary gathering.'

Referent: 'Thank you, Rhodopis. You are probably right. However, you possibly remember that patience is not my strongest attribute.'

Rhodopis responds with a warm smile.

As I sit looking into the fireplace, I am trying to elaborate on the answers and analyse the events that just unfolded.

The Life Puzzle

Is my birth a coincidence I can to my parents send?
Is life solely a one-time meaningless event?
Everything which has a beginning also has an end?
To whom can I my profound frustrations send?

My experience gained in the melting pot disagree.
A relief that makes me peaceful, happy and free.
Life is meaningful but requires you to seek your way.
Piece by piece, you build your own puzzle, so to say.

My puzzle can for you only set inspirations.
I am convinced as it arises from my convictions.
Are you ready to seek your own quest?
May you find convictions in which you can rest.

Each culture has its own truth invented.
Some even claim it is absolute and by God descended.
If you want to avoid the trap, trust your soul.
It is your connection which can your truth enrol.

Source: Senius

A Perspective in The Back Mirror

Senius: 'I have been at my home base for a while now. So let me offer you a sneak peek of my preparation. I met Oracle and some soulmates with one purpose—to define the call of my next life. I had the opportunity to see my next life in different scenarios.

'Nobody forced me to leave, but I felt a loving encouragement to get ready and join the family I have chosen as the best base for realising my call and also to complement the desires of this very same family.'

Oracle follows me to the launch gate, giving me the last instructions and filling me with love and compassion. The start of the journey is always a shocking experience, despite having performed it numerous times before.

It is time to leave, and I start to move away from Oracle faster and faster. The surroundings get blurry, the light fades out and everything else becomes dark, but still moving faster. Suddenly I stop moving, the surroundings become warm.

I merge with the physical body that has been expecting me. We become a team, and the borders of our entities become one. My consciousness is getting blurry and my memory is fading out.

Oracle returns. I look at him astonished and with a big question mark on my face. I then look at Rhodopis and notice that she has the same puzzled expression as well.

Oracle sends us a big smile and says: 'I can see the surprise and questions on your faces. You see, what is going on with Senius is transmitted to you via me as a moderator.'

Referent: 'This is overwhelming. Thank you. I look forward to the continuation.'

Oracle: 'Let me return to the continuation of Senius' experiences.'

Senius: 'The surroundings become active. I feel the pressure around my head, which comes in waves together with screams. Suddenly I see the light, and the pain makes me scream too.

'I am born. I am taking my first breath.

'In the room, my mother and midwife are present. As I am lying on my mother's chest—I can feel her and hear her heartbeat—I gradually calm down.

'My father shows up later without much excitement, probably because I am the third child my mother has given birth to within the last three years or so. I will have another brother about 1 year later, a total of four children within five years.'

Referent: 'His birth appears very vivid to me and confuses me at the same time. Oracle, how can we talk to Senius when he has lost the connection to his soul?'

Oracle: 'His soul remains the same, but he loses his awareness in the process of merging with his physical counterpart.

'He will have to rediscover his soul, a process that will take many years. But everything is recorded by the soul, which I can still access. I also have access to your souls at all times, which makes it possible for me to act as a switchboard between you.'

Referent: 'Amazing new world! I am impressed. Why do we lose our memories of former lives when we incarnate in the physical world again?'

Oracle: 'This is an important question. But you will gradually understand this in the same way as you have experienced it in your life until now. Therefore, you get many detours as you already have noticed, with a deeper meaning.

'Try to imagine how it would be if you knew your former lives. It would confuse you and make you focus on topics you are not yet ready to cope with until you are more mature. For instance, negative experiences (although they can be turned into opportunities) can harm your life, limiting your ability to experience life with new perspectives.

'Merging with a physical body would also become difficult. You will have to grow simultaneously. Likewise, new and mature souls are like oil and water seen from a young soul's perspective. The comprehension gap is enormous.

'With your current knowledge level from your present life, the distance in maturity is more than sufficient to create massive conflicts, which we will discuss more later.

'My dear soul, therefore, be pleased that you start with an empty board. Another way of saying it is to compare your situation to a new-born as that of a new computer. Like a computer, the mind depends on the only program installed, the operating system, which controls all the internal functions and making it possible to install the applications you want.

'Likewise, your memory and consciousness are empty but your operating system, the autonomy system, controls all your internal functions and keeps you alive.

'The way you learn programs is by copying the behaviour and views from all your close relations, which primarily happens during your childhood. It is a very efficient way to become a social being and to learn how to act in a social context, which is complicated. Besides, it is a flexible ability you can adapt to your chosen environment. In this manner, you prepare your reference during your early years, and this will colour your interpretation of how you understand the world.'

Referent: 'But why do we enter the physical world if it is just to go from one detour to the next?'

Oracle: 'I understand your frustration. The only way you can gain experience is to enter the physical world because it requires a physical presence. I think you need another break before we continue and give the word to Senius, who is becoming impatient to tell us about his life in brief.

'Please remember that Senius chose his frames of the incarnation with support from his relations in the spiritual world. The point in presenting his life, in brief, is that you can use the same exercise with your life to figure out what your call is.'

Referent: 'Why is the knowledge of the call so important?'

Oracle: 'If you do not know your call, you do not have a reference and cannot qualify your choices as appropriate or inappropriate for your development. When you know your call, you have a reference for your life and accordingly prioritise the thoughts and energies you focus on, thus helping you make better choices. The purpose of your life is to gain valuable experiences to heal the deficits in your knowledge.'

Referent: 'One last thing: Are you referring to karma?'

Oracle: 'Yes, but I deliberately did not use that word because many people misunderstand karma or associate it with other religions, like Hinduism and Buddhism, with different interpretations. The concept, however, has existed long before as a fundamental universal law and is linked to reincarnation. The principle is that everything you initiate with your thoughts will return to you and impact your next incarnation.

'A young soul would interpret it as a punishment—a reward mechanism, which is the most prevalent view. A more mature soul, on the other hand, would say it is about the kind of development you need to experience in order to gain the missing knowledge to heal your karma through your call.

'Karma has nothing to do with morals or ethics, which has been created by mankind. The Source does not judge. Karma is an impersonal law restoring balance and teaching you responsibility. And it does not mean that you will experience the same situations over and over again.

'Instead, your call should be a driver through bliss, raising your consciousness to your soul level. While recognising the Source, you get the power to dissolve the issues.

'You can also relate karma to your feelings as positive and negative sensations in the body. In spiritual terms, you can translate them to the energy of higher or lower frequency, respectively. It also explains why you feel blissful when you act at the soul level.'

The Deception

Who is the person I see in the mirror?
If I believe it is my true self, I get caught in an error.
The body ,thoughts and feelings are nothing but tools.
Relying on the ego and the mortal tools, makes us end up as fools.

You may wonder why we are taken over by our tools.
It is often because we get distracted by the wrong rules.
The need for recognition from others creates a distraction.
Peace and happiness we find only as an internal attraction.

What is the first step in finding the true self while being here?
Your soul is knocking on your door to see if you are there.
The ego carries on deceiving you with new surrogates.
You might think you will succeed with the next gadgets.

You feel the emptiness and realise you lost another round.
Your soul is in constant suffering and screams out loud.
It might sound straightforward, but what is true?
Is your chosen family and close relations the first clue?

Source: Senius

The Life of Senius in Brief

Senius: 'Close relations create the basis for my life, and as Oracle stated, it gives me clues to what I intend to master in this life. Therefore, I want to introduce you to my family and close relations.'

Family and Close Relations

Senius: 'My sister, who is the eldest, my two brothers and I were raised by our mum. The house was her responsibility, with all that it entailed. There was no washing machine, no dishwasher or other comforts whatsoever. Disposable diapers were not available either, and my mum had to wash them in a copper kettle.

'Spare time was scarce, but when available, she would often use it to knit clothes for us. My siblings and I spend a lot of time on our own. What a job for a mother who just turned 24 years of age when she gave birth to her last child.

'My mum was mainly occupied with all these practical issues and kept her personal views regarding the most significant questions of life to herself. Meanwhile, I learnt that she does not have any religious beliefs either. Now and then she would wonder what happens after death, but she chose not to pay much attention to the topic.

'On the other hand, we hardly had any affiliation to the church, except for the main sacraments. And apparently, Mum did not agree with her parents-in-law nor my father.

'My father was 3 years older than my mum. During the first few years of their marriage, he was working as a fisherman and was rarely at home.

And whenever he was home, he would spend more time with his hobbies than he would with his children. There is no accusation here, just a statement of facts—a behaviour he inherited from my grandfather.

'He loved being hands-on at work, and in his spare time, he enjoyed hunting, drawing and writing books and poems. He unsuccessfully attempted to get a manuscript published. Several years later, he still tries to get some of his drawings exhibited without much attention from the public. Besides, his curiosity for philosophy drove him away from classical religions and made him a freethinker.

'Times were tough, and the resources were few. My siblings and I slept in one room. During winter, the humidity was so high that it condensed to water running down the walls.

'My grandfather started a shipyard for fishing boats, and my father was eventually persuaded to join the company. One of my uncles started a sawmill that delivers wood for the fishing boats. Another uncle started another shipyard on an island; my grandfather was the architect of the whole operation.

'After World War II, my grandfather started the third shipyard in another town through the Marshall Help. In the beginning, they built fishing boats as on the other shipyards, but after a few years, they moved to building coasters, which soon became their main business. My aunt also joined the shipyard as an accountant.

'My paternal grandparents belonged to a right-wing Christian church; my grandfather followed a traditional patriarchal view. As the firstborn, my father had to take over the business after my grandfather. However, it was a pity because my father was not a businessman but an artist.

'My maternal grandmother took care of her home, just as my mum did. Whenever I visited them, she would always say the evening prayers with me, and that was how I learnt the Lord's Prayer at a very young age. We also performed daily morning worships.

'The last thing worth mentioning is that they had a picture Bible, which was shocking for me. All the violence and God's punishments were theatrical and vivid—quite scary for a young boy.

'Whenever my grandfather had to make difficult decisions, he would take his Bible, pick a random page and do what that page inspired him to do.

'My maternal grandmother raised my mother and her 12 years younger twins on her own. They do not share the same father. My grandmother was attracted to men who were of no good to her.

'Nonetheless, she managed everything on her own. To get the daily bread on the table, she runs an ice cream shop, which was part of their house. She was a very energetic, good-hearted and hospitable woman. For instance, she would have enough surplus to accommodate all of us for New Year's dinner, with a sleepover.

'When it came to beliefs, her views were as concealed as my mum's, and I believe my mum may have inherited her perspective from my grandmother.

'When we were under school age, we moved around frequently. After my first year at school, we moved for the last time as my father agrees with my mother that we will stay there until all of the children have completed high school. Despite that, I attended four different schools because I consciously decided to change three of them on my own initiative.

'My brothers shared the same interests and are very close to each other; they also shared our father's interest in hunting and nature in general. I, on the contrary, stood out by having different interests and lived most of my childhood on my own, mainly outside the family.

'Because of my grandparents' influence, I became quite religious in my early childhood. As an example, my father and I were once outside in the evening, shortly before Christmas. I suddenly pointed at the most prominent and brightest star and asked, "Is God living there?" He gave me a kind smile and a dilatory answer.

'As a teenager, I was still a practicing Christian, but I became interested in my father's way of thinking. It gave me a new and different perspective, which I primarily obtain by reading books belonging to many disciplines. This allowed me to have many meaningful discussions with my father.

'My siblings and I did not do well at school—we found ourselves in the same pattern as anybody else in our close relations. I realised that if I wanted to end that pattern, I have to change the environment and move to a private school. At the time, my parent's financial status was above average because of my father's position in the family company.

'I got their approval and went to a private school for 2 years, which turned out to be very successful. After finalising school, I started my higher education and got a diploma in engineering. As none of my siblings were interested in the shipyard, I took over my father's business.

'Unfortunately, a month into the role, the company went bankrupt, making it a very short career. But I managed to find another job in a large enterprise right away. At this time, my wife was also employed, which was remarkable, given the high unemployment rate during those years.

'My sister became a dental assistant, and my brothers chose to be craftsmen. A few years later, we headed in different directions, and I am the only one living in our country of birth.'

Working Life

Senius: 'At work, my core responsibility lay in the technical marketing area. The critical task is to ensure that the products match the needs of the customer segments. I then have to give the specifications for new products. To improve my skills, in my spare time, I got a bachelor's degree in marketing.

'In order to attend school and avoid frequent business trips, I decided to switch to a job with a site focus, and that was how I was able to take charge of the development of a maintenance system for handling the production machines and other internal equipment.

'Project management became one of my key competencies and acted as a springboard for many different professional areas. It also had an important impact on my way of thinking: I take it as a habit to always have an eye for improvements and challenge present perceptions, which also propagates to other life areas.

'Along the way, I joined a project management programme. In one of the modules, the instructor divides us into groups depending on our birth order in our family: only child, eldest, middle or youngest. The purpose is to describe our general lifetime so far.

'It was an incredibly eye-opening experience. While telling our stories, we realised that there are many parallels. In a way, I felt relieved to realise that most aspects of my behaviour could be explained based on my position in the family. I also learnt that this factor impacts the way we interpret communication.

'Some years later, I joined a process management programme, which was another eye-opening experience. In one of the modules, we were divided into groups and were asked to draw the other members of the group according to what we perceived as their key personal characteristics. My group members described me as follows:

'The first drawing is a small illustration of a lighthouse and some small boats floating around it. I am the lighthouse, and the boats are the other members of my group. A short caption states that my ambitious demands make me lonesome.

'Another drawing envisaged me like a bird labelled "active potential", escorted by two bobbles with an arrow between them. The first bobble described me as "a warm seeking soul" and the second one as "a cold observing sod". The arrow was labelled "development".

'The third and last drawing illustrated me as a sundial with the caption: "It is the same sundial that is sometimes bright and at other times dark".

'I will come back to what I learnt from these impressive images later. I have to mention that I fully realised the meaning behind these images only after returning from the course. To complete the session, they also describe me as self-aware and helpful, but also as a person who is hard to help.

'I realised that one of the main issues I faced during projects was to challenge my mindset and others. This realisation triggered my interest in human resources (HR). Besides, some of my upcoming projects are within the field of HR.

'My curiosity for this field led me to obtain a master's degree in business administration, where I wrote my dissertation in HR. I joined many HR development programmes and became a certified coach in connection with a job as the HR Director for one of my company's divisions.

'My work in HR was challenging but exciting, and I felt like I'm growing with my work. However, there were times I did wonder how I would want to spend my senior life. I got the answer to my question at a business conference I had attended with two of my colleagues.

'During the opening ceremony, the speaker asks us to talk to the person sitting next to us. I was sitting between my two colleagues. They both initiated a conversation with the person sitting beside them.

'In my loneliness, a question came to me: *What am I doing here?* All of a sudden I am hit by an infinite emptiness and see myself in another scene where I hold my last speech for my colleagues emphasising that I now want to dedicate my time to my passion. The vividness of the picture astonished me, and I realised it the following year.

'I lived out my passion through hiking, reading and writing, and whatever I learnt supported me in pursuing the quest of my life.'

Oracle: 'You have moved from one project to another within the same organisation. What made you move from one position to the next I wonder?'

Senius: 'First of all, it is how I feel when I go to work. As long as I am happy, I will keep the position. As soon as I get bored of it, I know it's time to seek new challenges. This happens on average every 4 years or so.'

Oracle: 'My point in bringing it up is to emphasise that this is the right thing to do. As long as you are positive about what you do, it reflects on the work you do through better outcomes. On the other hand, if you start experiencing negative feelings, you need to react. Otherwise, your passivity can lead to exhaustion.'

Senius: 'Good that you mention it. I experienced it once when I had a manager I did not choose on my own. The positive thing about it was that it pushed me to take the initiative of moving to another department for the first time. The move opened my eyes to a lot of new opportunities.

'In the back mirror, I am happy that it happened. I have subsequently used this lesson to help other colleagues and employees move to different positions that best suited their present needs. When a person is satisfied with her working position, it is a real win-win situation for both the employee and the employer.'

Oracle: 'I would like to bring your attention to the fact that you immediately gave a negative value to an event (i.e., you did not like the manager's behaviour), but what you perceived as "bad" turned out to be great at a later stage. What you may perceive as an obstacle in the short term eventually appears to be an opportunity.

'In more general terms, you should be cautious about adding value to any event. Instead, meet any situation with the same positive attitude and courage irrespective.'

Private Adult Life

Senius: 'I met my wife-to-be at a young age at a disco, but we did not get close from the first moment. I assume it was because we were a little shy and introverted back then. We met again after that, on our own, and after a short while, our love bloomed—what a fantastic time!

'Everything was bright and smooth. We got engaged the following year and then got married the year after that. A year after our marriage, our daughter saw the light of day, and 2 years later, our son was born.

'We got established as a family in our own house. Everything developed without any significant obstacles, probably because we implicitly have similar expectations regarding our family's objectives and roles. When our daughter started going to a private kindergarten, I became a board member, which I continued to attend until our son left kindergarten for school.

'But, without exactly knowing why, I had an undefined longing and feeling that something is missing. I can say that it was my soul trying to get through to me in the back mirror. After some research, I bought a book about meditation and yoga with a 30-day programme, where I had the opportunity to perform progressively advanced yoga postures and use the different senses for meditation.

'After the 30-day programme, I was supposed to continue with the three best techniques, and in the end, choose the one that I found most successful. On average, I spent 30 minutes per day practising yoga and meditation.

'I maintained a logbook to track my progress. However, after 7 months, I gave it up again: I did not harvest any benefit that could justify the time spent, and I felt that it drove my focus away from my worldly life. I decided to focus on my career and get a 4-year degree in marketing.

'Nevertheless, I still felt empty inside. I returned to the church and joined the service on Sundays and the annual church festivities. I met a pastor who knew my grandparents, and I became a member of the church board. My wife and I took part in a Bible circle with the pastor, his wife and some friends.

'However, after a few years, I felt restless again. My wife gave me a book[2] for Christmas which challenged the same old beliefs I have questioned previously. It is the drop that lets the cup flow over.

'It became a turning point. Seen in the back mirror, I can conclude, if you want to access the spiritual realm, you need to believe it is possible— the evidence shows up *after* you have realised it. I have learnt that this also applies to most things I am engaged in. Although the outcome would of course be different from what I read in the book my wife gifted, it inspired me to find my own way, just like I do hope that my experiences can inspire you.

---

[2] *Conversations with God*, Book 1, written by Neale Donald Walsch, Danish edition in 1997.

'I started to look for new perspectives once more. At the same time, our friendship with the pastor and the likeminded becomes awkward.

'I got out of the squeeze by saying I have to concentrate on my MBA, which I do in my spare time outside regular working hours. To manage that, I had to give up my hobbies and positions of trust, e.g., my Church Board Membership.

'In addition, I organised a private meeting with the pastor, to whom I had sent my point of view in the form of a metaphor before the discussion:

'Three men look at a wall and discuss its colour. The first one says it is red, the second says it is yellow and the third declares it as blue. An outside observer, however, sees that the wall is actually white and notices that the men are wearing glasses with a lens of the same colour they just mentioned.

'From the external observer's point of view, it is easy to understand why they maintained their view: they describe their own experience. What makes the situation more delicate is that they insist that the others have a wrong perception and want them to admit it. They cannot see each other's glasses and assess others' opinions through their own.

'To ensure justice, they decided to fetch some of their highly respected friends as credible witnesses. The friends, however, wore the same glasses as themselves; therefore, the friends could only confirm the same experience.

'The episode repeated itself and escalated to a point that the police had to separate the participants. Each group left the place in disagreement, believing that only their group was right and the others were unmistakably wrong.

'Each group returned to their people without any doubt and felt happy and strong of the supposedly right colour. The group members confirmed each other in their view and lived happily till the end of their days.

'I promised the pastor to return to him when I have solved the Gordian knot, revealing the white colour.

'In the same period, my wife gave birth to our second daughter. We have looked forward to her birth and made a lot of preparation. Our older children left home shortly before attending their respective educations.

'In a way, you can say that we became parents twice as there is a 20-year difference between the eldest and the youngest daughter. This gap allowed us to rethink how to bring up our child. She grew up in a more sophisticated environment and more enriched by her older siblings.

'A few years later, I started practicing meditation and yoga again. This time I held on to it for 9 months, and I ended more or less with the same feeling as the previous time. However, it was not fruitless. I became calmer and more reflective. Yoga improved the flexibility of my body.

'As seen in the back mirror, if you take the same route, you will probably end up more or less at the same point. I realised I have to find another way. I started studying various sources, and I gradually felt I was heading in the right direction.

'Meanwhile, our youngest daughter is now a teenager and introduces new inputs to our family. She influences our food consumption habits. We started as vegans but ended up as vegetarians.

'My wife does not share the new habit but is affected by it for practical reasons. When our daughter leaves home, I become more flexible, which my wife appreciates. From my point of view, it is another example of the rainbow perspective. Eating habits do not need to be black and white either.'

The First Clue

I have realised that we all have a call in being.
Our circumstances are signed off while seeing.
The first clue is to look at the close relations.
What do they tell about my constellations?

How do I tackle the contradiction I see?
Is the head- and tailwind my seed?
Can immediate contradictions be resolved,
and through my call of life be dissolved?

In the beginning, you may feel it as a trap.
How can your observations close the gap?
You have to design the puzzle pieces
until the picture from the pieces releases.

Source: Senius

A Perspective in the Back Mirror

Oracle: 'Now you know under which influences Senius has grown up. To make the discussion more comfortable for you, I will let Senius return to this room as you did before.

'You may wonder how Senius can be present here while being incarnated, and how come we can see his life in real-time pictures and scroll forward in his life if we are in the present.'

Referent: 'Yes, indeed.'

Oracle: 'We are non-physical, eternal and timeless souls. In other words, your stay here is the equivalent of zero in an Earth time scale. It means that once you return to your normal surroundings, nobody will be able to register that you have been here.'

Referent: 'Amazing!'

Meanwhile, Senius enters the room as nothing has happened since he left and retakes his seat. I wonder how the Oracle did this, but I feel that it is something I should let go.

Oracle: 'Welcome back, Senius. How do you feel?'

Senius: 'Thank you. I am fine but a little confused.'

Oracle: 'It is understandable. Just as the referent, your understanding is limited by the frequency band of your actual incarnation. Anyway, you have the benefit of remembering the meeting we had here before you left. Besides, Senius, this session takes place on your initiative. So where do you want to begin?'

Senius: 'Okay. As I remember it, we have stated that it is upon us to choose our family and its close relations to fulfil our call in life. On the other hand, we lose consciousness during the incarnation process.'

Senius: 'In my view, the logical question to this is: How can I derive the life call by looking at my family and close relations?'

Oracle: 'It sounds like a good point to discuss. However, let me tell you first that some people with a Christian background may question this concept. Mary and the apostles got their call from God or Jesus, which may lead you to think that the call is an external assignment.

'That is an exception, indeed. Most people find their call themselves, and it is a process that gradually matures during their life.'

Senius: 'The process we are going into reminds me of a quote from Søren Kierkegaard, who stated: "Life can only be understood backwards, but it must be lived forwards".

Concerning the question, I wonder if I should rephrase it: Which gaps am I trying to close?'

Oracle: 'I think it is a better starting point, as your karma represents the gap you want to close through your call.'

Gaps in Perceptions

Senius: 'The first thing that pops up in my mind is the gap between my grandparents' Christian faith and my father's view, which has created a strong dissonance in my life.'

Oracle: 'I agree. I suggest that you dive deeper into this dissonance.'

Senius: 'My grandparents' view is well-known, whereas my father comes from his research. I wonder who inspired him to do this. It seems to me that he has tried to fill a similar gap as I do.

As far as I know, though, there was nobody in his close relations who may have created that dissonance. Can you give me a hint?'

Oracle: 'I'm sorry, but I'm not allowed to inform you for a straightforward reason. It is your quest—you have to figure it out on your own.'

Senius: 'Okay, I will have to check that out then. Nevertheless, I can ascertain that this interest accompanied him for a significant period of his life. Even if I do not know what triggered his inspiration, he must have had the same longing to understand it as I do.

'In retrospect, I realise that even though he was a freethinker, he was not an atheist. He believed that there was some higher power that he could not define any further.

'The way I see it is that my call primarily consists of two topics. The first is to bring my father's perspective further, and the second is to merge his view with my grandparents' opinion on a higher level of acknowledgement.

'I realise that this is the primary call of my life. The rainbow portal with the church at the end of the path is a suitable image to portray this. The physical church represents my grandparents' view and the rainbow represents my father's.

'The sun behind the scenery is the Source that is guiding me, among others, to support more insightful souls. Rain is required to build the rainbow. Its drops represent the ocean of souls incarnated together with me.

'A few of them are my soulmates, some have a link to my destiny and quite a few need my guidance and support through my call, while the rest has a rare or minor impact.'

Oracle: 'I am glad you are interpreting the picture this way. The only souls you miss in the ocean of souls you mentioned are those who can help you, and this does not come as a surprise given that even your group stated you are hard to assist. I say this with a smile on my face, as you can see.

'I can acknowledge your conclusions as you have been struggling with both issues since your childhood.'

Senius: 'Thank you. I have also wondered why my research didn't impact my choice of profession. During my adult years, some of my friends often said that I spoke as a pastor. But seeing in the back mirror, it was good that my destiny made me choose differently.'

Oracle: 'Yes, things always become more evident in the back mirror. It also shows that what might look attractive short term may be cumbersome in the long term. As you interpret it, your destiny is an example of how the spiritual realm has supported you in a direction that is different from some of your short-term expectations.'

Senius: 'Am I controlled remotely?'

Oracle: 'No, nobody in the spiritual realm would interfere this way. The choice is always yours, and many impulses affect you. You have free will that allows you to choose whatever you want.

'Perhaps your intuition may have reminded you of your key priorities at the time.'

Senius: 'My take on this is that in the presence of a contradiction between my intuition and my desire, and I choose the latter, would it be counterproductive?'

Oracle: 'Yes. Intuition is always the shortest way to know what your soul wants. However, intuition should not be confused with gut feeling connected to your ego and your personal desires.

'What else can you derive from your family situation?'

Senius: 'The family I established is very classical; in the sense that it has a traditional structure—mother, father and children, all with well-defined roles. I see I have copied the same form from my parents without being conscious about it. I do not see it as a bad thing. It just came naturally to us. My wife is a single child and comes from a traditional family too.

'In a way, we have children in two different "pools" due to the age span between the two first and the last. I see that our upbringing in the first pool was more similar to my parents' than our youngest child's upbringing. I also inherited some behaviours from my grandfather as a patriarch, which fortunately lessened during the years.

'It allowed us to be more conscious of how we raised our last child. In addition, we have become more mature and have more resources.

'When it comes to my call, an essential part of bringing up children is that I have learnt to give up some of my personal needs. It helped me seek my call without being trapped in a hamster wheel.'

Referent: 'What do you exactly mean by "hamster wheel"?'

Senius: 'I will explain that in more detail. Imagine establishing a family. You can easily spend money with a significantly high burn rate. You may still have debt from your studies and may need family support to pay a deposit for your home, which must be paid back.

'You have rent to pay in addition to this, and you may need a car to get to work. On top of that, you decide to have children to fulfil your dream of what you consider as a family. Altogether, this increases your running operation costs and puts pressure on your monthly income requirement, which may devour you.

'Moreover, it may make you vulnerable and very dependent. This is how the hamster wheel can bind you for ages.

'Another way that leads to the same trap is marketing—marketing campaigns are trying to sell you a lot of things they claim can fulfil your life. The purpose of marketing is to create a dissonance in your brain, so you get a feeling that you need what they are showing you. And it works!

'Otherwise, companies would never spend exorbitant sums of money on marketing. Eventually, you will realise that all of these things are only a surrogate to fill the void for what you really need. You cannot buy your call for cash.

'Anyway, my life has fortunately, developed differently. First of all, my wife and I met at an early age, and she completed her education shortly after I started with my higher education, thus providing us with a stable income. Besides, we lived in a small yet economically affordable flat. We welcomed our first child while living there and even managed to live without seeking loans.

'Since early childhood, I have learnt to avoid spending more than what I earn. When I finished my education, we moved into a rented house in the neighbourhood where we work. The house belonged to my father's company, which went bankrupt as mentioned earlier.

'We then had to either move or buy the house from bankruptcy. We examined the alternatives, but after some negotiations, we obtained the house for a reasonable price. I should mention that my parents-in-law gave us the last 25% of the deposit we needed to buy the house.

'We had an old car that still functions well. All things considered, we benefited from the situation because our operating costs gave us enough room for my wife to work part-time, while I work regular hours.

'It also gave me enough spare time to search for information related to my questions about being here. But as you can see, it wasn't a straightforward process; it took many detours before I became conscious about what I wanted to obtain. Nevertheless, all those detours helped me to understand why other people have different perceptions and hold different beliefs.'

Oracle: 'How did your working life impact your call?'

Senius: 'In the beginning, unfortunately, I saw my work life and my spiritual interest as two independent and separate entities of my life. I understand that now but with annoying clarity.

'I had the opportunity to join the process management programme mentioned earlier where my group portrayed me with three images: the lighthouse, the bird and the sundial. In the back mirror, I realised that they were all part of my call.

'The lighthouse stands on an island on solid ground. It is a point of orientation for ships that need to find their way. Likewise, I act as a guide for souls who need help to find their way and want to go for it. In other words, I only attract souls whose needs I can support.

'The bird shows me that I have the gift of great potential. Whether I succeed or not depends solely on my ability to keep my soul warm and strike a balance between being a neutral observer and showing empathy. The latter is a point in development because, in my childhood, we were accustomed to not expressing our feelings.

'The sundial can only count the light hours. Correspondingly, I focus on having positive thoughts. Just like the motto: You do not fight darkness with darkness, but with light. I see it as a reminder not to overestimate the darkness I may perceive in my surroundings or my mind.

'An example is that I raise my energy level whenever I have to perform the coach role.'

Oracle: 'I feel happy on your behalf because you made progress during your latest years. You also see the value of reflecting in the back mirror. So, stay in tune. Is there anything else you can add?'

Senius: 'Meanwhile, I became a coach, thus improving my self-knowledge. It also deepened my knowledge of the power of beliefs and illusions. It becomes clear to me that many of them are unconscious, but if you can find a way to make them conscious, it is possible to break their power and replace them with new supporting beliefs.

'During coaching sessions, where I facilitated this very process, some of the outcomes often surprised me. The focus persons often found solutions that were different from what I expected. It brought me many new insights.

'My work as a project manager, not least within HR, increased my knowledge in inspiring participants to work on common goals and constructively influence people's mindsets.

'To answer your question, I can conclude that my work, first of all, paved the way to let my call bloom just now. I undoubtedly have the best time in front of me, because I have now the time to dive into my call. Furthermore, I can share my knowledge with those who have an interest in finding theirs.

'Secondly, my work motivated me to challenge my views and beliefs constantly. I, therefore, also realise why I cannot fully commit to any religion because they are all built on the premise that they are a solid, permanent and unchangeable truth. In my experience instead, everything evolves in all aspects of life.

'If you look at the Universe, you will come to the same conclusion. The respective positions of stars and planets change and never are the same forever. Nothing is static; everything is dynamic and is for now still expanding. On the other hand, I acknowledge that different people have different calls, and what they seek may be found in the religion they are affiliated to.'

Oracle: 'I love your passion. You are a fiery soul, and you demonstrated so when you accomplished your many projects. If you set your mind on an objective, you reach it fully. Besides, it is great that you have acknowledged that your call is yours only, and respect that others may come to different conclusions.

'What about your private adult life? Do you see any link to your call?'

Senius: 'First of all, I realise that my wife and I have an easy-going relationship, which among others can be explained by the fact that we generally share the same culture, values, expectations towards each other and our shared future. It has also been a lucky punch because it was not something we explicitly agreed beforehand. It just developed naturally.'

Oracle: 'Well, just a little teaser for you, it is not a lucky punch. I will let you know later in our conversation.'

Senius: 'You make me curious. I will look forward to your teaching. But let me get back to your original question. I see two aspects regarding my private adult life and the link to my call.

'First of all, we accepted that we do not need to do everything together. There is enough room to live out our dreams on our own.

'The second thing is that she was the one who triggered my need for finding my path. She did so when she gave me the book I mentioned earlier as a Christmas present. I sensed that the author's story complied with how he received the answers to his many questions.

'Still, I acknowledge that it is a subjective experience, just like mine and anyone else's. My take on this is that to make the process a reality, he must have had an open mind—a possible way to get access to the Source, which he has interpreted as God. It inspired me to try it out. To my surprise, I went into a flow, which made me very enthusiastic...'

Oracle: 'It is an excellent lesson. I can add that your soul's maturity or, as we label it here, your frequency determines who you can reach/make contact with. In the beginning, in your case, you did not sense with whom you were connected. But as you get more familiar with the spiritual world, you also develop your sensibility and thus become more aware of who you can join.'

Senius: 'Thank you. It makes complete sense. Anyway, before I get there, I have to go further back in time. Years ago, I felt a strong need to find my own way to overcome the dissonance between my grandparents and father's perception. I just needed to find my way.

'I found the answer to it while I was on vacation in the Gran Canarias about a decade ago.

'I am sitting on our terrace. I hear the waves hitting the rocks beneath me, while the sunshine is reflecting in the water in front of me. I literally see myself writing a book about my great passion, living a life that complies with my higher self, in delight and desire and alliance with my Source of life. However, I also realised that the time is not yet mature— not knowing why exactly.

'I did not make this vision a reality until I retired from my job, which was about 7 years later. I kept writing from early morning to late night for quite a few days. I wrote down the internal movie that was running in my mind.

'Whenever I took a break, say, watching the news or reading the newspaper, this external input would often trigger something related to what I was writing about, although the two things had nothing in common at all. In other words, I was in a perfect flow that became a full-time occupation. I later learnt that this state is called *synchronicity*. The book was later published in 2016 in my native language.'

Oracle: 'I can confirm this. It was hard to get in touch with you, and I tried several times. In fact, without you noticing it, your work swallowed more and more of your time while your professional responsibility grew.'

Senius: 'Gosh, how blind have I been!'

Oracle: 'Don't be too harsh on yourself. The only reason I bring this up is that it is a pervasive distraction. Most distractions are quite obvious when you look at them in the back mirror.

'Instead, let me suggest that since you now know your call, keep it in your heart always. Besides, you have made a lot of progress since you wrote that book.'

Senius: 'Thank you. I feel confident that I will do my utmost best to keep it in my heart and let it be the torch that enlightens my path henceforth. Meanwhile, I also realised that overcoming the dissonance of my grandparents and father's perception will not bring peace to the world.

'As long as egoism, nationalism, diverse religions and other excluding preferences rule the world, peace is just an illusion. Instead, I have to find my path, at least at a personal level, and share the fruits of my learning with my environment.'

Rhodopis: 'I recognise your distinct character, Senius. The sundial is a nice metaphor for your way of thinking, focusing on the light hours only.'

Oracle: 'Excellent observation, Rhodopis. What is your next move, Senius?'

Senius: 'Well, my next move is that you have met my request to have this event set up, which makes it possible to make this conversation public through our referent. So, I am very grateful.'

Oracle: 'You are welcome. It is in our mutual interest. I think it is time to hand over the word to our referent.'

Referent: 'Oh, I'm guessing that the scenery I saw on the Camino is something you orchestrated?'

Oracle: 'Yes, I did. But only because you requested it.'

Referent: 'I am not quite sure how I requested it. Can you please be more detailed in your answer?'

Oracle: 'When you went on the Camino, one of your questions was what to do about your writing, am I right?'

Referent: 'Yes, I was in doubt about what my next move should be. When I spoke with more pilgrims, I noticed that their interest was quite intense, and at last, I realised that I should write in English.'

Oracle: 'Yes. But didn't you also seek a way to discover a higher truth, just like Senius, without knowing exactly how to reach it?'

Referent: 'Yes.'

Oracle: 'That is my point. The scenery with the rainbow was my answer to that question.'

Referent: 'Hold on for a moment. Now I am confused. Do you mean that Senius had the same experience?'

Oracle: 'Yes, I could see that both of you needed the same perspective, so I let both of you share the same experience. It is not the first time I did this, but it is only because you are here together that you become aware of it.

'But let me get back to you, Senius. Another part of your quest is your character, which also influences your ability to carry out your call. It is what we will look into now.'

Personal Character

Oracle: 'Looking into the characteristics of your family, can you identify some of them that you have inherited?'

Senius: 'Yes, I can see that I copied some attributes from all members.

'Let me start with my paternal grandparents, as they connect to my main call. I received the gift of faith and felt the simple-minded bliss, and I can understand why somebody would want to keep this view. On the other hand, my dad's perspective has been a vital counterpart that forced me to seek new answers.

'My dad provided me with an open mind and made me curious about the big questions in life. In my working life too, I maintained the same need for asking questions. It became clear after receiving the drawings that represented me (mentioned earlier in our conversation). I also copied his role as the primary breadwinner, which, unfortunately, has also been an excuse to be less present at home.

'Despite being a child in a very competitive environment and four kids born within a short span of time, my mum did manage to give us a secure home base. It was a prerequisite that allowed me to be open-minded when I had to meet the world. In my case, there was also a portion of curiosity and sceptical reservation.

'My mum was very energetic and had a strong will. I merged the two into a strong drive to achieve whatever goal I set for myself. Besides, she taught me my first affirmation, which suited me well: "I am born under a lucky star". During difficult times, this affirmation convinced me that I would always succeed despite everything and no matter what the conditions were.

'My grandmother taught me hospitality and another affirmation: "Appreciate what you are capable of doing". When I performed boring tasks because I had to, she always said: "Be happy that you can".

'From my sister, I inherited confidence. When she struggled with some issues, she used me as an adviser, probably because she trusted that I would not disclose the information to anybody.

'My relationships with my brothers were limited. When we played together, I had to strike a balance to avoid being squeezed between them which taught me how to navigate tricky social relations.

'Compared to my siblings, I broke the family pattern of a short education and have conserved my thirst for new knowledge.

'My parents were not good at dealing with disagreements that could contaminate the atmosphere—not least at dinner time. This taught me to be very good at sensing the atmosphere, which has supported me in many social situations.

'I have had a strong relationship with my parents-in-law. They have always been there when we needed them and vice versa. Besides, they have been very supportive and regularly invited us for lunch and dinner.

'They treated me as if I was their son. If I had to highlight what they taught me, it would be the importance of being present and taking care of your relatives.

'Last but not least, my dear wife. On the one hand, we are complementary. On the other hand, we have enjoyed our marriage for so many years that we are more or less like two trees that have grown together into one. One of her strengths is focusing on our close relations and trying to mitigate potential disagreements because she dislikes disputes.

'Also, she gladly sacrifices her own needs when it comes to supporting our family. Our division of roles gave me time for my career and personal interests, where I have harvested knowledge and pleasure.'

Oracle: 'I am glad to learn that you have developed your ability to reflect and derive many attributes from your family. But where are your challenges?'

Senius: 'You are right. I have consciously chosen to focus only on my positive attributes. It corresponds to the feedback I got on the sundial, by the group and by Rhodopis. I try to deal with my challenges whenever they occur.

'Let me use the same metaphor you used previously, the new computer, to explain that the only program installed was the operating system corresponding to the autonomy system. While I stumble over a challenge in my present state, I attribute it to either of the two reasons: I have a program conflicting with my intentions or I do not have a program at all.

'As an example of the first case, I can say that I was stubborn when I was young. I realised that it was inappropriate and gradually turned stubbornness into persistence, which I believe, is a valuable asset if you have to deliver agreed objectives in projects. I have to admit, though, that it is a delicate balance.

'As an example of the second case: I can request help from somebody I know is good at it and eventually copy the program by practising.'

Oracle: 'I think your approach works well, at least for the cases you have acknowledged. I might add a chain of quotes from classical wisdom, which you can use in similar situations:

Be aware of your thoughts, because they become words.

Be aware of your words, because they become your actions.

Be aware of your actions, because they become your habits.

Be aware of your habits, because they become your characters.

Be aware of your characters, because they become your destiny.

My point is that the chain starts with your thoughts, as an old quote suggests: "You reap what you sow". Whatever issues you want to solve, you must start from your thoughts, irrespective of the level of the chain you have a problem with.

'Let's say you have a bad habit of always looking for a flaw in others to criticise them and you now want to turn that into looking for something you can make a compliment about, you can do the following:

'Shift your focus from blaming to complimenting. Two things happen: first, you famish the old thought, and secondly, you start learning to see positive attributes of other people instead of their faults.

'I know it sounds simple, but in reality, it takes time to learn, because you have to build new paths in your brain. You have to be very conscious of every event. Otherwise, the old program takes over through your subconscious mind.

'The more links down the chain, the more profound the tracks you have to overwrite with the new application. Therefore, the earlier you can become aware of your issues, the better.'

Rhodopis: 'Your statement, "You reap what you sow", reminds me of another metaphor: Thoughts are like seeds in your garden. If you pay attention to them, they will flourish like small plants. You begin to see the outcomes of your thoughts.

'Some plants are weeds, and others are useful. It is time to nurture the useful plants while ignoring the weeds, the negative beliefs, which will make them wither.'

Oracle: 'Rhodopis, it is a poetic metaphor that demonstrates the power of your thoughts.'

Senius: 'I agree, and it reminds me of a statement from Matthew 13:31-32: He told them another parable: "The kingdom of heaven is like a mustard seed, which a man took and planted in his field. Though it is the smallest of all seeds, yet when it grows, it is the largest of garden plants and becomes a tree, so that the birds come and perch in its branches".

'Both your inputs and the Bible's statement reinforce my belief that I have to focus on positive thoughts. I have had issues that were hard to replace. Among others, I remember that as a child, I was shy and insecure.

'At the time, I did not know how to deal with it, and it was not a topic for discussion at home. I did not have a program for dealing with it and had no idea where to get the application. I never realised why I felt that way.'

Oracle: 'What did you do?'

Senius: 'I can hardly remember all my attempts, but as I moved through my higher education, I think I grew, wherein step by step I gained small successes, such as solving problems and presenting solutions for my fellow students. They expressed their acknowledgement, which was a new thing that rarely happened during my childhood days. When I got my diploma, I felt I was ready to conquer the world, and I was full of confidence.'

Oracle: 'The great thing with your example is that even if you do not know the root cause of an issue, it is still possible to solve it because you do not let it stop you. That requires courage. Do you have any other family members or friends who have had an impact on you?'

Senius: 'I did not have any other family members who had an impact on my character. I did have a few friends at the different schools I attended during my childhood, but the friendship faded away as soon as I completed them. My conclusion is that they were only relevant in the context of the situation I was living in.

'On the other hand, it may also be part of my nature. I rarely live in the past, mostly in the present, and when required, in the future.'

Oracle: 'You establish your ability to make and sustain relationships in your childhood. In your case, there has been a strong competition to draw the attention of your primary caregiver—your mother. Your relationship's trigger was primarily personal needs, say, food, a dry diaper and comfort when you were crying.

'When you grow a little older, your mother reads books to you and your siblings. You play games together. You brought this into your adult relationships. For you, relationships need to be purposeful in your way, which means that they have to cover a specific need or task for you.

'In return, you are very loyal and supportive of their needs. Therefore, as your context changed, your friends changed too.'

Senius: 'Thank you. It is a new perspective for me. I have always seen it as a typical trait of men that the relationship is often linked to a specific activity performed together. But let me get back to your original question. I have a friend who has a strong intuition, and her attitude has given me a higher awareness and confidence to use my intuition as a guide in my life.'

Oracle: 'That is interesting. Since intuition is above experience and memory, how do you use it?'

Senius: 'I use it in the creation process, which we will return to later.'

Oracle: 'Fine. Is there anything Rhodopis or our referent wants to add?'

Rhodopis: 'Intuition is one of my main capabilities. It is my guiding star in most of the things that I do and my main source of inspiration.'

Oracle: 'I love your awareness and usage of intuition, Rhodopis. It means that you have a strong connection with your soul, which is a link to the spiritual world.'

Referent: 'I feel I use it in the writing process. It is as if I got connected to a higher power, which lets the thoughts flow through me all the way down to the paper, and I am often surprised with the outcome.'

Oracle: 'It is an excellent example. Intuition is useful in many ways. But the core is that your thoughts connect with the inner dimension of your subject. Their frequency has to match.'

A Life Journey

When you think you are on your own and feel alone,
you have forgotten that the spiritual world is your home.
If you have been caught in what your eyes can reassure,
you have lost sight of your never-ending life of treasure.

If you can accept that you chose your circumstances,
you can see your life with more positive stances.
You will never be a victim but a free and open soul.
Whatever happens, you can with a smile let roll.

When do you know your call and what to do next?
What can support you in reaching out to your life's nest?
Can your common sense and conscience be your light?
And is anybody else bringing you perseverance and delight?

You have to build your convictions on your experiences.
The rationalist will become short in the law of sciences.
That is the essence. Nobody can their life state as rational.
Instead, use your subjective experience as your rationale.

I cannot tell you what you have to do to live your call,
But I hope to inspire you through what I can recall.
Therefore, let us look into what I have used on my journey.
I hope you find inspiration for your incredible life journey.

Source: Senius

On the Life Journey

Oracle: 'Senius, when you look at your life journey, you have found your call and a reference and have harvested beliefs, values and convictions to support you in getting there. Could you share these topics with us?'

Senius: 'Sure, and as you stated, I spent a great part of my adult life figuring out my call to prioritise what I value and evaluate my beliefs. If affirmative, fine, and if not, there is a task in replacing the old belief or rather overwrite the old program.'

Valued Life Areas

Senius: 'Based on our discussions, the absolute number one priority is my reason for being here—my call. The call has two derived focus areas as preconditions:

- Health to have the focus, energy and durability.
- Personal resources as the drive to achieve and contribute out-of-box thinking, development and so on.'

Rhodopis: 'Don't you think that somebody would argue that you are either egocentric or selfish while addressing your own needs first?'

Senius: 'Well, you may argue that but if you consider it in more detail, I am sure that you will see it differently. If you aren't capable of taking care of yourself, you are not capable of taking care of others. Just as it is for love, if you do not love yourself, you cannot truly love others.

'On the other hand, if you fulfil your call, you can master both. Love is the foundation for your call, and your ability to see your relations as they really are will help you understand what they need, although it may be different from what they expect from you.'

Oracle: 'I agree with what you say. It is an essential question, and I want to express it in a metaphor to make it crystal clear. You can compare it to the act of buying a house. You cannot share it with others before you have acquired it.

'And the same goes for love. You can only share it if you have love for yourself. Please proceed.'

Senius: 'Thank you for emphasising. My second priority is my family. Here too, there are preconditions:

- Health is also valued here to live up to my obligations.
- Wealth by having a career to create security and freedom.

My third priority is my relationships. In a way, you can say that "relationships" are too generic. In that case, I will distinguish between my family, close friends, professional relations, neighbours and other acquaintances.

'And here, I will only focus on the group of close friends to whom I feel an outstanding commitment. Besides, some of my friends belong to more than one of the groups.

'Even though I restrict my description here, I have obligations for everybody. We all should help each other whenever we can, besides our respective calls, which is our specific focus area.

'Another side of my valued life areas is that they all give me joy, inspiration and now and then worries, which is an equally essential prerequisite to grow. You may see them as unfavourable, but they are an alarm clock that you can act upon and turn into the light and derive a constructive outcome.

'Whether you consider worries as unfavourable or opportunity for development is a matter of your beliefs, convictions, values and matureness. Alternatively, if you are in a harmonic state with divine love, you can turn worries into compassion.

'My experience, however, taught me that prioritisation is dynamic and very dependent on my actual context. For example, if I am contacted by a friend who needs help, I will automatically prioritise that person's needs. 'Let me go through the prioritised valued areas from an end apart from the personal resources that we have already dealt with previously.'

The Call

Senius: 'Let me summarise my call from the section, "Gaps in Perceptions", illustrated by different pictures:

The Rainbow:	Together with the church, they represent my call as a merger of rethinking my dad and my grandparents' views, freethinking and religious faith.
	The sun behind the scenery represents the Source guiding and supporting me through more insightful souls. The raindrops represent the ocean of souls incarnated together with me.
	A few are my soulmates, some have a connection to my destiny, others support me, and quite a few more are souls who need my guidance and support through my call. The rest have a rare or minor impact.
The Lighthouse:	Stands on an island on solid ground. It is a point of orientation for ships that need to find their way. In the same way, I act as a guide for souls who need help to find their way and have a desire for it. In other words, I only attract souls who have needs that I can support.
The Bird:	Illustrates my gift of great potential. Whether I succeed or not depends on my ability to be a warm seeking soul and strike a balance between being a neutral observer, and at the same time, show empathy.
The Sundial:	Expresses that I primarily count the light hours and focus on having positive thoughts that make me attract what I need to accomplish my call. However, I must also scan my feelings to be aware of negative emotions before they grow and become an issue.

'If you look at my example, the first thing that strikes me is that the most important one has come to me like the last piece of the puzzle, until now! I have flirted with philosophies, religions and spiritual things most of my life. Seen in the back mirror, I do not think it could have been any different.

I have realised that, at least in my case, I needed to grow in terms of maturity to be able to cope with the dissonance that the different inputs have caused in my mind during the transition of understanding.'

Rhodopis: 'I think it is a natural development. To me, it shows that as you become more mature, your call will also change character and direction.'

Oracle: 'I agree with you, Rhodopis. The call is not a static destination. As it matures, it will bring new branches to your call. Another way to put it is that you can nurture your call your entire lifetime.'

Senius: 'It sounds reasonable to me. In my opinion, we all have to contribute something to the world to find meaning in life. This meaning is built upon unconditional love—a concept that can be found in any true religion.

'This is basically what the call is all about. In a way, the lighthouse finely expresses this and may also be used by others, because you can be a lighthouse in many different ways.

'During my search, I also realised that having a call is not a new idea. It is, among others, expressed in Vedic philosophy, which originated from ancient Vedic religion between 2 and 1 millennium BC through a generic purpose consisting of four objectives: Dharma, Artha, Kama and Moksha[3].

'When I talk with people, there is a tendency to put their understanding into what I present as my call. In this way, they colour my call so it fits into their view. You can see this as another example of the metaphor I used in my letter to the pastor—the three men with glasses of three different colours.

---

[3] Source: VedicGranth.Org, Teachings of Vedic Granth, 4 Objectives of Human Life.

'On the other hand, I do something similar when I get new information. There is a significant difference though. When I find further relevant information, I change an old brick in my building and replace it with a new one. In this way, my view is coherent.

'In my opinion, you can imagine your convictions as a building that you have to build from the start with the foundation before making the walls and so on.

'I have practised a part of my call at work; the central piece has been in my spare time, which I probably have inherited from my dad. Meanwhile, I have made it to my primary occupation. But with my knowledge today, I believe for quite a few it is possible to turn your call into your work.

'As an example, I had a colleague who was very happy with his job. I could feel his passion, which is a good indicator showing that he acted out his call. So even though he already passed the average national age of pension, he continued working until he died. I believe it was the right thing to do in his case.

'Another thing worth mentioning is that the group that made the three drawings of me had only known me from the three modules in the process management programme. If you doubt your call, you can invite some of your close friends and ask them to draw a picture of you on a flip chart. And if they care for it, you can make a drawing for each of you.'

Referent: 'You can find additional information in Appendix I, "Exercise 1: Your Personal Drawing".'

Senius: 'Do you have any questions?'

Oracle: 'Well, as your guide, I feel quite happy. Please continue presenting your learnings.'

Senius: 'Okay, and thank you for your appreciation.'

Health

Senius: 'Health is an important topic for me. My body is the temple of my soul, which I honour and respect. It is also a prerequisite for my ability to realise my call.

'In general, if you do not take care of your health, it will lead to an increased risk of diseases and you will have to accept them as a consequence. Therefore, why not take care of it in the first place?'

Oracle: 'You may be right, depending on what the actual call is about. On the other hand, the purpose is not about creating guilt. A disease is a flag indicating a possible imbalance in your life.

'Therefore, change your thoughts and actions while you can. In addition, you have to be aware of the additives present in different kinds of food, e.g., pesticides, chemicals, genetically modified fodder and medicine, among others.'

Senius: 'Thank you. I got your point.

'My rule of thumb is that you should feel good about the choices you make. As Hippocrates (460-370 BC), an ancient physician, stated: "Illnesses do not come upon us out of the blue. They developed from small daily sins against nature. When enough sins have accumulated, illnesses will suddenly appear".

'I want to live long, keeping my capabilities to the end of my life. To accomplish this, I need to keep my body strong and flexible, feed it with healthy food and maintain my mental health. It calls for inspired action.

'Therefore, when I think of health, three things come to mind: physical fitness, diet and mental health. It is not a comprehensive overview, but the main guidelines I use. Besides, it is only a snapshot, which I now and then make new adaptations.

'You can use it as an inspiration to adapt what fits into your context. Let us delve into each one of them.'

Physical Health

Senius: 'I have a general belief that what you do not use, you lose. For instance, the older you are, the more apparent it becomes and the harder it is to rebuild your lost capabilities. My rule of thumb is to walk at least 10,000 steps a day.

'I love hiking and I hike most days, which is definitely not difficult for me unless I am writing or am assigned to other big projects. Hippocrates said, "If you are in a bad mood, go for a walk. If you are still in a bad mood, go for another walk".

'However, to maintain fitness, I find it necessary to get my pulse higher than the one I would usually obtain by hiking. Therefore, I primarily jog or sometimes go for row spinning twice a week. In addition, I perform some high-intensity training every morning as part of my morning rituals.

'Nonetheless, this is only a snapshot and may change. But the need for high-intensity training remains. To keep my body flexible, I practice yoga and other stretching exercises every morning. I also incorporate breathing exercises to the session to increase and maintain my blood oxygen level.'

Diet

Senius: 'The primary purpose is to keep the body light. To achieve this, it is necessary to avoid consuming heavy foods, such as meat. Vegan foods can help achieve this.

'I started being vegan more than five years ago, but I must admit that being vegan is too fundamentalist for me. Nevertheless, I respect those who make this choice as long as they acknowledge that others are in a different development stage.

'I am a vegetarian, but I am not religious about it. It is another example of the rainbow view once again. In reality, I am indeed a flexitarian, which complies with my fundamental life view. I can eat what I feel like.

'For me, it makes a huge difference. It is a voluntary decision without any rules I have to obey which fits well into my general understanding of personal freedom. The only rule I have is that I want to feel good with the choices I make.

'I use intermediate fasting most days which means that I skip breakfast to elongate my body's time to repair. The only thing I have in the morning is a glass of water with lemon juice (half lemon) to cleanse my body.

'For lunch, I usually start with a smoothie which consists of a mixture of fruits, vegetables, ginger, turmeric and fatty acids like omega 3, 6 and 9. This gives my body what it needs and improves my immune system.

'I often have a piece of rye bread (a national tradition) with cottage cheese which I mix with a spoonful each of flaxseed oil and wheatgrass powder. It is a variant of the German biochemist Johanna Budwig's recipe to protect the body against cancer. It also gives me a lot of proteins.

'If I care for more, I mostly indulge in some vegetarian food. Now and then I eat pickled herrings, which is another national dish.

'On special occasions, I eat meat, primarily fish and chicken. During some of our family traditions such as Easter and Christmas, we eat lamb and duck, respectively. I ensure that the fish I eat is sourced from the open seas and not from fishing farms, and that chicken, duck and lamb have lived free-ranged in their natural surroundings.

'I rarely eat processed food and fast food. Healthy food has to be produced from the basic ingredients without any artificial additives primarily organic vegetables, nuts and fruits, and meat products should be based on ethics.

'I drink a lot of water. During the last two years, I have also produced my version of kombucha—fermented tea. I use less sugar than the standard recipe prescribes, and I have chosen my variants of green tea mixes to boost my immune system.

'I do not use any food supplements, other than the ones mentioned above, or vitamin pills.'

Oracle: 'There is an old quote that states: "If you want to live longer, you should make your meals shorter".'

Referent: 'You can find the recipes in Appendix II.'

Fasting

Oracle: 'You mentioned you use intermediate fasting. Can you elaborate a little further on this?'

Senius: 'I use this tool to give my body more time to repair itself as it prolongs life. The intermediate fasting I follow allows me a window to eat a maximum of 6 hours. In the remaining time, I drink water, tea and coffee without any additives. I have chosen to skip my breakfast.

'My first meal is at lunchtime and dinner is my last meal. I end my day with a glass of water with a little Himalayan salt, juice from half a lemon and a spoonful of apple cider vinegar or fire cider. The latter is a mix of healthy pickled ingredients where apple cider vinegar is used as brine.

'I know that some Buddhists skip their dinner instead. Others' practices can be extreme wherein they eat only one meal a day. For me, it is too radical. Generally, the purpose is to find a set-up that fits well with the individual needs you have.'

Oracle: 'If you want to boost your health once in a while, the intermediate fasting may be complemented by prolonged fasting[4], where you fast for a prolonged number of days.'

Senius: 'I have done some research on this and found many different types of fasting. Do you have any recommendations?'

Oracle: 'It is very much dependent of what you want to obtain. As it is the key driver for your motivation, it is worthwhile to be clear about this from the beginning. For example, it could be a way to reduce excess fat in the body, which is a far more efficient way than reducing the number of calories.

'The reason is that the latter does not change the way your body utilises energy. Another reason could be to repair the body to obtain better health and longevity.'

Senius: 'From my perspective, the purpose is to clean the body for toxins, reinforce the immune system and replace damaged proteins to improve the quality of my life. Besides, I'm fine with achieving longevity too.

Prolonged fasting consists of four phases:

- The Planning Phase entails searching about what you want to obtain and how you want to carry it through.

---

[4] You can find a YouTube video by Dr. Berg DC, which gives an excellent overview of the benefits and the processes during prolonged fasting:
https://www.youtube.com/watch?v=vhmtoAYVRSo&t=279s

- The Preparation Phase consists of things you can do to create motivation and make the transition smoothly.
- Fasting Phase is where you fast and have considered the frames you want to carry it through.
- Refeeding phase is where you gradually switch back to a normal diet, maybe with some new healthy habits.'

Referent: 'You can find more details in Appendix I, Exercise 2: Prolonged Fasting.'

Mental Health

Oracle: 'The cornerstone in mental health is peace and happiness, which are qualities you can find only within yourself. This inner state makes you independent of your external circumstances. A precondition to obtaining this state is that you surrender to absolute forgiveness to both your fellow human beings as well as to yourself.'

Senius: 'Conceptually, I completely agree with your clarification. But in my present state, I find it hard to realise it. Why do I feel this gap?'

Oracle: 'The major reason is your unfulfilled desires; there is something you want to possess or achieve, and this lack of something disrupts your internal peace and happiness, which then erodes your mental health and result in diseases. It breaks the balance between mind and body. It also disconnects you from the Source, thus filling you with emptiness and making you feel even more miserable.'

Senius: 'It makes complete sense. On the other hand, if I have no desires, where is the inspiration to do anything and thus fulfil one's call stem from?'

Oracle: 'I understand your scepticism. You're mixing your desires with your call and both represent a gap. But there is a major difference between the two gabs. A desire is a craving that stems from your ego.

'The call, on the other hand, is a vocation to heal your soul. And my usage of "you" in connection with the soul is your true self, which you probably know already.

'Peace and happiness are not purposes in themselves; they are prerequisites to fulfilling your call. But let me come back to your view. What do you do to maintain your mental health?'

Senius: 'I have realised that there is an interdependence between body and soul. Therefore, I practice yoga to keep my body flexible and help focus my mind on meditation. I use *The Five Tibetans*[5], which is a form of yoga exercise.

'The purpose is to balance the seven main chakras[6], which means that the energy can flow unfettered through them. It supports both physical and mental health and prolongs your life.'

Oracle: 'Meditation and yoga are other important disciplines to maintain mental health. However, I will leave it aside for now as we'll come back to this topic later.'

Senius: 'It's fine with me. I hike almost daily. It is also a form of meditation for me when I do it on my own. When I do it with others, it is mostly an inspiration to reflect upon the big questions of life. For example, my last Camino experience brought a vital puzzle piece to my call.

'My writing helps my mental health as well, and it is a great pleasure and playground for drawing the full picture of my puzzle. Hopefully, it is also a source of inspiration for those who have the chance to read my story.

'Another encouraging activity is to watch documentary movies on YouTube on subjects I find interesting and read great books.

'I have started to learn a new language, Spanish, for two reasons. I usually visit a Hispanic-speaking country every year, and in some places, I know people who talk only in Spanish. I would appreciate having a conversation with them. Besides, it maintains some of my essential brain capabilities.

'Finally, I maintain my mental health by exchanging experiences with my family, friends and people who share the same interests as mine.

---

[5] If you want to learn how to practice these exercises, you can look up 'The 5 Tibetans Rites' on YouTube

[6] The chakras are described later as a section in 'Foundations.'

'When it comes to friends, I am very selective. I primarily choose people who are concerned about their self-development. Besides, I work on reducing negative discussions as they bring our frequency down and attract more misery.

'It is far better to have a constructive approach that raises the frequency and builds mental energy. It means seeing them as opportunities to grow.'

Oracle: 'I agree. Generally, people consider a problem unfavourable. But if you choose to see it as an opportunity, it is converted into a favourable challenge that has the potential to bring you new insights and improve your development. Another way of saying it is that you have attracted the issue to heal a gap in your call.

'Therefore, do not meet issues with resistance, but with gratitude. It will also make you calmer, constructive and improve your ability to master the new challenges whenever they pop up.

'There are also tougher incidents. You have managed to get through life with some severe knockouts. And those you did have, you chose to process healthily. But people who get severely hit by them are at risk. For example, job loss, divorce, severe diseases, loss of close relatives, and so on.

'The point I want to make is how you choose to respond to different events in life. It is about resilience, which is linked to your beliefs about your actual situation. I will come back to this topic later.'

Wealth

Senius: 'At the beginning of my professional life, I focused on taking over the responsibility of my father's company, but the situation changed rapidly. I then joined another far larger enterprise and kept improving my skills and abilities by specialising further within the different professional areas I was in through various project undertakings.

'This was not something I had to do, but I did it out of sheer interest, which was the driving force. In fact, one of my directors could not understand why I would spend more years to obtain an MBA on top of the education I already possessed.

'Nonetheless, he accepted my decision and the company funded the programme. I must admit that with time, you may forget why you wanted to work in the first place; in my case, the reason was to gain security and financial freedom. In the process, I got caught in the hamster wheel during the last few years of employment.

'My income, however, had exceeded way more than we needed. This, however, was not driven by revenue but by a commitment to deliver my assignments on time and as intended; the workload was significant. On the other hand, this gave my wife and I the economic freedom to do what we want.

'In the back mirror, I also ran my private economy the same way one would do with a business, which has added to our economic freedom. First, I made a monthly balance that showed my planned and actual operating costs, which I suppose many households do too. But the most valuable part for me has been the balance between assets and liabilities.

'I did set a goal for the annual development in equity. Through this exercise, I learnt how to optimise income, debt, assets, pension schemes, tax and investment. In addition, I was more comfortable to have a balanced dialogue with my bank and pension advisor.'

Family

Senius: 'I will, in this context, see childhood through the role of a parent. My experience tells me that any family is dysfunctional to a greater or lesser degree. However, I believe that parents do the best they can. And remember, parents have been children too in the past and have inherited many traits from their close relations.

'As we were waiting for the birth of our first child, I was reading about raising children and had meaningful discussions with my wife. We had a pretty good idea of how to give and do the best for her. When our daughter was born, reality hit us.

'Among others, our baby had colic and issues with her ears. It was hard to comfort her and get coherent sleep, making it difficult to live up to the grand intentions as we had discussed.

'When parents have issues and tend to pass on their frustrations to their children, the children often hold themselves accountable for everything that is going wrong. As a result, this gives birth to a negative self-image. Therefore, as one of the many countermeasures, remember to let them know that they are appreciated and make them feel acknowledged. It is essential to compliment them when they do great things and not only for their initiative.

'At one end of the spectrum, some children grow up to be modest and choose the last row, which may have them attracted towards the feeling of being "wrong" or "unworthy". This in turn becomes a breeding ground to attract other life situations that make them feel the same way—"wrong" or "unworthy".

'On the other end of the spectrum, you have children where parents allow them to believe that they are "perfect" and second to none, which potentially makes them intolerable egocentric. In many cases, when faced with the realities of life as adults, they feel inadequate.

'My point is that any extreme rarely makes any good. There needs to be a natural balance between the individual and the community to create mutual respect.

'As already stated, my wife and I have had the pleasure to be parents in two pools. In the back mirror, we raised our first two kids in a similar way as our respective parents did, basically unconscious copy-pasting of programmes where we corrected a few things.

'When they were children, I believe it was vital for them to have clear and loving frames. It also means that if you have said no to one of their wishes, it is non-negotiable. It creates peace and easy-going relationships—a topic where my wife and I have at times disagreed. And our kids utilised that.

'Depending on the issue, they knew whether they should ask Mum or Dad. On the other hand, it is also part of their social skills. One of the unfortunate issues with our way of raising our kids was that if they crossed the line, the consequence was punishment, without a pedagogical explanation of the reason behind it.

'With our youngest daughter, we were more engaged in her activities and encouraged her to become more mature emotionally at an early age. But I also believe it was part of a significant change in time due to technological advancements.

'The need for passing the border of the agreed rules was rare, but when it did happen, it was with less tension. Another way of saying it is that we were more comfortable and appreciated our role as parents and what we did was more of advises, even though it was not perfect. But I think it is part of human nature to use a trial-error learning process.

'The children also learn that their parents are not perfect either. This approach may also make the individual more robust and forgiving of themselves and others.

'In our case, with time our beliefs have also become more mature and more balanced. And we did what we could to be good parents. We tried to hand over some of our experiences that she could use to qualify her own choices. However, in many cases, I have to admit that the transfer of skills is rarely successful.

'In most cases, children have to learn their lessons on their own. Nevertheless, I suppose most parents try anyway.

'Through my culturally coloured glasses, I think the most important qualifications we can give our children are that they can live as independent adults and that they are able to balance between their self-esteem and skills.

'When they become adults, it is every parent's desire, I believe, that their children consider them as their confidential friends with whom they can share their joy, worries and seek support in times of need.

'Nevertheless, all our children are doing well in their own ways, which is a great pleasure for us as parents.'

Close Relationships

Senius: 'I think it is essential to distinguish between close or real friendships and just friendly relationships. The first category refers to friends who encourage you to live out your dreams and always support you in difficult times. As I often say, whenever you are in trouble, you will realise who your real friends are.

'The second category refers to friends who benefit from knowing you and your network. If you choose to do something different and leave your highly respected position, they are gone.

'For example, when my dad went bankrupt with his shipyard, his greatest disappointment was that most of his friends turned their back on him. Even friends, he previously had helped out during their difficult situations.

'Another category is people you meet for a reason. It is often people you have attracted to help you solve one of your questions. It also goes the other way around; people you meet to resolve one of their issues.

'And then you have those who you meet for everyday experiences, such as pleasant memories, but you only meet them in that context, e.g., vacations, concerts and exhibitions. The friends I talk about here are close friends only.

'My wife and I have spent most of our time with our own little family and my parents-in-law. However, we both have a few close friends who we meet with separately. My wife has known hers since her high school and apprenticeship.

'In my case, most of them are colleagues from my former company. We do not meet very often, and when we do, it is mostly one-to-one. Nevertheless, I find it inspiring and appreciate that we can discuss whatever topic we are occupied by at the time of the meeting. Most importantly, they are there whenever you need them.

'One of them is a particular case because it was as if we had known each other for years when we met. When this happens, I believe we have met in an earlier incarnation or have something to share within our calls.'

Oracle: 'I agree with your statement, which I will return to later. In addition, I can add to your presentation that there are two prevalent topics in people's minds when they are dying; things that they did not manage to accomplish when they could and issues in connections with family members or friends.

'But I have a few other things to add. When you talked about your childhood, you told me that you felt that you had a secure home base. This element is crucial for your ability to create and maintain relationships, whether temporary or permanent. Relationships are an essential part of bringing quality into anybody's life.

'You also benefit from this in your choice of partner, who has had the same benefit as you have. Both of you are comfortable and allows you to rely on each other. For you, it likewise leaves space for individual interests like travels or hikes.

'A final remark is that your secure home base has given you confidence about being on your own. Therefore, you never feel lonesome. Relationships are active opt-in for you.'

Senius: 'Thank you for your comments. It makes me feel very fortunate.'

A New Challenge

Dear friend, have you found inspiration for your call?
If not, do not give up. It is there for you to recall.
If you are trustful, you cannot miss the dream of your aim.
The more focused you are, the earlier you can your call claim.

Remember dear seeker, you are never on your own nor alone.
As soon as you respond to your soul, the door will open.
The light from above will your lighthouse bright ignite.
Soon the light will bring your call in your mind delight.

With your call, you a reference for your life have found.
Now you can get about your valued life areas around.
Suddenly you realise what you have to prioritise.
Prerequisites to your call, which you need to realise.

With your call in mind, you need to checkout each belief.
Do they support your call, and are you ready for release?
Which values have your beliefs in your mind generated?
Do they fit with your call, or do they need to be regenerated?

Source: Oracle

The Community

Oracle: 'Until now, we have been occupied by life from a personal standpoint. When it comes to the national and international community, it is interesting primarily from two perspectives: the impact on each of you and the impact you can have on it. But it also shows that most people still act from an ego standpoint.

'To set the community into this context, I feel a need for addressing the real issues from a holistic point of view. As this discussion is up to your alley, Rhodopis, I think you should unfold this topic.'

Rhodopis: 'Thank you. I really care about this topic.'

Key Challenges the World Is Facing

Rhodopis: 'Let me start by saying that what I want to present to you is the overall picture in brief. Of course, you will find some exceptions, but they do not change the overall picture. Besides, the perspective can be observed from different positions.

'The first position is from a personal view and the second is where you watch others. These are extremely different perceptions. For example, in a war, a patriot is considered a hero among his own people.

'The enemy, however, will perceive the same person as a terrorist. And both stakeholders believe that their perception is the truth. I intend to present the outside perspective, the third position, which is a neutral one.

'At present, the climate has gained a lot of attention for good reasons. Meanwhile, populous countries have gained higher living standards, such as China, India, Indonesia and Pakistan, to mention a few of the significant ones. This accelerated the pollution to the extreme. It is not to blame anybody as they strive to achieve the same standard of living as they see in developed countries.

'However, it is just the tip of the iceberg; CO_2 is only one factor of the many types of pollutions. Chemicals, pesticides, particles, micro-plastic, escape of radioactivity from nuclear reactors, resistant bacteria, new dangerous viruses, etc. pop up due to human irresponsibility.

'The pollutions have mainly appeared within the last one and a half-century; a short period when you take the Earth's age into account. Moreover, pollution is multiplying because of the dramatic growth of consumption worldwide. On top of all this, the world population is growing with untenable annual growth rates.

'This development is unsustainable. The more people, the higher the consumption of everything causing the depletion of our natural resources and eventually the destruction of the environment.

'The other side of the consumption is the over-exploitation of the natural resources, which took nature millions of years to provide, such as crude oil.'

Senius: 'What about farming?'

Rhodopis: 'A similar development has taken place within farming to improve productivity. Farming is going through industrialisation, and it is a significant shift in production.

'The animals lose their freedom and are deported to overcrowded stalls or open fields without their natural surroundings, which are far away from their natural environment. They are fed unnatural fodder, such as genetically manipulated corn, and additives, such as artificial vitamins and minerals, to grow faster. Many animals are vaccinated pre-emptively to avoid diseases. And all of this ends up on your plate.

'The industry makes processed food containing ingredients with low nutrition and many additives, such as sugar, salt, saturated fat and preservatives, to mention a few. Overall, the outcomes are diseases such as obesity, cardiovascular diseases, and type 2 diabetes. These additives, combined with the increasing pollution, have become a breeding ground for the dramatic increase in cancer.

'The medical industry profits from these situations. They introduce new medicines that reduce the symptoms of people affected with diseases as a result of consuming mediocre food.

'It also keeps the healthcare system busy, while trying to ward off the most significant damages. In a way, the system should be renamed to "disease system" as it deals mainly with diseases that are nothing but symptoms. Healthcare employees are not to blame. They do what they can.

'Another very potent risk is the storage of nuclear bombs, which has the potential of laying waste to the entire world. In terms of figures, Russia and the US detain 90% of all nuclear weapons.

'However, although the rest of the world has far less atomic bombs, they remain a threat to the entire world. Just one delusion of grandeur and other worldliness of a leader with access to an atomic bomb can start a nuclear war with consequences that affect everybody.'

Senius: 'I understand your analysis. On the other hand, many businesses see your analysis as an opportunity for new business areas. It is only a matter of time.

'What is the root cause of this situation in the big picture?'

Rhodopis: 'You hit the critical issue with your question. The main reason is that most people act on behalf of their ego which is primarily interested in what is in it for me or on a great day, maybe my nation. The misery is created by a mindset that acts upon the ego at different levels.'

Senius: 'What is the medicine to overcome all the key issues you have mentioned?'

Rhodopis: 'I like your constructive question, Senius, and it is the next topic I want to raise.'

Countermeasures to Key Issues

Oracle: 'Before you continue, Rhodopis, I would like to set the scene. Based on the last century, my observation is that potentially many more souls will increase in maturity in this millennium, which will accelerate the evolution and impact people's views regarding morale, ethic and wholeness.

Spiritually, it may evolve into a global network.'

Senius: 'It reminds me of an old trinity: liberty, equality and brotherhood from the French revolution (initially "or dead" as an appendix). If that spreads to the world, it would help a lot.'

Rhodopis: 'Fine with me, but a millennium in the context of pollution might be far too late. Besides, Senius, the sundial really fits you.'

Oracle: 'Dear, Rhodopis, I think you are still too pessimistic. As I told you, you need to shift focus. More souls will mature and supersede the ego, resulting in a new awakening that will convince most that existence depends entirely on your co-existence on Earth.

Besides, the pollution you mentioned as well as the other global issues will reduce the old arguments' power. Please continue.'

Rhodopis: 'Thank you. The first step in any countermeasure is to agree upon the goals to overcome the obstacles we have just discussed. Here, there seems to be light at the end of the tunnel. The UN has formulated 17 Sustainable Development Goals that were agreed upon in 2015:

#1: No Poverty
#2: Zero Hunger
#3: Good Health and Well-being
#4: Quality Education
#5: Gender Equality
#6: Clean Water and Sanitation
#7: Affordable and Clean Energy
#8: Decent Work and Economic Growth
#9: Industry, Innovation and Infrastructure
#10: Reduced Inequality
#11: Sustainable Cities and Communities
#12: Responsible Consumption and Production
#13: Climate Action

#14: Life Below Water

#15: Life on Land

#16: Peace and Justice Strong Institutions

#17: Partnerships to Achieve the Goal

'Furthermore, they have concretised targets by 2030, thus making the ambitions clearer. It is a great starting point for the required transformation.'

Senius: 'I fully agree with the intentions, and I also see some progress. Do you think they can be realised?'

Rhodopis: 'Well, I feel you imply that it could be a challenge, which I agree to. Anyway, as Oracle said just before let us see it from the bright side. It is a significant step in the right direction, and if Oracle's prediction holds the situation will improve.

'In compliance with Oracle's prophecy, the situation will change. People who get elected will operate at the soul level, ensuring a wholeness view or at least a holistic view across the different borders. It will also break up the populists selling simplified messages in an increasingly complex world, which increases the gap between its citizens.'

Senius: 'Seen in this big picture, I believe that generally speaking the citizens of any country will prefer an evolution instead of a revolution. It gives everybody time to understand the changes and adapt to them. It also leaves time for business to turn some of the key issues into business opportunities, which can be supported by the respective nation's governments and public services requesting the products and services.'

Rhodopis: 'Thank you, Senius. Your comments bring me in a better mood.'

Oracle: 'I am glad about observing the development in your dialogue. It is like a coin with two sides. When you started with the "as is" situation, you spoke about the backside of the coin. By the Law of Attraction, you will attract more which can confirm you in that view.'

Rhodopis: 'I apologise. Now when you point fingers at it, I must admit that I also feel bad about it, which confirms your ascertainment.'

Oracle: 'I am glad that you recognise that your feelings pulled you down on a lower frequency in the beginning. It is also an illustrative example. The positive question Senius asked you at the end triggered you, Rhodopis, to look at the coin's head side. To reinforce the energy, I wanted to set the scene to ensure that you kept your focus on the head side of the coin.'

Community's Impact on Individuals

Rhodopis: 'It is prerequisite making a community work, that there are rules to make it operates. As a consequence, individual rights get restricted. Let me illustrate this with a visual example. You have to decide whether cars have to drive on the right or left to avoid chaos.

'In general terms, each country has a constitution that describes the rights and duties its citizens have. It also explains to what extent a nation wants to distribute its power. Many different perspectives can characterise it. I can illustrate this through a few examples.

'The power may be regulated based on confidence or control. In the first case, it is built on values, and the latter on bureaucracy. The trend is more control while the world becomes more complex. It is a Gordian knot that is hard to solve.

'Freedom of speech can be more or less valued, or even unwanted. The threefold division of power with arm's length is fundamental: Executive, legislative and judicial power. This principle is enforced in most nations, while others want to centralise control. It depends among others whether you live in a democracy or a dictatorship, respectively.

'It will be interesting to follow how the UN's 17 Sustainable Development Goals will be incorporated and how they will address the issues discussed in the beginning.

'Another significant issue is that none of the present social science models faces these crucial challenges. While consumer growth has been an option on a national level but not globally. It creates many new dilemmas that also require significant paradigm shifts.

'Unless you take part in this through development or interest organisations, it is something where you have a minor impact. Therefore, I will suggest we look at what you can do on your own.'

Your Responsibility Towards the Community

Rhodopis: 'At a personal level, the best thing you can do for the community is to be an excellent example for your surroundings. You may think this is nothing but a negligible drop in a vast ocean, but that is not the case. Let me illustrate using an example.

'In your country, Senius, during the last years, people have become more convinced that they should eat less meat. A few have of course chosen the ultimate shift to be vegans or vegetarians. It is excellent! But the most significant impact comes from the bigger group of people who have implemented meatless days during the week.

'It has been a movement from the bottom. The effect has been strong enough to cause a remarkable drop in demand for meat. Besides, it has created a market for vegan meat substitutes. As it is processed food, I see this as a transition solution to support a change of habits.

'Meanwhile, health authorities have come up with new dietary guidelines recommending you to eat less than 350g of meat per week. It reflects a general movement towards the consumption of vegetarian food in your country.

'One of the main issues in these kinds of changes is the change of habits. In a traditional western main dish, three main ingredients are on the plate: meat, vegetables and potatoes, pasta or rice. The challenge is to change this view is in your old habit and realise that it can look differently, and support is at hand.

'It is easy to find many recipes on the internet if you want to change your habit and get better health. Another source of inspiration can be food from other regions of the world, e.g., Asian cuisines.

'My point is that your consumer behaviour impacts the producers. So much that they spend a lot of money on marketing to influence your practice. Your contribution can be to consume food that lives up to your conscience, e.g., make food from raw materials to avoid unhealthy additives.

'You can spread this to all other kinds of consumption and impact your social circles. In other words, you become a political consumer.'

Senius: 'For the most part, I implement this in terms of what I consume. I have also seen extreme cases of minimalism, for example, which I think is great but hard to implement in the existing building heritage.'

Rhodopis: 'You are right. Some initiatives are nearly impossible to implement, like minimalism for most people. But they can inspire you and create more awareness, so you redirect and reduce your consumption. The preceding example also illustrates this. Besides, there is considerable potential in consuming less in rich countries, reducing waste, and buying sustainable products.

'For example, when you buy furniture for your home, instead of buying economical furniture using the concept "buy, use and throw away"; you can purchase second-hand sustainable furniture or new ones that can last your entire life. It would mean a lot for the overall consumption and pollution.'

Senius: 'I see your point, but for people with low income, it would be hard to implement. Wouldn't it?'

Rhodopis: 'You are right, but if those who have the resources buy sustainable furniture, the market for second-hand durable furniture also grows to more attractive prices. It can be an alternative to buy economical unendurable things.

'This applies to food as well. The more people shift to organic food, the more farmers will move from conventional farming to more sustainable agriculture, which will drive prices down to a more competitive level.

'From a health perspective, it will also improve peoples' health and reduce demand for medicine and health care. This is good news for people and nations who contribute through funding to both areas. On the contrary, this is bad news for the corresponding private industries whose market is that of treating symptoms. It will require new social science models that fit into different forms of national governments.'

Oracle: 'Thank you for your contribution, Rhodopis. Let me end this topic with a more general statement: Focus on what you want, because that will manifest what you desire to experience.'

Your Contribution to the Community

You know your call and have your valued life areas found.
Besides you from your call beliefs and values get around.
It reinforces your personal integrity as an energetic shield.
But make your efforts and aims to your community yield?

The world is facing many and complex encounters.
But who on Earth can create countermeasures?
The nations set their own agenda as first priority.
The world is suffering while all choose their territory.

UN is the only organisation who can the world rule.
But for now, it has only collaboration as a tool.
UN needs a mandate if the root causes are released.
But do you think that the nations are pleased?

A naïve request to raise and condemned with dignity.
Nations do not voluntarily hand over sovereignty.
While the nations discuss, nature is suffering.
Is there an alternative for you surrendering?

You might think it is like a drop in a big sea,
but you will wonder when you the result see.
It is like you make a snowball on a top of a hill.
When you let it go, nobody can ignore your will!

Source: Senius

Foundations

Oracle: 'As mentioned earlier, your reincarnation starts with an empty board where you uncritically copy your beliefs from your close relations. This gradually creates the reference of how you interpret your environment and act in it. On the other hand, it is not a coincidence because you have chosen the frames yourself.

'Another way to put it is that you have selected these frames based upon your level of insight, consciousness and maturity, combined with the discussions you had with me and your remaining relations here.

'The luggage you bring with you from your past lives is stored in your soul and is a potential resource that may create excellent opportunities for you to realise your call in the frames you have chosen. The barriers between the call and the resources represent the experiences you have to gain in this life. Altogether, it can bring you to the destiny you are seeking.

'In the following, we will look into some basic frames and foundations that can give you an understanding of how some critical factors in your life play together.'

The Cognitive Diamond

Oracle: 'Our perception has an enormous impact on the quality of our lives. I know you are familiar with this model, and I think it is a great way to explain some of the critical interactions between thoughts, feelings, behaviour and body. As we will come back to this topic several times throughout our discussions, it is worthwhile to delve into it now as we advance.

'Do you mind unfolding your experience with the model?'
Senius: 'Sure. I learnt the model in connection to my certification of becoming a coach.

Figure 1. The Cognitive Diamond

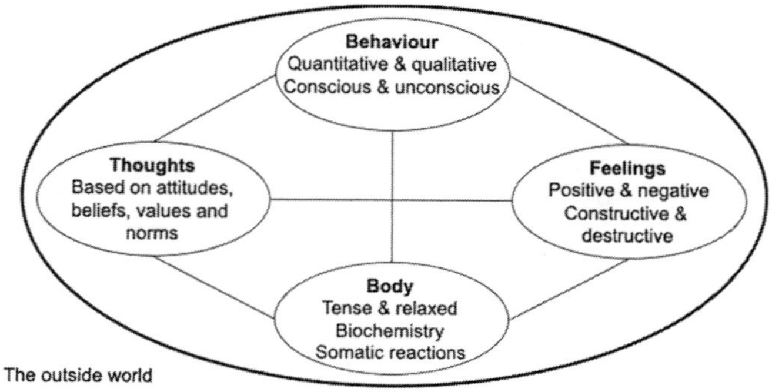

Behaviour
Quantitative & qualitative
Conscious & unconscious

Thoughts
Based on attitudes,
beliefs, values and
norms

Feelings
Positive & negative
Constructive &
destructive

Body
Tense & relaxed
Biochemistry
Somatic reactions

The outside world

Source: Axept Coaching Programme, Module 1 by Birgitte Jepsen, 2007 in Denmark

To me, it was a fantastic eye-opener. The cognitive theory has presupposed that thoughts come first, which also fits the classical wisdom you referred to previously:

Be aware of your thoughts because they become words.

Be aware of your words because they become your actions.

Be aware of your actions because they become your habits.

Be aware of your habits because they become your characters.

Be aware of your characters because they become your destiny.

'What became very apparent to me was that our upbringing, culture and religion impact all the four factors indicated in Figure 1. It also explains why we experience massive dissonances between people with different upbringings.

'In coaching, a significant part of the focus is to look into beliefs and behaviours the focus person perceives as inappropriate compared to what he or she wants to obtain.

'Our thoughts and feelings have a significant impact on our behaviour, whether it is optimistic or pessimistic. We can think of our body as health or disease depending on our perception.

'Another way of saying it is that our thoughts and feelings are our compass that helps to navigate our lives. Therefore, whenever a negative feeling shows up, we need to convert it into an opportunity. Otherwise, there is a risk that it turns into something that will create barriers and even diseases.'

Oracle: 'I can confirm that both sufferings and joy originate from what perspective you choose to bestow your focus. You are the creator of your reality.

'Anyway, I believe it is an excellent introduction to the model. It gives a great overview of how your ego operates. On top of that, there is a spiritual dimension. It is your most precious part—the soul, which we already have mentioned quite a few times.'

The Soul

Oracle: 'The soul has more synonyms like superconscious mind, the self and so on. In a nutshell, the soul is your "true self" or "I". The former model can be portrayed in a triangle, shown in the figure below, on the left side. The triangle becomes the basement of a pyramid with three sides, where the top represents the soul.

'From this level, your ego is just a tool, which you will leave behind as an empty holster when you die. The soul contains your memories from all your incarnations and remains eternal.'

Rhodopis: 'I see that the soul has connections to both thoughts, feelings and body. How do we secure that the soul has the lead over the ego to fulfil its call?'

Oracle: 'It is an essential question. Thank you, Rhodopis. As you can see in Figure 2, the soul communicates with all three tools via your intuition.

Figure 2. The Links Between Ego and Soul.

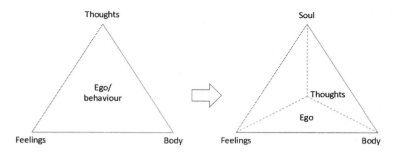

Source: Own interpretation of relationship between ego and soul

'As an example, the soul sends ideas that pop up in your mind. In the beginning, you probably believe these ideas came from your ego. But as you become more mature, you start seeing a clear distinction.

'Thoughts from the soul are pure and founded on divine love, compassion and freedom. Ego desires are short-term positive feelings and often create cravings or guilt afterward.

'When you do something that complies with your call, even if it may be unconscious for you, the soul will send you great feelings distinctly different from what you can obtain through your ego desires. You feel blessed. However, it also works the other way around. When you get a negative feeling, it can be because you violate your call, which is a message from your soul.

'Alternatively, your ego desires make you break the norms of your society or other learnt behaviours. Most ego pleasures do not last as they often intimidate others.

'The most unmistakable sign for the body for receiving sensations from the soul is that you feel lighter. You can get a similar sensation if you exercise as the body creates some of the same chemicals, making you feel happy. However, the feeling from the soul is more profound and lasts longer.

'The last and most critical issue is your free will. Whenever you choose to use your will for egoistic purposes, you compromise your call! Intuition is always the shortest way to the goal.

'However, it takes time to build up relying on your intuition. Like any other skill, you have to develop it through praxis to build confidence through experience.'

Rhodopis: 'This gives me a new insight into a line in the Lord's Prayer, Matthew 6:10: "Your kingdom come, your will be done, on earth as it is in heaven". As we decide to replace our will with the will of the Source, our respective calls can flourish.'

Oracle: 'It is a nice way to describe the divine will as the Source is always there for you. You just have to tune in by raising your frequency to be able to receive whatever you decide.'

Senius: 'It triggered some of my memories from my first Camino Francés in 2017. While visiting the Cathedral in Santiago de Compostela, I got a contrast-filling feeling. On the one hand, the experience was lavish and beautiful, quite overwhelming.

'On the other hand, I imagined all the sacrifices that had been made to realise this place. I felt a compelling encouragement to move on to the end of the world, Finisterre.

'Furthermore, a pilgrim I met earlier on the trail said to me after our discussion: "Your goal is not Santiago de Compostela, it is Finisterre". The incident confirmed my feelings.

'I got ready to leave for Fisterra—as it was spelt on the first array stone I found. On my way, I started reflecting on what is required to let the soul become an instrument for the Source. Maybe it is the connection between the Source (God), the Spirit (the Holy Spirit) and the soul (God breathed into Adam's nostrils the breath of life, and the man became a living being).

'The soul became conscious as Eve and Adam ate from the tree of the knowledge of good and evil. I decided to let it stay open and realise the answer when the time is ripe.

'Later on the journey, I realised that it is about whether I dare to believe what I want or not, as Rhodopis expressed. While the soul is a mouthpiece for the Source, it requires nothing else. But to get there, I need to practice my call with unconditional love in order to tune into the corresponding higher frequency. As a practitioner, I am getting into the Source and becoming an intermediator.'

Senius: 'Do you agree with my derivations?'

Oracle: 'Very profound derivations, but I am not sure I have the insight to unfold it for you. Can you add further comments?'

Senius: 'As I see it, the ego cannot stand in between, because the soul is above the ego. But I believe that the ego will try to tell you something else as it does not want to lose control. I don't think that the ego can surpass the soul's consciousness, as the soul makes itself more and more available to the Source.

'That means it is now my soul's actions complying with the divine Source. So, the only thing I have to do is to let go of the ego, which means what is in my human nature that resists, disguised as vices.'

Oracle: 'Thank you, Senius. I am very impressed. But I am sorry to say I cannot give you a comprehensive explanation as you bring me to the limit of my knowledge. But I assume that you will get another chance to get it evaluated later.

'I can, however, explain a part of your question. Your soul is contained in an energy centre labelled *Soul Star* that is situated above your head. It holds your essence with two components. First is the divine part, e.g., divine love and compassion which contains your potential for enlightenment and unity.

'The second component is, among others, your soul, including former incarnations, spiritual capabilities and karma. And karma represents what you want to experience in your present incarnation through your call.

'To execute your call, you are required to fully understand and trust your "true self" or "I". It is the only way you can create harmony in your life. It takes strong faith to execute your call fully.

'The Soul Star is also bridging the spiritual world and your ego as represented in the former pyramid in Figure 2. At the same time, it is another view of your ego, which we will look briefly into now. It is denominated as *chakras* in Sanskrit, meaning "wheels" or "spinning energy discs".'

Chakras

Oracle: 'Another way to understand the concept of the connection between your soul and your body is through energy centres. You have seven main energy centres in your body, labelled as *chakras*.

'They start below the Soul Star. It is your connection with the Source, and through this channel, it potentially connects you to all other souls. Although not an exhaustive description, Table 1 shows some selected features of chakras, and additional information can easily be found on the internet.'

Table 1. Characteristic Features of Chakras

Chakra	Location	Colour	Function	Inner state	Physical ex.
Crown	Top of head.	Violet	Understanding psychic capabilities	Bliss, Spirituality	Pineal gland, Brain, Nervous
Third Eye	Centre of forehead above the eyebrows	Indigo	Visualisation Intuitive capabilities, Knowing	Imagination, Intuition, Wisdom	Neurological systems, Ears, Eyes and Nose, Pituitary gland
Throat	Throat	Bright blue	Communication, Creativity, Inner voice	Expression, Ideas, Will power	Neck, Throat, Thyroid, Jaw, Mouth, and Teeth
Hearth	Centre of chest just above the heart.	Green	Love cardinal point for other chakras	Compassion refining of humanity	Heart, Thymus, Circulatory system, immune
Solar Plexus	A few centimetres above the navel.	Yellow	Will Power	Joy and anger, Energy, Self-worth	Central nervous system, Liver, Digestive tract
Sacral	A few centimetres above the navel.	Orange	Desire, Sexuality, Pleasure	Emotional Relations	Reproductive organs, Large intestine, Kidneys
Root	Base of spine.	Red	Survival, Grounding	Stability, Stillness	Spine, Rectum, Arms, Legs, Feet, Bones
Source: The author's interpretation of information gathered from several public websites					

Senius: 'The colours of the chakra remind me of my experience with the rainbow because the colours are identical from the Root to the Crown chakra.'

Oracle: 'Your associations also fit into your description of your call, where you used the raindrops in the rainbow to portray the ocean of souls incarnated with you.

'Any imbalances in the chakra will manifest in the part of the body the actual chakra controls. We will later return to how the knowledge of chakras can be utilised to improve health and mood.'

Beliefs

Oracle: 'Your resources, combined with your experiences, create negative/limiting and positive/motivating beliefs and deliver input to build your values. Another way to express it is that your values are a consolidation of more experiences and beliefs.

'As I said through the chain of quotes from classical wisdom, "Every action starts with a thought and turns into a reaction/behaviour", which also works the other way around. You get exposed to others' actions, where you develop a particular reaction/behaviour.

'In the first instance, you can get a different reaction to your behaviour than you expect. For example, if you are used to challenging opinions in your environment and then meet a person where adults' views are unquestionable, you will probably experience a clash.

'In the second instance, the situation will work in the same manner—the opposite.'

Senius: 'It reminds me of an example from my working life as an IT professional. I had a manager who was very loyal when dealing with IT projects in a standardised way. Another colleague was very pragmatic and loyal to his customers' needs.

'They both were very persistent if not stubborn. They did have many passionate discussions. For the remaining of us who attended these meetings, it was more or less fruitless battles because the gaps between the two views were inconvertible, inwards versus outwards. At the end of the day, it is the customers who fund the organisation, but if an organisation gets big enough, it sometimes become a purpose in itself.

'At a later stage, a successor in a reorganised role managed to close the gap. He delivered what the customer wanted and at the same time, keeping the quality assurance intact. But his efforts were not honoured as he was laid off after a relatively short period of employment.'

Oracle: 'An interesting example is when you have clear preferences. However, it is not a question about who is right or wrong but a matter of perception; perception is not the same as the truth, but an interpretation of it. In general, there are three aspects in the interpretation of events: the subject or self, the object or non-self and the apprehension of the object. I can illustrate this with an experiment:

Fill water into three cups with a temperature of 0, 10 and 20°C.

'In your part of the experiment, first put your finger into the water with 0°C, then immediately place the same finger into the water with 10°C. You will perceive the water as warm because you come from a colder reference.

'In my part of the experiment, I first put my finger into the water at 20°C. I then immediately put the same finger into the water at 10°C. Because I come from a warmer reference, I will perceive the water at 10°C as cold.

'The conclusion is that we perceive the opposite outcome. Since we know the entire experiment, we can understand that both results are possible because we have a different reference. Another way to express it is that the outcome is also given if the reference is given beforehand.

'When it comes to our respective beliefs, it is a whole different story, because we often only know our own references and tend to be pretty fixed with our views, therefore unwilling to accept contradictory views, especially if the topic goes beyond the present life. This holds particularly true when it comes to religions as they are the most cemented perceptions.

'For most of us, people who we socialise with have the same references as ours and can therefore confirm us in our opinion. The point is that you need to be curious about contradictory perspectives to expand your own view and become wiser.

'Seen from another perspective, it also means that we should endure listening to views that do not fit with our own and may even contradict our experiences. And who knows, maybe the prerequisites for our experience have changed.

'Another perspective on this small example is the scale. It is a common standard reference that enables us to understand the outcomes and repeat the experiment with the same results.

'The benefit of natural science is that it is possible to measure the outcomes objectively. When it comes to religion and humanity, we can only embrace them by our beliefs.

'Within the field of religion, you can only know by experience. And experiences are gained within specific contexts. The risk in this process is that you might generalise a particular context and apply it to where it may not be valid.

'If you choose the old religions, you base your knowledge on old thoughts that were relevant during a different context of time and space. I recommend you to connect with your inner self, your soul, because that is the way to revelation.'

Senius: 'I guess I understand your point of view. On the other hand, I feel it is hard to throw all my religious ballast overboard. That is why I try to interpret the statement of the Bible in a more contemporary view.'

Oracle: 'I understand your perspective. Naturally, you make that connection because it has been your starting point. Besides, there are many wise statements in the Bible, especially if you read them with love as you do.

'But let me return to the original beliefs from the beginning of our talk about beliefs. Whenever you have a clash, it is worthwhile to stop and reflect upon the situation. The reflection can bring new insights that can improve your development and behaviour.

'If the reflection process is unconscious, you miss the potential learning and you risk developing beliefs that do not support your call. The views you gain can be divided into negative and positive feelings that impact your notion about yourself and the world around you.

'A negative belief creates a barrier, which often prevents you from executing. Whenever you get a negative feeling, you can choose to react in different ways.

'Let me start with a few examples where you prevent the event from happening:

- Ignore or displace the action. It may give you other issues if it is something you are supposed to do.
- Escape the situation by letting somebody else act for you.
- Postpone the action and possibly procrastinate more.

Avoid making decisions that can prevent action.

- Deny it even if the issue is real.
- Suppress the unacceptable feeling and turn it into a physical symptom.

'If you do not act upon the negative feeling, the barrier grows and turns into a bad habit. It can negatively influence health and wellbeing, which is enforced by the chain of quotes/thoughts already mentioned a couple of times. In the worst case, the habit turns into your character and finally into your destiny.

'Many firm beliefs have their roots in childhood. Let me illustrate this using an example.

'A child who experiences neglect may interpret that he is unwanted. This belief may result in many barriers in his adult life. It can create insecurity, thus making it hard to be accepted in his relations, because there is a tendency that the surroundings mirror his expectations.

'It means that his relationships will overrule his needs the same way he experienced them as a child. His self-esteem will erode. He may start becoming less social and feel lonesome. It can eventually turn into another negative behaviour, including developing compulsive eating as a substitute. It turns into a destructive spiral.

'This child will need professional help as he quickly plays the role of a victim.

'For less cemented beliefs in your mind, it is possible to choose a more constructive reaction. The point is to acknowledge the unpleasant feeling and see it as an opportunity to make the belief visible and the earlier the better before it becomes an insurmountable barrier as the example before.'

Senius: 'A simple example from my daily life is that I tend to procrastinate a lot until I recall my grandmother's affirmation: "Be happy that you can". Furthermore, if you do the task right away, you minimise the attention the task demands of you. When you procrastinate, the noise will remain until you are done with the task.'

Oracle: 'Yes, affirmations are a tool that we will come back to later. Regarding procrastinations, the best solution is often to get things done immediately. For now, I'll continue with the other side, the positive beliefs.

'A positive belief is a stimulus that creates inspiration which generates a feeling of passion and energy in releasing an appropriate action. Based on your previous experience, you feel convinced that you can manage just like you have done in your many projects.

'It does not necessarily mean that you are inside your comfort zone. You have managed other projects where you did not know how to get there, but you trust that you can design a process that fulfils its purpose.'

Senius: 'Yes, you are right. I find it very appealing to do projects where you cannot just use a standard project model but have to build the frames and processes together with team members and stakeholders.'

Oracle: 'Great experiences create positive beliefs, which can spread like rings in water. Instead of barriers, you create opportunities that can form great characters that will ultimately bring you the destiny you seek.'

Senius: 'It makes good sense to me. But what is the determinant for whether the negative or the positive belief wins?'

Oracle: 'That is a great question, but hard to give an unambiguous answer to because it depends on the call and the frames you have chosen for your childhood. Your mind absorbs whatever behaviour you observe in your environment.

'The call represents your level of consciousness, which depends on how you have lived in the previous life (karma). The outcome of the actual incarnation depends on how you choose to use your free will.

'If the balance of beliefs tips to the negative side, it can form a worried and pessimistic view that can bring it to a dark mind. A soul in this state will need support from other souls to get a more tolerable life and better options to improve development during the incarnation.

'There is also another aspect of negative input. During your childhood, you create your reference and a self-image. If somebody challenges your self-image, you will suppress the threat and choose defence mechanisms as mentioned earlier, e.g., through procrastinations.

'Correspondingly, if the balance tips to the positive side, it will typically form a happy and optimistic mind. If the person uses his will to live his call, there are excellent opportunities to accelerate his development. However, such a soul may risk missing his call.

'For example, if he uses his potential success for his own sake of winning or moving the focus of the call's altruistic nature into a personal need for recognition. Such a soul can also need support from other souls.

'It is also essential to state that the person's mind does not determine whether he is successful or not, but it explains why some appear to have a more easy-going life than others. On the other hand, responsibility comes along with your abilities. Nobody is on freewheel.'

Senius: 'I understand that you cannot determine success or failure without knowing the call. But it appears to me that our destiny, to a great extent, is given beforehand. Isn't it?'

Oracle: 'No. What you can say is that your karma gives you the frames for your life. You still have free will to decide whether you choose to follow your call or to live in your ego. Karma is impersonal. If you observe beliefs from this perspective, you will not distinguish between bad and good beliefs, but between beliefs, you should improve in order to grow, and those you should nurture to sustain.'

Faith

Senius: 'From our previous discussion, I noticed that what we believe depends on, among others, when and where we lived and the maturity of our soul. Isn't there something more constant over time?'

Oracle: 'Hmmm. Exciting question. In fact, yes, there is something more constant—faith. It is how you believe as an outcome of the intrinsic human need for finding meaning with life, and in your case, an inner longing that you experienced on the Camino on seeing the rainbow.

'It is universal and goes across borders, as well as across different religions, and it is for real independent of whether the things you believe in are real. Faith is about something more significant, wiser and more sensitive to supernatural phenomena—your soul. Faith is an intrinsic conviction in correlation with your soul, whereas belief is an extrinsic frame of understanding, e.g., a religion or an alternative human view inherited from your environment.'

Senius: 'I am not sure I fully understand your distinction. Let me try to elaborate a little on what you said.'

Oracle: 'Please go ahead.'

Senius: 'As I understand you, it means that we potentially have an intrinsic inspiration and an extrinsic motivation that triggers a "belief process" resulting in outcomes that for the latter are dependent on the former factors of time and place, including culture and maturity?'

Oracle: 'Yes, you may express it that way. I like the distinction you're making between inspiration and motivation to separate the intrinsic and extrinsic sources of input. As a consequence, humans inherit the extrinsic view first during their childhood.

'However, in your case, you have lived between the dissonance between your grandparents and your dad's views which have created an awareness of your soul and opened the door to the intrinsic view. You have realised that you are not a body with a soul, but an eternal soul with a temporary residence—your body.

'Concerning the cultural issue you mentioned, I can add that culture is about common views that you don't question because it is something you are born into and take for granted. Therefore, it is something that first becomes visible when you meet other cultures that have created different views or praxis on the same issue.'

Senius: 'What about the longing?'

Oracle: 'The longing you felt on the Camino came from your soul, who became homesick. This longing comes from your being consciously aware of your soul.'

Senius: 'You mentioned that faith is a personal conviction that results in action. Does it mean that if people believe in something different than religions, then everyone would act selfishly?'

Oracle: 'You get sharp and bright. With your background, you would immediately assume that without God, you would be a doomed and selfish sinner, which other religions will claim too. However, religions are just one way of practising faith.

'Still, the personal conviction can be as sincere as in any religion, which means you would still do what is right even if you cannot justify your action on a rational basis. Instead, it requires that you find your fellow human beings trustworthy, which is a cultural trait.

'A part of the illusion is that you are separated from all other human beings, which is right for the ego only. Your soul knows that it is not like that and transmits that to your ego, thus creating a feeling that supersedes your thinking. If you think about it, you will probably realise that whenever there is a dissonance between your thoughts and your feelings, the latter wins for the most part.

'And that is great if it's your soul initiating it. In case it is created from your lower thought, you should let go as it is always about your ego's desires.'

Senius: 'What about atheists. Do they have faith too?'

Oracle: 'Yes, they have. They have decided to believe that there are no religions, and this firm belief is still faith, which brings me to an important message. If you do not believe that there is something beyond what you can sense, not being open-minded, you will not be able to see it. Simply put, you can only see what you focus on.'

Senius: 'What you just said contradicts what most people believe. You need to be convinced about something before you can believe it. This precondition reminds me of something I have read in the Bible, Matthew 19:14: Jesus said, "Let the little children come to me, and do not hinder them, for the kingdom of heaven belongs to such as these".

'The way I read this is that you need to be as naive as a child to get access to the Kingdom of God, which I translate as the spiritual world. Is this actually confirming what you are saying?'

Oracle: 'When it comes to the child, you need to have an immediate faith to get access to the kingdom. The point is that belief is about what you cannot know but have confidence that it exists anyway.'

Senius: 'You didn't comment on my interpretation of the Kingdom. Was that deliberate?'

Oracle: 'Yes, I intend to bring it up later because it is not directly connected to our present theme. It is more connected to the evolution of the religions, which I will address later.

'Another perspective is that you can hardly speak about faith without considering doubt as you cannot prove your faith.'

Oracle: 'Senius, could you tell how you have experienced this during your life?'

Senius: 'Looking back, I see I have had two different kinds of faith: faith as a child and as an adult. As a child, my faith in God was naive as my grandparents preached to me with both love and fear. The latter was reinforced by the picture bible, filling me with fear.

'As I grew older, I started to question this through discussions I've had with my dad, creating doubt in my mind that I could not solve before I realised what my call was about.

'The transition period was a difficult time. While being in the bible circle with the pastor, I experienced it as the truth. When my wife gave me this book for Christmas mentioned previously, it felt all apart again.

'On the other hand, I felt a strong attraction to seek my own truth. During that period, I experienced a new reality which step by step transformed my doubt into the convictions I have today. I wonder whether you orchestrated that?'

Oracle: 'Well, I would rather state that I was a catalysator for the enlightenment you were seeking. But your story contains more important recognitions. The dissonance you have perceived between your grandparents and your dad's view has created doubts in your mind.

'No wonder it was a difficult experience for you because you considered and experienced both the views as truths. However, there are some distinctive differences. The faith of your grandparents is something you have inherited, and you have tried to interpret your experiences to fit into that context.

'When it comes to your current view, it is your own personal experiences built upon your connections to the spiritual world. In this way, your doubts have been transformed into convictions. In other words, your faith is built on your personal experiences, which is more solid ground.

'Another characteristic feature of your present spiritual view is that it also includes peak experiences, letting any remaining doubt vaporise. An example you also find in Acts 9:3-19 where Saulus, later known as Paulus, had a very strong peak experience:

'As he neared Damascus on his journey, suddenly a light from heaven flashed around him. He fell to the ground and heard a voice say to him, "Saul, Saul, why do you persecute me?" "Who are you, Lord?" Saul asked.

'"I am Jesus, whom you are persecuting", he replied. "Now get up and go into the city, and you will be told what you must do".

'The men traveling with Saul stood there speechless; they heard the sound but did not see anyone. Saul got up from the ground, but when he opened his eyes he could see nothing. So, they led him by the hand into Damascus. For three days, he was blind, and did not eat or drink anything.

'In Damascus, there was a disciple named Ananias. The Lord called to him in a vision, "Ananias!" "Yes, Lord", he answered.

'The Lord told him, "Go to the house of Judas on Straight Street and ask for a man from Tarsus named Saul, for he is praying. In a vision, he has seen a man named Ananias come and place his hands on him to restore his sight".

'"Lord", Ananias answered, "I have heard many reports about this man and all the harm he has done to your holy people in Jerusalem. And he has come here with authority from the chief priests to arrest all who call on your name".

'But the Lord said to Ananias, "Go! This man is my chosen instrument to proclaim my name to the Gentiles and their kings and to the people of Israel. I will show him how much he must suffer for my name".

'Then Ananias went to the house and entered it. Placing his hands on Saul, he said, "Brother Saul, the Lord—Jesus, who appeared to you on the road as you were coming here—has sent me so that you may see again and be filled with the Holy Spirit".

'Immediately, something like scales fell from Saul's eyes, and he could see again. He got up and was baptised, and after taking some food, he regained his strength.

'What I want to emphasise with my long answer to your question is this:

- Here your doubt is used constructively in contradiction to what happens in Genesis, which I will address later.
- The peak experience always happens at some point in time in any spiritual awakening.

'The unfortunate thing is that many Christians conclude that revelation is an experience only for those who God promoted as prophets and therefore do not seek the experience themselves.'

Oracle: 'Can you share some of your peak experiences with us?'

Senius: 'I had my first peak experience during the 30-day meditation programme I had mentioned in "Private Adult Life". During the session, as I was meditating, I saw a vision of myself. During a meditation session I saw myself from the outside, on the floor in a lotus posture. It was a scary experience I could not cope with, and it never occurred again.'

Oracle: 'Yes, I recall your experience and must admit that it was too early for you. Anyway, it raised new questions for you and inspired you to search for more knowledge. Please proceed.'

Senius: 'While I was in the Bible circle, I frequently went to church for Sunday service. During one of the services, I saw a bright staircase that led straight up from the floor to above the altar. At the top, somebody reached out to me. I got up and climbed up the stairs into the unknown. The staircase disappeared and so did I!'

Oracle: 'How did the experience impact you?'

Senius: 'The experience happened shortly after I read the book my wife gifted. It stands far clearer for me now. I now realised that I could have my relation with God or the Source as I prefer it to be—a direct experience without needing anybody as a mediator in this world. Besides, I now see the peak experiences I have had since, bringing my faith to a new level.'

Oracle: 'It makes me happy that you now completely understand how doubt, experience and faith play together in a constructive way.'

Values

Oracle: 'Values are the principles, norms and actions that characterises human beings. They are meaningful and considered as worth obtaining. Besides, many of them are above the personal level and the strongest ones are manifested in religions.

'They are hard to change because their foundation is built on strong feelings. Values are the strongest motivation to act.

'Values are generally cultural traits. In the western world, culture is primarily derived from Christianity and flavoured by national history, immigration and family. There is not a sharp border between all of them.'

Rhodopis: 'I can add that some values you consider as Christian values were already prevalent in ancient times. For example, *The Golden Rule*[7]: "Treat others as you want to be treated yourself". It is, among others, mentioned by Ancient Egypt (2040 – 1650 BC) and Confucius (551 – 479 BC). It has inspired many religions, such as Buddhism, Christianity, Hinduism, Judaism and Taoism, with slightly different interpretations.'

Oracle: 'Thank you, Rhodopis. It is a good example of how humans have inherited ancient values from former cultures. How do you look at your values, Senius?'

Senius: 'Well, I can recognise that in some cases, it can be hard to tell, wherefrom they originate. But let me try anyway.

'Faith is the first value that comes to mind. However, in my case, it has changed from inherited faith to convictions built on my experiences, which have grown from reciprocity between my grandparents and my dad's views and from which my call derived.

'Unconditional love is the foundation to overcome most of the issues we inflict on others. I honour this value, but it is also an ongoing point of development.

'Curiosity means a lot to me and is the prerequisite to bring me wisdom.

'Trust is essential for me to have open relations where you can grow. It also relates to loyalty, which may stem from my grandfather's patriarchal view. One of his quotes was: "A word is a word; otherwise, a man is bullshit".

'I value responsibility and hard work to fulfil my commitments to my employers, employees, colleagues and family. I think I have derived them from trust and loyalty.

---

[7] Source: https://en.wikipedia.org/wiki/Golden_Rule

'On the national level, my nation pays tribute to freedom of speech, which should be understood literally. Sometimes it is blended with sarcasm, which can be offensive or even shocking for other nationalities, and some may even require an apology. The reaction here could be to say you are too huffy or self-important.

'In the old days at a king's household, you had a jester, who should master humour and tell jokes that also contained spruce of truth. In Denmark, people interpret irony and satire as a modern version of this role, whereas many foreigners perceive it as sarcasm. Humour is another value that can also act as self-irony that helps us deal with difficult topics.

'Social responsibility for our citizens is another principal value. In Denmark, we have a welfare model that secures social rights. It gives people access to a home, food, education, healthcare, etc. The funding comes through the tax system, which means that in Denmark we have one of the highest income redistributions.

'As a country, we are among the happiest people globally and well educated. In addition, we have a low power distance between people, low poverty, low crime rates and healthcare is available to everybody. The backside of the coin is that we have very high taxes and more people are receiving and less are contributing. This imbalance can be a democratic dilemma as every citizen can vote at elections.

'Being humble is also a common national trait. Particularly in the western part of my country, you do not use big gestures, which is in contrast to the American culture. I think you should celebrate successes, but just like anything else, it is a matter of striking a balance.

'It reminds me of a Norwegian novel from 1933, *The Law of Jante* (Janteloven[8]), written by Aksel Sandemose, a Danish-Norwegian writer who wrote about the working class. It is a dark description of how we treat each other, which is far cry from *The Golden Rule*:

---

[8] Sources: 'Den Store Danske' and the Danish Wikipedia.

1. You're not to think *you* are anything special.
2. You're not to think *you* are as good as *we* are.
3. You're not to think *you* are smarter than *we* are.
4. You're not to imagine yourself better than *we* are.
5. You're not to think *you* know more than *we* do.
6. You're not to think *you* are more important than *we* are.
7. You're not to think *you* are good at anything.
8. You're not to laugh at *us*.
9. You're not to think anyone cares about *you*.
10. You're not to think you can teach us anything.

'The Law of Jante is universal and not just valid for the original fictive town, Jante. If his pessimistic description is right, it shows that the people lived in their egos. I hope we are beyond this viewpoint today.

'The last value, I think, I can recall right away is that my nation is a country that has the most individualistic standpoint in the world. It has also impacted my view. One of my values has been to raise my children to be independent of us parents as adults, which also goes the other way around.

'As a parent, I feel pleased that I am not dependent on my children for support. However, it does not mean that we do not help each other. On the contrary, we voluntarily help family and friends in need.

'The point is that everyone has the ability to manage on their own, but support makes life more comfortable and strengthens our relationships.'

Oracle: 'Thank you, Senius. Your interactions with other cultures imprint your awareness. An interesting observation is that you define many of the values with their opposite. To illustrate the span, we can take your individualism as an example. On the other end of the spectrum, you find India as the most collective society.'

Roles

Oracle: 'When you interact with others, you play many different roles as husband, father, friend, neighbour, colleague and so on. There are a set of appropriate behaviours, expectations from others and a social norm that makes socialisation work for each role.

'The way you act is a result of how your parents raised you and of the surrounding culture and religion. Altogether, these inputs have formed your personality and created several attitudes and preferences that impact your way of interacting with others.

'A way to discover your preferences is to differentiate behaviour into different roles whose relevance can vary depending on the context. Models have their limitations as they describe stereotypes that ignore individual divergences. On the other hand, they can give you some point of reference.

'Meyer-Briggs type indicator[9] is a very generic one and handy. It consists of four indicators that have two options each:

- How do you appear in interaction with others: Extrovert or introvert?
- How do you seek information: Sensing or intuition?
- How do you make decisions: Thinking or feelings?
- How do you live your outer life: Judging or perceiving?

Each indicator can be combined with all others, giving a total of 16 different possible personalities.'

Senius: 'I know the indicators from the projects. We often used Meyer-Briggs type indicator as a teambuilding exercise, which gave a good insight into the individual's preferences. It is helpful to understand which tasks fit the different profiles.

'Besides, it is also important in communications. The different personalities interpret information differently. It is also a great tool when considering the kind of job you should go for.'

---

[9] If you want to learn more about this tool, you can google MBTI.

Oracle: 'That was my point. There is also a more specific tool for other specific tasks, e.g., team roles where Belbin's theory of the nine roles is widespread.'

Senius: 'I have used them as well. Most people have one or two of the roles as preference. In my case, it was different. I took the role needed to complement the project team's preferences.'

Oracle: 'But in our context, I would like to present you to different kinds of generic roles. The roles are often unconscious dynamics between the family members. In its essence, it is about competing for attention from the parents.

'Let me use the first one in Meyer-Briggs type indicator as a starting point. Quite a few have a clear preference to either be an introvert or an extrovert, but some are in between—ambivert.'

Senius: 'I know that there are ongoing discussions about whether this indicator comes from nature or nurture. So how is it?'

Oracle: 'It is both, but they are hard to separate. There are differences in the brain, suggesting that some have a dominant preference when they are born. But it can be either reduced or reinforced depending on how the parents stimulate the child.

'In the case of your wife, she had predisposal from nature to be introvert. This trait encouraged her parents to keep asking questions to get her attention. Over the years, it has made her aloof even if she is a single child.

'In your case, it is different. You are one out of four children born within 5 years. The competition about the parent's attention is very intense. As an in-between child, you have to navigate both with your parents and your siblings.

'It means that sometimes you need to take the lead to be heard, and in other situations, you are better off by being resigned. This combination has made you ambivert.'

Senius: 'I can recognise your explanation. I have wondered how my wife became aloof. As a single child, she got all the attention she wanted from her parents. In my youth, I was shy and insecure, which I have misinterpreted as being aloof.

'She has sustained her role as aloof, whereas I have become the one who makes the inquiries. It made it easy for me to adopt both the role as coach and the way I often invite people to problem-solving.'

Oracle: 'That makes sense because an aloof couple will get challenged in their social relations. There is another thing worth mentioning regarding your wife and her parents. She has inherited her nature from her father, while her mother has played the counter role as an inquirer. It also fits with their preference as introvert and extrovert, respectively.

'The above roles also exist in a less harmonic version. The parents may have a tense relationship, and often it is a fight between an extrovert and an introvert. For example, the extrovert cannot relate to what is unspoken, and the introvert expects the partner to know what the issue is that the introvert has already processed in mind. The extrovert tends to "think aloud", which the introvert may perceive that the extrovert questions everything.

'In case they have a child, there is a risk that the child, unfortunately, feels accountable for the quarrels between the parents and makes himself or herself "invisible" by acting like a victim. In more challenging situations, the parents transfer their shortcomings to the child where the victim is challenged.

'In that case, the child will build up rage that can develop into a hostile behaviour, which gets released by attacking the parents. In all cases, you bring your role with you into your adult life.

'The victim role is the most unfortunate situation because the person feels some sort of guilt that the parents have imprinted. In his/her adult life, the person continues to attract situations that make him/her feel like a victim. *Like attracts like.*

'The conviction paralyses your options for action. The problem originates from the outside, which is also beyond the person's control.

'Your possible way out is to recognise that your thoughts and feelings are negative. Negative emotions are always a warning or a flag telling you to shift focus. To break the destructive cycle, look at the former argumentation. Try to examine why you experience the situation from this point of view.

'Next, you can look at it from the outside, i.e., without involving your feelings. Finally, consider why your parent's relationship has been dysfunctional. You will realise that it is not about you. This may be your way out of the trap.'

Senius: 'Wouldn't it be better to take out the steam of the parent's attack and put words on what they did?'

Oracle: 'It would be a far better reaction, and it would take away the power from the parents. However, in your childhood, it is hardly an option, unfortunately. It is something you can see as an adult if you are brave enough to face your youth with clear and objective eyes as just described.

'Then you can challenge the view of your parents when appropriate.'

Senius: 'From what you have told so far, I understand that the circumstances we have chosen to be born into is to have the right frames for obtaining the experiences to heal our soul, and the shortest way to achieving that is through our call without letting our will get in our way. Did I understand this correctly?'

Oracle: 'Yes, that is very precise.'

Senius: 'Somehow, I still feel that I am missing something in order to comprehend why it is necessary to struggle with the tension it creates on a personal level. As I see it, this tension also creates issues in our relations with other people.

'Isn't there a way out of this tension?'

Oracle: 'It is an essential perspective. When you are in your ego, you need to be seen by your surroundings as a social individual. You use the pattern you have learnt while growing up to cope with your fellow beings surrounding you. These patterns also apply to anybody else.

'The way out of the situation is to live out your call. Your call builds upon love, and your awareness of your soul will grow. If you stay focused, you will gradually become your soul, and the ego will diminish. Then you will radiate love in all situations and see the world as it really is.'

'Senius, with a thoughtful look on his face: 'Wow! I feel that it brings order in my understanding. It is as the fog disappears when the sun is shining in the morning.'

Oracle: 'I am glad that it brings light on your understanding.'

Rhodopis: 'Sorry for putting cold water on everything, but a person like Hitler also believed he had a call, in which innocents were slaughtered on the streets in the name of a hideous ideology.'

Senius: 'If this is a call, I miss an explanation too.'

Oracle: 'Fundamentally, a call is always constructive, voluntary and based upon the foundation of love. A violent roll out of ideology is outside the concept. On the other hand, it does not prevent anybody from believing something different. They have free will to do what they want, just like you.

'But let me return to the topic of discussion. There is also a different layer of roles that I want to share with you.

'The first one is the business role where you are accustomed to setting objectives, realise them and set new ones. One of the challenges, however, is that the goals can be short-term and based upon choices that are built on a shortage of capacity (scarcity) and competition (separation) for your own benefit. If that is the case, the motivation for the objectives is set based on your ego.

'Another risk is that you project your present moment into the future and live in the future. It becomes a means to an end postponing your happiness. From a development point of view, you are moving in circles in a horizontal plane in your ego.

'If you choose your call, the circle becomes a spiral, as you will still have your detours. Besides, the spiral will also bring you upwards in a vertical plane to benefit your development.

'Finally, the last role is the altruistic role where you see your life in the long-term view. It is independent of results and founded on principles.

It is built upon ethics, compassion and love. With this as a starting point, it is far easier to find and carry out your call.

'Please notice that none of the roles are "wrong", but the perspective should be to evaluate them with the experiences your soul wants to gain. Since you have been in different roles in different contexts, you already know them by hearth.'

Senius: 'How do I ensure to remain in my call?'

Oracle: 'As part of your call, you have the image of a lighthouse. It can be generalised to everybody as light represents purity, goodness and positive and protecting energy. It is a symbol of the Source, and the soul is a little reflection of that light.

'The lighthouse becomes a symbol of your call. And just like the lighthouse, your call has served to help others in one way or another.

'In this way, you receive another clue regarding your call. You have to consider what brings light to your lighthouse. When you do something that is in line with your call, you will feel enthusiasm, joy and peace in your state of mind, which then influences your relations.

'Everyone likes to be together with a person who loves his call and describes his activities with enthusiasm. You become thrilled yourself.'

Senius: 'How do I maintain this enthusiasm in practice?'

Oracle: 'I can mention a few examples for you: You can stand on your right to follow your call. Do things that you love.

'Know that you are here to make a difference.

'What you don't use you lose. Therefore, engage your full capacity to realise your call. Be mindful of your thoughts.

'In addition, there are a few things you should avoid: Do not compromise your personal integrity.

'Do not please others to gain their recognition if this betrays your call.

'Do not take responsibility for more than you can cope with.

'With your experience, you can probably add more topics to the list based on your own understanding. I will return to tools that can help you fulfil your call.'

Your Compass

With your call, you are with your destiny gifted.
Besides, you have an idea of how it should be lifted.
The great question is how do you get there
with the knowledge, you have gained from here?

You need an instrument to find your way.
Actually, you have a compass right away:
Your common sense and your consciousness
as shining stars in the night in brightness.

Your compass has you from trips returned
while your beliefs and values get fine-tuned.
Your personal integrity shine as a star at night.
Your love and compassion are to everybody's delight.

Under your journeys you many harbours dock
And know countless views which other people rock.
As you are in crowded international water,
you have, in return, met them with laughter.

As an experienced captain, you know how to navigate
and from the different deviations to compensate.
You have experienced which roles you can play
and find confidence and balance to find your way.

Source: Oracle

Tools to Release Your Call

Oracle: 'We have now spent time to identify your call and what you already possess in your luggage that can support you to realise your call. Now it is time to look into the supporting tools.'

The Creation Process

Oracle: 'In connection with your call, do you remember that you used the sundial as a symbol to create positive thoughts to create what is needed to accomplish your call?'

Senius: 'Yes, I do.'

Oracle: 'It is both a method and a law, labelled as the *Law of Attraction*. A straightforward way to define the law is that *like attracts like*. It is the creative power of the Universe.

'One way to interpret the Universe is in terms of matter as energy, and energy has a specific frequency. A thought represents an energy with a particular frequency. In other words, your thoughts attract whatever you focus upon, and your surroundings will mirror this to you.

'Furthermore, the longer you concentrate, the more other supporting thoughts you will attract and add more momentum to your creation according to the Law of Attraction. For example, if you want to lose weight, you start seeing everything in your surroundings that is about losing weight. It is as simple as that.

'Whether you believe in the law or not does not matter; it works like any other law. For example, the *Law of Gravity*. If you jump from a tree, you will hit the ground irrespective of your beliefs.

'The only difference is that it is more difficult to prove the Law of Attraction as it is impossible to isolate the thoughts that created a specific event. This obstacle makes many conclude that the Law of Attraction does not work.

'The central point is that whether you are conscious or unconscious about your thoughts, you will manifest the dominant thoughts. What you are now is what you have been thinking until now. And what you think now and from now on will determine who you become in the future. The law mirrors what you think and sends it back to you, which will bring you to your life circumstances.'

Senius: 'It complies with my experience. The biggest issue is to get our thoughts under control. Most of the time, the subconscious mind runs the show.'

Oracle: 'You are completely right. Whenever you do all your routines, your subconscious mind has a program that does the job for you. In fact, consciousness comes into play for most people only if there are conflicts as consciousness has an overall overview.

'The conflicts are often between thoughts and feelings, where the feelings often win. It can also be a conflict between what you want short and long term. But most of the time you have thoughts you are not aware of running in the background. These thoughts can be either positive or negative and will manifest a corresponding outcome.'

Senius: 'How do we break this lousy circle?'

Oracle: 'The first exercise is to sit down and consciously stop the stream of thoughts. You might have to experiment with a posture to find one where you feel relaxed and comfortable. You will probably realise that you cannot keep your thoughts away for more than a few moments in the beginning.

'But be patient and try to do the exercise for about 5 – 10 minutes. The time needed to master it depends on your ability to concentrate. You probably have to do it every day for at least a few weeks.'

Senius: 'It reminds me of meditation because that was what I did when I started. To make the concentration process easier, I focused on my breathing. Furthermore, I tried to maintain my posture in the same position throughout the session. And every time a thought popped up, I returned to my breathing.'

Rhodopis: 'Actually, the first step is to become aware of your unconscious thoughts. The second step is to refrain from attaching to these thoughts and the emotions possibly associated with them. But it is hard in the beginning because we are very good at attaching to them.'

Oracle: 'It is a good suggestion, and you are right. We are talking about reprogramming the subconscious mind. The key thing is that you train your ability to be conscious about your thoughts and only think when you have a conscious purpose.'

Referent: 'Just another practical hint. You will find this exercise in Appendix I, 'Exercise 3: Thoughtless Presence,' which also contains further details.'

Senius: 'When I hike on my own, I now and then focus on observing what is around me while walking. Then I am present and suppress my thoughts. Besides, it sharpens my senses. Suddenly I smell, see, hear and feel my surroundings.'

Oracle: 'It is a great remark because it supports you to implement it as a new habit. Besides you benefit from the exercise by being present, which is another important ability.'

Rhodopis: 'To underline your statement: When you think you are inside your mind.'

Oracle: 'However, until you master controlling your thoughts, there is another more passable road for you. You can ask yourself how you feel. If you feel good, you will attract more of what makes you feel good. And the higher the vibration, the better.

'If your frequency is high enough, you are potentially in alignment with the Source. Then everything is possible for you.'

Rhodopis: 'This is up to my alley and is far easier for me to practise.'

Oracle: 'Yes, I agree. It is a self-reinforcing process. The more you act at that level, the more you attract for your creation.'

Visualisation

Oracle: 'Visualisation is a creative process where you deliberately attract a desire. It requires faith to work.

'Given your background, I can relate to what Jesus stated in Matthew 17:20 (part of the paragraph): "Truly I tell you, if you have faith as small as a mustard seed, you can say to this mountain, 'Move from here to there,' and it will move. Nothing will be impossible for you".

'You cannot attract anything consciously if you do not believe that it is possible. If the process is new, I recommend you start with something that makes you feel more confident. As you experience and your faith grows, you can start manifesting more extraordinary things.

'The first step is to choose a desire with care and formulate it with positive feelings. This means that you hold your desire up against your call and make a sanity check to ensure that you are on track with your soul.

'Here, there could be a pitfall if you sneak in a negation. Please remember that "no", "none" or other disclaims do not work. For instance, if you state: "I do not want to get sick", it gets translated into "I do want to get sick".'

Senius: 'I can support you with an example from one of my hobbies. Once I was playing golf and had to send my ball over a small lake to hit the green. My thought was: I have to avoid the lake. I hit the ball, and it ended of course in the lake.

'The negation "avoid" has sneaked in and translated my desire into "I hit the lake". Instead, I should have seen the ball hit the green. The conclusion is: "Visualise what you desire and do not use negations".

'I also struggled with what desire I should focus on, and I realised that having too many balls in the air at the same time does not work either. In the beginning, it can be quite overwhelming. So, it is a good idea to write your statements down and follow up on them. This will also help you to improve your phrasing and reinforce the associated feelings.'

Oracle: 'I can easily follow your experiences, although it might look chaotic in the beginning. But as stated previously, start with something where you feel more confident.'

Senius: 'It reminds me of my first deliberate creation:

'Early morning at around 4:30 am, I wake up to birdsong while camping with my youngest daughter in our garden. For a while now, I have been tumbling with the big questions of life. I can feel how the puzzle pieces are starting to fall into place, and I am filled with joy, gratitude and energy.

'A little before 6 am, I get up and put on my jogging shoes. I move faster and more effortlessly than usual.

'The essence that pops up in my mind is: You are what you have thought, and you become what you think. It may sound rather abstract to you, but for me, it is concrete. Most will say, based on our present situation: This is me.

'But this is the me I have thought in the past. If I want a different me, I can change my thoughts now. In other words, who shall form my day— me or my surroundings?

'The key to being a master in your own house is to decide it: I am the master of my thoughts and feelings and I create my life through them.

'One day I had a desire and I decided to start small. On our way to an amusement park, I visualised a butterfly with red wings and black dots and told myself that I would like to see it by the end of the day. While sitting in my daughter's favoured carousel, I saw a butterfly on a butterfly bush that opened its wings, and it was precisely as I had visualised it. I did not see any other butterflies that day.

'I was delighted! Because I was convinced that it was possible to create what I desired. Until then, I had only known it intellectually, but this was the first time I had experienced it and understood it.'

Referent: 'I got very captivated by your example. But somebody may call it a coincidence?'

Senius: 'I understand your reservation. But this is precisely the point. It is a subjective experience that has created a confirmation to me and turned it into a personal conviction. Besides, I barely have any knowledge of butterflies.'

'So, I did not even know whether the butterfly I imagined existed in the real world! To me, it was a breakthrough.'

Rhodopis: 'This also illustrates the difference between the methods of science and experience. Although it cannot be proved by science, but it can be a personal experience that works in the context you have created.'

Oracle: 'Thank you, Senius, for your great example. I think your experience is a good example to visualise something which you find possible to happen. And thank you for your comment, Rhodopis. The more you experience, the more faith you create in the process.'

Senius: 'In principle, you can do the visualisation whenever you care for it. Based on my experience, it is excellent to dedicate time to it every day thus setting a new productive habit. I have named this timeslot "The Wishing Well".'

Oracle: 'I agree it is a good idea, but it also demonstrates that you work in a very structured way, which may be difficult for others. The main takeaway is that you find a form that fits for you.'

Senius: 'It becomes far easier to use the Law of Attraction as soon as you get a successful experience. But I have made more attempts before that, and many others might have resulted in unsuccessful outcomes as well. So, why do we fail to create what we desire?'

Oracle: 'The Law of Attraction always works without exception, and you create as long as you think, which everyone does. There is no stop button unless you stop thinking. And you have probably also received outcomes that you do not want but have created unconsciously.

'The first step is to become conscious about the process and then get your thoughts under control. Besides, it is not sufficient to express a desire, because only passion can create that desire. You need to trust the process too. The next step is to visualise as you already have it, feel it and be grateful. Appreciation attracts, and allow yourself to possess it as you are worth it.

'The third step is to leave the state and focus on all you already have and appreciate it. Finally, you can turn your focus to your other tasks with the certainty that the Universe will figure out the "how".

'Sometimes you will be inspired to do actions. When this happens, you will feel joyous because you are tuning into the corresponding frequency, which is another expression of love through action.'

Senius: 'In my experience, it is a good idea to plan your day beforehand in the morning. When I wake up, I say a few affirmations:

- I appreciate that I did wake up to a new day and feel happy.
- Thank you for the new day I can use to comply with my call.
- It will be an amazing and inspiring day.
- My soul and I are one, and the Source will elevate me in love and wisdom.
- These gifts power my lighthouse to benefit those who seek my support.

'Next, I feel that I had sent energy in front of me, which in turn will realise my desire to fulfil my call. In addition, it sets my mood in a positive state of feeling, which helps me to succeed.'

Oracle: 'I fully agree with your recommendation. It is also an excellent way for a beginner to start using the Law of Attraction.

'I want to add that the Bible also mentions this law. Hence, a Christian believer may find this as a supporting reason. As an example of the Law of Attraction, you can find the essence in Mark 11:24: "Therefore, I tell you, whatever you ask for in prayer, believe that you have received it, and it will be yours".

'Another way to present the Law of Attraction is as the Law of Love, 1 John 4:8, stated: "Whoever does not love does not know God, because God is love".

'As God is second to none, this statement describes the highest power in the Universe, the highest frequency and level of consciousness. In other words, the closer you can get to embrace all your thoughts with love, the better you can transform your life and be a lighthouse for everybody.'

Senius: 'I am amazed! On my grandparent's tombstone is engraved: God is love.'

Oracle: 'Concerning your previous question, it is also essential to be aware of your desire: Is it build on fear or love. Fear is connected with lack and will attract more shortages. Love is associated with abundance and attracts more abundance.

'As an example, Jesus expressed this when he healed the blinds in Matthew 9:29: "Then he touched their eyes and said, 'According to your faith, let it be done to you".' Please notice the last sentence: "According to your faith, let it be done to you".

'So, what do you expect? That determines your outcome.'

Referent: 'In Appendix I, you find instructions for "Exercise 4: Visualisation".'

Coincidences in the Big Picture

Oracle: 'We have discussed this notion multiple times. The first time was in "The Melting Pot", where I stated that there are no coincidences, generally speaking. When you believe it is a coincidence, it is because you are missing an insight.

'And as you just replied to the referent, Senius, a coincidence is a subjective experience that confirms a belief for you. As you get conscious about them, they appear more often, turning into a personal conviction for you.

'It is an important tool. However, from the time you begin noticing the coincidences until you experience them and turn them into a conviction, there is quite a way to go. Therefore, I think it would be a great idea if you can share some of your experiences with this tool.'

Senius: 'Sure. What immediately strikes me is that it was an unconscious use of my intuition and the Law of Attraction: *Like attracts like*. Let me mention a few major ones in time chronological order.

'As I told before, the butterfly example was the experience that convinced me. Besides, both you and I mentioned the chain of quotes from classical wisdom that starts with our thoughts and ultimately becomes our destiny.

'In the late '90s, I became restless again, and it triggered my wife to give me the book mentioned previously. What seemed to be a coincidence became the drop that let the cup flow over once again. Due to my MBA study, I didn't have time for much reflection, which brings me to the next example.

'I went to a learning session with my MBA classmates. At the centre, we had to write our names on the nameplates. The quotes from the classical wisdom already mentioned were written on the other side. I thought it was peculiar and brought it back home with me. It still adorns my home office.

'After a while, I was reading my wife's union magazine, and suddenly the same quotes appeared again. I found it very weird and couldn't put it into a meaningful context. Time passed by and one Sunday, my wife and I went to service in our church, and guess what happened?

'The pastor used the quotes in his homily. I was astonished, and it became clear that it contained a message for me.'

Oracle: 'It is a great example in many ways. When it happened the first time, you were very busy—your MBA programme on top of your normal working hours. Despite that, you were also seeking information about how some of the spirituals could fit in. The answer was right there, but you were so occupied, and it did not reach your attention fully until you experienced it three times. However, the important outcome was that it became the trigger for you to join a coach training programme a few years later.'

Senius: 'I am overwhelmed. I haven't seen the full picture until now. But when you explain it, it becomes self-evident.'

Oracle: 'This is the beauty of it. What you have seen as independent events fit into the big picture of your call if you take a higher helicopter view. And it does not stop there.

'Can you see the connection to where you are now?'

Senius: 'I am not there yet, but let me try to enrol the storyline. I realise that the focus persons I have been coaching brought about experiences that broadened my perspectives. Simultaneously, it carried me into different fields of spiritual topics.'

Oracle: 'Yes, exactly. What do you see right now?'

Senius. 'It reminded me of the vision mentioned previously, the one I had when we were at Gran Canarias. My wife and youngest daughter went shopping, and I was on our terrace where I was daydreaming about writing a book—a book about my great passion, living a life that complies with my higher self and in delight, desire and alliance with my Source of life.

'A few years later, I went to a conference in London. During the opening session, I saw myself in another scene saying goodbye to my former colleagues. Among others to write a book about my passion. It saw the light in 2016.'

Senius: 'Did you orchestrate this too?'

Oracle: 'Yes, it was my response to your longing.'

Senius: 'After that, I was in doubt of what the next move should be.'

Oracle: 'Yes. Then the answer came to you on your last Camino in 2019. The rainbow emerged in front of you, encircling your path with the church at the end. To get your full attention, I contacted you beforehand via your intuition to let you know that you needed time on your own.'

Senius: 'I now understand how everything plays nicely together. First, I send a message to find my next step. You reply by letting me know via my intuition that I have to be on my own to get my full attention. Then you display the fantastic scenery with the rainbow, which initiated this gathering.

'Furthermore, you have brought the incident into the big picture. I am sincerely grateful.'

Oracle: 'I feel happy you do.'

Senius: 'All that you have said confirms my conviction that there are no coincidences. It is a matter of being conscious every time something unusual happens and consider how it fits into your situation.'

Rhodopis: 'Your derivation is also meaningful to me and easy to follow. I think it is harder to accept if somebody gets injured or affected by diseases. Then on top of whatever happens, you add guilt to the person's already unhappy situation.'

Oracle: 'Well, it depends on how you see it. A disease is signalled because of something that you did, thus creating an imbalance in the body. The body generates many signals before it gets so far. Furthermore, you cannot blame anybody for being unconscious about the correlation. We will come to this later.'

Rhodopis: 'I understand your response. But how do you explain about how somebody gets involved in an accident, for example where more cars collide?'

Oracle: 'You need to be on the same frequency to take part in the clash. The Law of Attraction always works. For most people, it is outside of their awareness. The ones who take part in the accident can be involved for many different reasons—one might be distracted; another might see it as a serious message to change behaviour and so on—just to give you some ideas about what I mean.

'What can immediately be interpreted as awful circumstances can become a blessing if you use the event constructively. It is confirmed by the Law of Attraction too. Please remember, likes attract likes without exception.'

Affirmations

Oracle: 'Affirmations are positive statements for future incidents stated in the present tense. They have a profound influence on your feelings, your conscious mind and support the reprogramming of your subconscious mind. You have already met a few of them from Senius' experiences.

'They can change your state of mind and speed up, delivering what you seek. It is faith used in practice.'

Oracle: 'Senius, do you have any practical input?'

Senius: 'Yes. In the beginning, I did not realise that I used affirmations. As an example, the one from my mum, "you are born under a lucky star". I was just a child, but it worked anyway and has become a conviction through confirming experiences.

'On the other hand, it is hard to transfer experiences as you probably know. You must try it yourself and gain your skills. At the same time, being realistic is equally important. When the gap between what is and what you want it to be is too wide, the process may become counterproductive.

'Therefore, you must have positive feelings about what you want to happen.

'If you are unfamiliar with the tool, it can seem a little awkward in the beginning. But as far as my experiences go, I recommend you try it anyways. Besides, if you dig deep into your memory, you probably use some affirmations already, unconsciously.

'Some of your beliefs are affirmations, but often ones that do not support you. As an example, "I am no good at getting up in the morning". That is a negative affirmation. Affirmations work whether they are positive or negative.

'It is a prevalent belief in the western world to claim that time is a scarce resource. Imagine the negative affirmation before. Due to that, you have to rush out of bed and start your day by being late. It might generate fear to get to work late.

'As like attracts like, you will unconsciously form negative expectations before you arrive at work. You might even complain and state that you do not have enough time. This is another negative affirmation, and the outcome must inevitably deliver your request.

'My point is that the snowball started to roll down the mountain with your affirmation, "I am not good at getting in up in the morning". It emphasises that it is good to start the day with positive affirmation and probably reinforce it by visualisation, as mentioned in "Visualisation". They support each other.

'When you write affirmations, it is always in the present tense. In the beginning, it is often a good idea to write it down with a pen on paper several times while you consider each word. It helps to reprogram your subconscious mind.

'If you want to reinforce your affirmations, you can try to speak them out loud in front of a mirror. It is very transgressive, but if you can overcome your resistance, it is efficient and rewarding.

'Many affirmation statements start with "I am", which the above affirmation from my mum is turned into when I use it. But others will do as well. There was also a strong affirmation in my example with the butterfly: I am master over my thoughts and feelings and create through them my life.'

Referent: 'I can recognize this too. For example, I would write: Whatever I need to know will be revealed to me when I need it. In doing so, my energy level would raise, making me feel happy. This supports my experience that affirmations reinforce the Law of Attraction.'

Senius: 'It is a nice example, which also supports your conviction that it works. I have a similar example. Before I go on vacation or hiking, I use affirmations that send out positive energy ahead of me. Besides, I believe that it attracts great experiences and makes me more curious and open-minded.

'When I return from a journey, I feel grateful for the great experiences I have had. It reinforces my conviction because I get my affirmations confirmed.'

Referent: 'You will find another exercise in Appendix I, Exercise 5: Affirmations.'

Birth Order

Oracle: 'When you spoke about your work-life, you mentioned that it was a big relief for you to realise that some of your characters and behaviours are related to your position in your family. I believe this eye-opener can be interesting for the readers and it can be an additional view that can reveal new sides of a person's personality.

'Can you give further information about the birth order?'

Senius: 'Yes, it is another interesting perspective. But one of the challenges is that it depends on more variables. The first one is that there is only approximately 1 year between each child in my case. It intensifies the competition between the children.

'If there are about 4 years between the kids, the dynamics may be quite different. The order of gender also has a significant influence on the characters. So, like any other factor, you have to be conscious about the fact that we are talking regarding stereotypes with a high degree of variation.

'The combination in the family I am born into is sister, brother, me and another brother. I can see I have inherited some of the typical characters from my position in my family. What brought me the relief I mentioned earlier is that middle children typically establish their relations outside the family. Until I realised this, I felt guilt regarding my family as I did not have any unresolved issues in the relationship with any of them.

'To be stubborn is also a typical trait for a middle child, as well as being very performance-oriented. In my case, I have been able to convert them into persistence and drive to achieve my goals.

'Besides, I am good at reading a situation and mediate divergences.

'Furthermore, I focus on creating a positive atmosphere, which is another typical trait. Whenever I can, I contribute with a positive inspiration. I do not believe that threatening people is motivating. It is, in my view, poison for creativity.

'On the other hand, somebody confuses my constructive perspective with people-pleasing, which would compromise your personal integrity.'

Oracle: 'Interestingly, you mention it, because being a people pleaser will often contradict your call. In your childhood, you have learnt what pleases and annoys your close relations. As you want to feel well, you will mostly choose to satisfy your relations expectations. If you bring this conditioned learning into your adult life, you risk leaving your way and contradicting your call.

'However, in your case, you have been surrounded by close relations who have had high personal integrity which you have inherited. It is an excellent gift supporting your call.'

Senius: 'Thank you for reminding me. Anyway, let me return to my considerations.

'Additional attributes I have inherited is independence, and I also sometimes use ways to reach the target, which can be perceived as rebellious by others. Simultaneously, the required rules are just indicative and are bent if it can be beneficial to reach the destination easier but still be ethically acceptable.

'I also mentioned we did not speak about our feelings in my childhood, which was also a typical trait for most families those days. My relation to my sister has moderated the effect. On the other hand, it may have been the reason why the group saw a risk for me when they drew the bird: The chance of being a cold sod.

'Even if my dad was the firstborn, he did not have most of the typical traits of a firstborn. However, he was curious, a feature I inherited. He took the responsibility to be our provider, which I somehow inherited as well.

'As my mother did not work, my father expected her to be responsible for all the work at home—a pattern copied from his grandparents and how it was in most families those days, and which I partly did too.

'My mum was the firstborn as my dad. She had two siblings, twins, who were 12 years younger. In this context, she is virtually a single child and was very close to her mum. She grew up with her mum only.

'It was during a difficult time. Fortunately, she did not have responsibility for her siblings. At 14, she left home to assist an aunt with her guesthouse and avoid her two siblings' father. Due to her life circumstances, her traits as a single child have been less characteristic.

'She was energetic and responsible, with a reserved personality. She sacrificed her needs for the benefit of the family.

'As mentioned earlier, I inherited her energy level and strong will transformed into a strong drive to achieve.

'When it comes to my two brothers, my situation is classical for a middle child. It is a typical "either-or" role. In my case, I went more or less unscathed through my youth and got the best out of it and became a strong negotiator.

'In general, I am trustful, which is atypical for a middle child. On the other hand, I act upon disloyal people, which fortunately is rare. But to be trustful is also a Danish national trait.'

Oracle: 'It is quite a few traits you have been able to derive from your position in your family.'

Rhodopis: 'And typical you, Senius. I agree with your interpretation, but I also see that you repress some of your negative experiences.'

Senius: 'What do you exactly refer to?'

Rhodopis: 'None of the mentioned attributes is negative. The sundial really fits you, Senius.'

Oracle: 'I can be a little more specific. As an example, you sometimes have felt that your parents and your siblings mistreated you.'

Senius: 'Yes, you are right. It has happened, but I do not interpret it that way. As I see it today, I feel fortunate to have got the possibilities I brought into my adult life. So, I do not repress anything.'

Thoughts

Oracle: 'With our thoughts, we reveal how we perceive ourselves as we talked about "Beliefs". Most of them are based on values we inherited in our early childhood. And as we have seen, this luggage tends to determine our present thoughts, thus determining our future. That is fine if it fits with our call, but it is obstructive if it does not.

'Another way to put it is that you are what you have been thinking until now and you become what you think right now. On the other hand, thoughts are just perceptions, which are interpretations of reality and can be changed as they are in your control.'

Senius: 'What is it you are aiming at?'

Oracle: 'Well, Senius, be a little patient. The idea of going through your past was to become crystal clear about your call. It has given a solid reference for your life.

'Furthermore, it allows you to consider whether your thoughts support that. You know that everybody has something in their luggage, the karma, which potentially can be healed through the call. This challenge is, at the end of the day, caused by the lack of love.'

Senius: 'Do you mind being more specific please?'

Oracle: 'Since you haven't received unconditional love in all situations in your childhood, you have inherited limiting beliefs. They can have many disguises. Let me give you an example from your childhood.

'Before you went to school, you did not always get the support you needed. Four children born in a span of 5 years is quite a task for your parents. You were very curious and had many questions that you wanted to get answered mostly from your dad.

'However, he did not always take the time needed to give you a suitable answer due to their situation. Instead, he said that you should not bother or gave you the impression it was above your ability to understand. As you wanted his attention, you sometimes became stubborn, which just ended with a more decisive rejection. It made you unhappy and you felt unaccepted, which contributed to feelings of unworthiness and guilt.

'Your dad did not intend to hurt you. Nevertheless, it made your ego think about what you did, and it harmed your self-esteem, which you did struggle with during your younger days.'

Senius: 'Yes, it becomes clearer to me how my childhood formed my personal character or rather how my ego interpreted the situation.'

Oracle: 'It is fine that it gives you an understanding of how your past has formed your ego. But it also demonstrates that thoughts are conditional, where the ego personalises events with judgements. In a broader perspective, your past thoughts are fuelling your ego, thus keeping it alive. It also applies to imaginary thoughts concerning the future, as you saw when we spoke about setting goals for the future "Roles".'

Senius: 'I notice a shift in your notion of the ego. What is the purpose?'

Oracle: 'As we have stated more times, you are not your ego. The ego is your tool. Whenever you are in your thoughts, you are inside yourself. It can be either in the past or in the future, and disconnected with your soul.'

Senius: 'It brings further understanding to what you stated previously about the chatter of thoughts running in the background without our awareness.'

Oracle: 'Well, actually more than that. How do you get aware of this chatter?'

Senius: 'By observing my thoughts.'

Oracle: 'Exactly. And what is it you use to observe your thoughts?'

Senius: 'My soul.'

Oracle: 'I agree. But to be more specific, it is the consciousness of your soul. While you do this, you are outside your ego. The ego cannot relate to consciousness or store it. It is simply conceptually out of reach for the ego and thus your way to freedom.'

Senius: 'It is exciting. I assume that it also works for what I observe outside myself?'

Oracle: 'Yes. It implies that you are in the present moment with your consciousness, which enables you to see what you observe as it really is without judgement.'

Senius: 'Let me summarise what you said to ensure I got it right: We went through my "Life in Brief" to derive my call. However, without identifying myself with the ego, which is nothing but a tool to carry out my call. The perceptions I gained are based on my ego's thoughts connected to the events that occurred to me. The clue is to be conscious and fully aware of the present moment.'

Oracle: 'That's how it is. It will also strengthen your awareness of how you feel while focusing on what you do. Furthermore, your ego is always thirsty for more thoughts to fuel its existence. Maybe you now understand why I previously stated that peace and harmony are not a purpose in itself but a precondition to observe clearly with your soul's consciousness.

'You can compare it with looking into a lake. You can only see the bottom when it is calm. It is a prerequisite to fulfilling your call.'

Rhodopis: 'It suddenly strikes me that there could be a complete picture: While being an embodied soul, we experience consciousness with the ability to see the whole through our own entity of being.

'Does it mean that we, through this perspective, can get access to the entire picture?'

Oracle: 'It is a very bright question, Rhodopis. And yes, in principle, you can. The consciousness of the Source pervades everything. It is another way to see the raindrop compared with the vast ocean as mentioned previously.

'The possibility to access the Source lies in your ability to tune into your highest possible frequency related to your development sphere. I will return to this discussion when we come to talk about "Supporters".'

Senius: 'Is that what is meant by "Don't you believe that I am in the Father, and that the Father is in me? The words I say to you I do not speak on my own authority. Rather, it is the Father, living in me, who is doing his work", as written in John 14:10?'

Oracle: 'Yes, I can confirm this. It also means that it is potentially accessible to anyone. It is what enlightenment and spirituality are about, and is the ultimate test of your faith.'

Senius: 'It also puts a new light on Matthew 19:14, which we spoke about in "Faith": Jesus said, "Let the little children come to me, and do not hinder them, for the kingdom of heaven belongs to such as these".'

Senius: 'If I understand you correctly, it means that anyone is in the Father and that the Father is in anyone?'

Oracle: 'I can confirm this. It was also the reason why I said it is the ultimate test of your faith. If you truly believe this, it will be revealed to you right away.'

Feelings

Oracle: 'Our feelings are the most vital tool to create our lives. We talked about how the soul communicates, among others, through your feelings as a way to discover your spirituality. It is the feedback mechanism or part of our compass that tells us whether we are on the right or wrong course of action, telling us so with positive or negative feelings, respectively.

'There are only these two sets of emotion—positive or negative feelings. However, please be aware that positive and negative feelings are not the same as good or bad feelings. These designations are subjective judgements of the ego.

'Positive and negative emotions are equally good if you treat them well. You can continue nurturing positive feelings, while negative feelings are gaps or development areas.

'They are signals that should make you look deeper to figure out why you feel like you do.

'In general, most people want to be happy and praise the good emotions, whereas bad feelings are something they want to avoid even if development potential lies in them.

'When you are more mature, your mood is more aligned with your soul. You notice the beauty around you, filled with love and less dependent of the perspective of others.'

Senius: 'I can use the Law of Attraction to secure that I attract only positive feelings.'

Rhodopis: 'In theory, you are right. But is that what you experience in your daily life?'

Senius: 'No. I have to admit that negative thoughts occur and sometimes I am even not aware why I feel as I do.'

Rhodopis: 'That is exactly my point. You are not in control of your feelings, even if you have perfect intentions.'

Senius: 'You are right, unfortunately. But why am I out of control?'

Oracle: 'Because your mode of feeling is dependent on what happens around you or in your mind. Let me start with the incidents in your surroundings. If somebody acts in an unrespectable way that does not fit your view, you automatically react with a negative response that does not only impact your conscious mind but also your subconscious mind.

'It can also be something that's happening elsewhere, e.g., when you watch television. Most of the time, news is negative. Catastrophes create the biggest headlines.

'You might say that it is not something you attracted yourself. Okay, but you also agreed to expose yourself to the broadcasts when you decided to watch the news. Another way to express it is that as long as you do not master the Law of Attraction perfectly, your reactions are dependent on the events around you.'

Senius: 'I see your point. Is there any way out of the trap?'

Oracle: 'Fortunately, yes. Let me refer to Matthew 5:43-45:"You have heard that it was said, 'Love your neighbour and hate your enemy.' But I tell you, love your enemies and pray for those who persecute you, that you may be children of your Father in heaven. He causes his sun to rise on the evil and the good, and sends rain on the righteous and the unrighteous".'

Senius: 'I know these quotes, and I agree. So far, it has been hard for me to forgive business relations who have misused my trust even if I know that it is the only way I can get peace within myself. It is far easier if the relation is less relevant to you.

'You can even apply a different perspective: "Out of sight, out of mind". Can you give me further inspiration because I still feel trapped?'

Oracle: 'Sure. You can start to see these relations from the outside view. You know that he/she comes from the same Source as you do, and both of you will ultimately return to the same destination. Furthermore, you can see your enemy as a teacher who can teach you to deal with his or her kind.

'When you judge others, you point at yourself. In your view, you may find their behaviour inappropriate because you would expect it differently. A situation like this is an option for you to extend your knowledge. Alternatively, you create karma for your next incarnation.

'Besides, you should know that nobody can be obliged above their level of development. Finally, if negative feelings are absent, you may also lose sight of further development.'

Referent: 'Senius nods.'

Senius: 'Yes, when you point at somebody, three fingers point back at you. Once I parked my mast while sailing my boat to the mast crane, another sailor drove his mast into mine crashing my top light. As I came, he was upset and blamed me for leaving my mast behind.

'I stayed calm and asked him whether he could agree that my mast was parked and that he drove his mast into mine. As I did not respond to his aggression, it was as if the air slipped out of a balloon. And we got the situation settled. If I had reacted by aggression, it would not have worked out.'

Rhodopis: 'It is a good example of an appropriate reaction to a negative situation, although you could not mount the mast before you bought a new top light.'

Oracle: 'Let me get back to your *enemy* who has a more or less conscious call. Please remember it is not up to you to judge. Your example is excellent, as Rhodopis mentioned. Responding to an insult with another insult or any type of aggression will only bring more fire to the conflict, creating a negative mirror image for yourself.

'If you want to maintain your peace, you can do what you did or try to clarify why he reacts that way. A misunderstanding may cause it, or maybe it is not about you, but you became a lightning rod for his frustration. Instead, try to help the poor guy and try to stay calm to avoid getting contaminated by his mood.'

Senius: 'I understand your reply so far. However, I think it can still create a gap between the right behaviour and how I feel about myself. Isn't there a risk that it will appear false and unworthy?'

Oracle: 'It is only true if you hate your *enemy*. That was why I started by saying that you should see the situation from the outside. Because in doing so, you disconnect your feelings. It should then be easier for you to deal with the issue. If you join his attack, you create a conflict in your mind.

'You can also use your experiences from your past related to how you handled it yourself. Let me illustrate this with an example. Try to imagine a situation where you know the right thing to do, but you do not implement it right away. It is called cognitive dissonance".'

Senius: 'Well, I did smoke in my younger days, and I attempted to quit way more than once, but the temptation was too strong. Besides, when I tried, I became annoyed, which went beyond my surroundings.'

Oracle: 'Excellent example showing emotional reactions that have nothing to do with the people who were affected by your mood. There are plenty of these cases. Anyway, how did you get out of the bad habit?'

Senius: 'When my wife got pregnant with our youngest daughter, I got a strong motivation for stopping. The hard thing is to take the serious decision to quit. Furthermore, I started jogging to do something that did not fit with smoking, and that worked out for me.'

Oracle: 'Perfect. Apart from this approach, there is another method. I will get back to this when we address meditation.

'With this awareness, you learn about the consequences of feelings you are worried about or negative emotions that you are scared of, which by itself creates bad feelings. Another affirmation can alleviate it: It takes many negative thoughts to cancel positive thinking. The fact that the power of love supersedes the power of fear confirms this as well.

'Furthermore, God, Source, Universe or whatever label you attached to it has been so wise that in the physical world, there is a time delay between the feeling and the manifestation. It offers you time to do mitigation measures.'

Senius: 'On the one hand, it is pretty obvious that bad feelings are unattractive, so why choose them at all? On the other hand, nobody can state that they never have had bad feelings.'

Oracle: 'Immediately, you are right. It seems irrational until you manage to love everything and everybody. It is the most exquisite spiritual development level, which is far beyond where you are at present. And if you were, you would not choose to incarnate.

'Until you reach that state, what you designate as negative feelings are triggers showing you potential development areas. It gives you opportunities to look inward and learn who you are and why you react as you do.

'It is also important to process trapped feelings as they can be triggered when you experience situations that reminds you of them. For example, if you are filled with grief from the death of a dear relative which you haven't processed, it will appear whenever you experience something that reminds you about him. You have to find a way to deal with it to let it go, e.g., by talking with somebody you trust and who is willing to listen to you. Joy cannot coexist with grief.

'It also has another meaning. You are in the physical world to gain experiences. To make this possible all feelings, as well as attributes, are defined and realised by its opposite or antithesis.

Let me illustrate this with some examples: you do not know what good feelings are if you do not know what bad feelings are. The same goes for attributes like high-low, thick-thin, narrow-wide, short-long, life-death, etc. Each of them is each other's prerequisite.'

Senius: 'What is your point?'

Oracle: 'My point is that you can only define your feelings and attributes if their opposites exist. If it were singular, you wouldn't be able to get it as a conscious experience. If you look at the examples mentioned before, you will realise this, it also goes for actions and reactions to others' actions.

'Is has already been described in ancient Chinese philosophy through Yin and Yang as intrinsic dualism. It can be described as seemingly opposite or contrary energies which are interrelated and complementary.

'Let me bring it a little bit further as stated God is love. But you cannot understand it if its opposite does not exist.'

Senius: 'Does it mean that fear needs to exist to let me experience love?'

Oracle: 'You hit the nail on the head. Love is like the light which covers all colours apart from black, the absence of light.'

Senius: 'I am confused. As I understand, God did not invent fear by himself?'

Oracle: 'Well, to meet you where you are, I can refer to The Fall in Genesis 3:1-5: Now the serpent was more crafty than any of the wild animals the Lord God had made. He said to the woman, "Did God really say, You must not eat from any tree in the garden?"

'The woman said to the serpent, "We may eat fruit from the trees in the garden", but God did say, "You must not eat fruit from the tree that is in the middle of the garden, and you must not touch it, or you will die".

'"You will not certainly die", the serpent said to the woman. "For God knows that when you eat from it, your eyes will be opened, and you will be like God, knowing good and evil".

'Pictorially spoken you broke the command of God. So, fear was brought into your world by you.

'This illustrative example also shows another impressive view. In the beginning, the serpent saw doubt in the mind of Eva. The second attack represents a lie which blamed God and was intended to awake suspicion to his motive and pave the way to Eva's pride.

'Both attacks are toxic for our ability to realise our desires. With doubt in your heart, you will fail to create your desires, and you will miss your call with pride. Besides, doubt is used negatively in this context which has caused many Christians to perceive doubt as a negative concept. However, doubt can also be used constructively as we did when we discussed faith previously.'

Senius: 'What do I do with my fear?'

Oracle: 'We will come to it soon. However, there is another topic I want to address first.'

Referent: '"Exercise 6, Switch Feelings," is described in Appendix I.'

Intuition

Oracle: 'The rationalist will be sceptical to this tool as it does not comply with the ego's illusion of being in control. But if you look closer into it, your ego is far less in control than it thinks. It believes it makes decisions based on facts only.

149

'But in reality, it does not have access to the required information nor can it predict the consequences of its actions. Besides, in social interactions, we let emotions more or less consciously impact our decisions. You have an objective uncertainty that you overrule by an inner certainty—your intuition. The more aware you become of your intuition, the more confidence you will ascribe to it.

'If you look at history, you will find a lot of different definitions of intuition by philosophers like Plato, Descartes, Hume, Immanuel Kant and others, as well as by various religions. Quite a few have had an awareness of its presence. The interpretations of intuition vary as they are coloured by their personality and time of living.

'Intuition is your internal voice that originates from your superconscious mind—your soul. It is the link that connects us. If you are a religious person, you can see it as a divine gift. The gut feeling often gets misinterpreted as intuition. Gut feeling is belonging to the ego, therefore your lower thoughts and desires.

'Do you remember that in our previous conversation I used the computer as a metaphor to describe how the mind of a new-born works?'

Senius: 'Yes, even though I am not sure I can recall the metaphor in detail. Why do you ask?'

Oracle: 'Because I want to extend it a little bit further to give you an understanding of what intuition is. So, let me repeat what I said earlier. Just like a computer, the mind is dependent on the only program installed, the operating system, which controls all the internal functions and makes it possible to install the applications you want.

'Likewise, your memory and consciousness are empty, but your operating system, the autonomy system, controls all your internal functions and keeps you alive. The operating system corresponds to your subconscious mind. Your memory and your application programs match your conscious mind. The extension I want to make is to include your soul—your superconscious mind.

'In the computer, it corresponds to two areas: online memory and communication applications. The first area or the online memory

150

corresponds to your consciousness, the one you use to relate to the physical world. The second area or communication applications give you a potential connection to the spiritual world. Furthermore, it gives you access to your former lives, which also requires programs to be installed, just like the former application programs.

'The point I want to make is that you can download the application programs in the online memory by observing and interacting with the external physical world, which is immediately accessible to anyone. You cannot miss them nor control them, at least not in your childhood.

'Another way to put it is that it is a subject, you, who observes an object, something in the outside physical world. When it comes to the communication applications, it is very different, because it is something that occurs within you, a subject observing itself.'

Rhodopis: 'Sorry, you lost me.'

Senius: 'I, too, am wondering what you're getting at.'

Oracle: 'Be a little patient. A part of the communication programmes consists of monitoring what goes on and act if something doesn't operate as it should. You have practical experience with this when you decide to observe your thoughts. But it can also be an inner voice that gives you an idea you may act upon. This is an example of your intuition.'

Senius: 'What do you mean by "may act upon"?'

Oracle: 'Brilliant observation, Senius. You have free will, and are therefore, free to act or not on what your intuition suggests you to. Remember when you envisioned your first book, I couldn't get in contact with you and you were annoyed because you didn't listen to me. In this case, for example, you used your will.

'This leads to another important general conclusion: Intuition is always the shortest way to your aim. If you want to embrace your call, don't let your will get in the way.'

Senius: 'I think I understand your point. But when it is something that is coming from you, then can it be a "subject observing itself"?'

Oracle: 'It is a correct derivation. It is another communication application to stay on the computer as a metaphor. It is a monitoring programme that gives you access to the spiritual world. It was my response to you which you chose to ignore when you looked into your future at Gran Canarias about a decade ago.'

Senius: 'I see this clearly and am still annoyed over my reaction at the time.'

Oracle: 'It was not the reason for me to bring it up. To your excuse, you were in the initial phase and more or less unconscious about this ability, simply because you were not fully aware of it as an opportunity to get your question solved. Out of this, I would like to underline:

- If you do not consider intuition as an option, you will miss it.
- You can use your intuition in two ways: either by the ideas you didn't ask for or by asking for them. It corresponds to an action initiated by me or another supporter in the spiritual world or by yourself, respectively.

'Summa summarum, if the process has to work for you, you have to trust the process. And this has been an issue for you because the so-called "self-appointed wiser" have convinced you that you cannot trust your inner voice, which is a significant error and may have mixed it up with gut feeling.'

Senius: 'Yes, I can confirm that I was influenced by the rationalists.'

Oracle. 'It is a classical barrier that made quite a few lose their way.'

Senius: 'Fortunately, one of my friends has a strong intuition that gave me the awareness back again, and I now feel more confident with my intuition.'

Oracle: 'Yes, you are fortunate to have such a soulmate as a friend. I want to elaborate a little on your experience. The reactions from your environment triggered doubt in your mind because you did not fully develop your intuition at the time. It initiated a dissonance between your soul and your ego.

'Your soul wants to accelerate your spiritual development while your ego wants to use its will to maintain its dominance. Simply put, the will is the ego domain while the soul is the intuition domain.

'A way to overcome this seemingly is to gradually gain experiences that the ego cannot disapprove of. Another way to cater to the resistance is to ask yourself why you feel reluctant. In this way, you use your doubt to convince your ego constructively. But let me return to you, Senius. What did you do?'

Senius: 'Well, it depends on the situation. If I know what question I want to get solved, then I keep it in my mind and be open-minded for a response, which can be conveyed through different channels, e.g., frequently through an intuitive thought or other people.

'For example, I can present a recent question, in which I wanted to know if I should attend a meditation programme in Sweden. I raised the question just before I went for a walk. As I was walking, images showed up in my mind—images of me getting infected with Covid-19 and how I was struggling to return home.

'When I returned home from my walk, I watched a press meeting on TV where more restrictions were introduced due to the infection surge in Denmark and other countries. I did not have any doubt in my mind and cancelled my participation.

'If the incident is less present, it is still possible to acknowledge. A while ago, I met an acquaintance while walking, but I was deep in my thoughts and didn't take any action and neither did he. We met again half an hour later as we were walking towards each other. However, this time it was hard to overlook. Nevertheless, we had an exciting talk, and I realised that he had a message for me, which I didn't realise until I came home.'

Rhodopis: 'They are great examples. The first one speaks for itself, and both are classic examples. I can add to the second example that whenever you meet somebody twice, you both have a message for each other. In more general terms, this also applies to strangers.

'If you made eye contact with somebody, say, in a restaurant and it happened twice, be curious and try to contact that person. You will probably be surprised by the outcome.'

Oracle: 'It is a great point, Rhodopis. Besides, it also demonstrates that you receive messages by being alert through your consciousness.'

Senius: 'I agree even though it can be somewhat transgressive in the beginning. When I am in doubt about something, I concentrate on my feelings. If I feel love, then I know it is the right thing to do, and if I feel something else, I am sure it originates from something of a different nature, and I will skip it.

'I use this approach in many other situations. For example, during my Camino journey, I arrived at a hostel together with another pilgrim. The hostel was closed, and we took our place in the queue.

'Suddenly I was hit by a feeling telling me that it was not the place I should stay. I told my fellow pilgrim that we should leave the hostel without giving any proper rational argument. But we left the hostel.'

Oracle: 'It is a beautiful example. And I can add that you can always trust your intuition when you are connected to your feelings as you described it. Besides, when you are in doubt, it is still appropriate to ask questions like "Why does the situation affect me negatively when I have no evidence supporting it?" It is a question that calls for guidance. And you will get advice from your relations in the spiritual world irrespective.

'Some may say that it is not their experience. The issue is that you sometimes are not aware of the answer because it can come in a way different from what you might have expected. It can be in the form of a whim, a memory, a feeling or an inspiration, for example. The roads are many.

'You also know it from the Bible, e.g., in Matthew 21:22: "If you believe, you will receive whatever you ask for in prayer". Another way to put it is that when people pray to God, they get a response in the same way as you do. This also explains why people get confirmed in their faith independently in the name of their God.

'Furthermore, you also did have a great role model in your grandfather. Let me refer to what you told earlier about him. When he had to make difficult decisions, he looked into his bible, picked a random page, and did what that page inspired him to do. It is also a great example of using intuition. Due to his strong Christian faith, it was his way of utilising his intuition.'

Senius: 'I haven't seen it from that perspective before. I am amazed.'

Oracle: 'It is also a classic example of childish ignorance, which you remember without seeing this great ability from an adult perspective. You have kept it as a weird character of your grandfather in your memory. But don't blame yourself. I do mention it only to let you understand that you have many memories from which you can harvest new opportunities if you reflect upon them with the insight you now have.'

Senius: 'Thank you for bringing up this new insight. Anyway, let me return to the time when using my intuition was relatively new; the responses I received were contaminated by my fear, confusing my feelings about the answers, which sometimes surprised me.'

Oracle: 'What did you do about it?'

Senius: 'I used my intellect to ask questions until I realised what it was rooted in, e.g., insecurity. I rarely experience this trap nowadays.'

Oracle: 'That is excellent. As you grow more mature, you will also learn to distinguish which sources supply you with information.'

Senius: 'Is this important?'

Oracle: 'Not so much at present, but probably in the future. Try to imagine that you work in different areas of development. This attracts other souls who are interested in what you do, and they will support you.

'As you develop, somebody may also replace me, and you may even attract souls at a higher level, e.g., the master of your field of interest who will occasionally help you.

'When you get support from such different souls, you can get different answers to the same question. So, in order not to be confused, it will help you to know who the source of the message is.'

Senius: 'It makes perfect sense to me. However, when I look at the people dominating my rational environment, they will probably shake their heads and assume I am from a different planet. For example, it is outside the cognitive psychology, which is the foundation for my coaching praxis.'

Oracle: 'I can confirm your observation. But whether a person is aware of his or her intuition or not, does not matter. Everybody receives guidance and support.

'However, the person who is conscious about these connections will strive to bring himself in line with his soul, which will strengthen the ability to further growth, peace and happiness by serving a higher purpose.

'There is another perspective to what you just said. Do not let people contaminate you with doubt as you did in the beginning. Fortunately, you have re-acknowledged your intuition for good. To return to the computer metaphor, you cannot immediately use other people's data.

'You have to align it with your personal reference. If you copy-paste, it will create a clash that will cause a malfunction: There will be tension and dissonance in your feelings and your body may respond with a disease.'

Dreams

Oracle: 'Dreams are a magnificent tool that you can use in different ways. In your case, your other followers and I have planted ideas there, which you can choose to act upon.'

Senius: 'To my knowledge, it is not the channel that I have been most aware of during my adult life. But there is one dream that stands out crystal clear to me that I would like to share with you, even if its content is something we will return to later.

'One early morning, a big detonation breaks the peace. Bad weather exposes itself with a big thunderstorm accompanied by heavy rain, drumming against my bedroom window. The abrupt wakening reminds me of a dream that took place right before I abruptly got awakened.

'I was drawn back through time—before the beginning of the Universe precisely. It was very vivid, and I felt as if I had been there on the entire journey.

'I do not know how it is possible, but it is as if my life and experiences came into a more immense and unbroken context without being frightening—more like the pieces of an enormous puzzle being laid. In the puzzle, you, the reader, I, and anybody else can join with their contribution. I think it is most comfortable to grasp the concept if I describe my dream in a chronological order.

'I am in something that appears to me as a whole which I perceive as pure consciousness without any form. I experience myself as being part of this, together with an endless number of others without limits. We all are in profound harmony, togetherness and timelessness. I feel unconditional love, perfection and deep peace. The whole or "we", is all there is.

'Indeed, I feel that something is underway. Something that I can best decode as a desire or more precisely a wish to experience what "we" are. The wholeness is changing, and I hear a tearing crash. I see a huge flash, and in a split second, I lose my consciousness.

'In the next moment, I see the event from a different perspective, as an observer from outside the event. I realise that I have just participated in the "Big Bang" and moving forward while the Universe develops itself.

'I feel a resignation of the former togetherness and harmony. At the time, I feel a break-up between my now physical presence and my non-physical being. I exist on more levels, so to say.

'The dissonance reinforces the fact that my physical presence is part of the perishability of life: birth, growth, decay and death. On the long journey through space and time, I see myself in countless figures, gender, roles and with progressive insights that fit into a more significant evolution.'

Rhodopis: 'Wow, Senius, I would like to join you on that journey.'

Senius: 'I think anybody else does too, Rhodopis. The only difference is that the dream reveals my deeper needs for understanding why I am here.'

Oracle: 'In a way, I can confirm your statement. Your dream is unique and a great gift. It is an example of a peak experience, as we have discussed previously[10]. It has a great connection to your call and what you are dealing with right now.

'Besides, it lifts your faith to a new level. There is a vast difference in believing something and experiencing it even if it is a dream. On the other hand, your dream is also in harmony with other beings in your time of living. In this sense, you are still part of the wholeness even on the physical level.

'Another essential point that your dream can demonstrate is this: Allow yourself to be the one you are and allow anybody else to have the same freedom. In this way, you do not judge anybody but acknowledge that they are in a different stage of their development process.'

Oracle: 'But I think you need to explain: how did you attract your dream?'

Senius: 'I remember that I have been struggling with what should be my next step to bring joy and benefit to other people who have the same desire to understand what they should be aiming at.'

Oracle: 'As you did not have any expectation to how I should contact you, I chose the dream to inspire you through the big picture.

'In the beginning, you said that dreams are not the channel you have been most aware of. The reason is that you, for quite a few years, have ignored suppressed feelings from your childhood. By building up such a shield of your inner self, you also tend to ignore your dreams.

'You haven't made a systematic clean-up of your suppressed feelings, but only treated them one by one when you realised that it was something preventing you from doing what you wanted. Due to this, you have also been detached from your dreams for quite a while.'

---

[10] In the chapter about 'Faith.'

Senius: 'I see your point clearly and realise that I still have something to do in this respect.'

Oracle: 'You are right. But the first step is always awareness. And with the tools you have at hand, there is also a way forward. It is a necessary step to fulfil your call, which contains unconditional love to yourself as to anybody else.'

The Wishing Well

Oracle: 'You previously mentioned your "Wishing well", and earlier I said that it might not work for all, but I think it can be a source of inspiration. Do you mind sharing it with us?'

Senius: 'With pleasure. "The Wishing Well" is my daily moment of processing my visions. It is where I put the Law of Attraction into conscious creation to realise my call.

'I set up my annual objectives, which are mostly derived directly from my call. To each of them, I write why I want it and why I will receive it. Some of the topics may require inspired action. Then I break them down into intervals to a level that makes sense for the individual objective, which at the lowest level is monthly.

'When I start my daily Wishing Well, I start with a few affirmations to get into the right mood. Then I take a look at my objectives one by one and let my inspiration decide what I desire to do about each of them.

'The outcomes can vary significantly. It can be affirmations, visualisations, intuitive inspirations and so on. The level of detail depends on how close I am to one of my objectives, which is made easier by the fact that I usually break down an objective into smaller tasks.

'The main thing is that I give them awareness, and this brings them further in the creation process. For me, it is an experimentation laboratory, get started and let your inspiration fly and try out whatever comes to your mind.

'Remember, it is about your visions, your deep-felt desires at the soul level. Therefore, you will feel joyous, which also is the fuel to your ideas and what can bring them to life.

'It takes some time to get the Wishing Well established, but when you set up the essentials, a quarter of an hour is sufficient to keep it flying.'

Oracle: 'How is your experience so far?'

Senius: 'In the beginning, I was very excited about it as any other new interests catching me. But it came as a surprise to me that it was only a few visions I could get down on paper in the beginning. For me, it was a new way of thinking.

'Besides, the Wishing Well was a minor part of an entire model of how I would spend my time, and I wrote all my experiences down in a diary to be able to follow my progress.'

Oracle: 'It sounds great but also a huge step to take, isn't it?'

Senius: 'Yes, indeed. Even I have been deflected many times in the same way. In recent years, I have been hiking and doing other inspiring journeys for one month every year. I also kept a diary on the hikes, but very different from what I do at home.

'It is only about the inspirations I receive and other noticeable experiences. I get out of my daily routines for practical reasons, and when I get back, I do not return to the routines. They appear too overwhelming.'

Oracle: 'What do you intend to do about it?'

Senius: 'I am in the process of reinventing my tool in a lighter version. In this context, I will focus on the Wishing Well. What I said so far about it is still valid, but there is one more thing that is hard for me to understand. It is about an experience I have and to share with others who are aware of their call, which I would like you to address the topic.

'Once we know what our call, contribution to humanity, is and that it realises the highest meaning and joy for us, why is it that we often get distracted?'

Oracle: 'Well, a starting point can be what you learnt from Christianity, particularly the above-mentioned *Fall of Eden*. I summarise the tale in three points:

- The serpent saw doubt in the mind of Eva.
- The second attack of the serpent is a lie that blamed God. The

purpose was to wake suspicion in Eve and use it for its own purposes.

- The use of suspicion to make Eva feel pride.

The classical conclusion is *never even start listening to the serpent.* All the three attacks are toxic for your ability to realise your desires. With doubt in your heart, you will fail to create your desires and pride is what will make you miss your call.

'In the classical view, the serpent represents the devil. In the modern interpretation, the serpent represents the mortal human ego, our lower thoughts and feelings, which we have to overcome. Our call of life is a step towards our original state.

'As the ego loses power in this process, it will fight back in the beginning. If you are persistent, the ego will have to obey your soul.

'Another common distraction is all your daily tasks. If you feel you are under time pressure, it is easy to convince yourself that you can postpone this task until tomorrow. If you do so, you risk starting a destructive cycle that occurs the next day.

'What you decide and do now forms your future. The main driver of this decision is your ego. The countermeasure is to ask yourself: If I am my soul, what is the right thing to do?

'The last thing I would like to add is that there is an ongoing fight between your soul and your ego, especially in the beginning. When you start to awaken, your ego will try to suppress your soul because it knows it will lose its power. Sustaining your soul requires that you use your will to focus your thoughts at the soul level. You will experience setbacks but with time, you will see that they become less prevalent.'

Referent: 'You can find inspiration about 'Exercise 7: The Wishing Well' in Appendix I.'

Time Planner

Senius: 'In my experience, time is a very volatile concept, like sand between your fingers, and time can easily be wasted. This is especially true for a truly independent person. If you have fixed working hours, it helps you to keep structure on your working days.

'To get the most out of my day, I divide my working days into eight timeslots of 2 hours each for different activities, and I decide in the Wishing Well how I want to spend the day. Some will probably claim that this tool is killing their creativity.'

Rhodopis: 'Yes. I am one of them.'

Senius: 'I apologise, Rhodopis. Your answer does not surprise me. However, to me, it works the other way around. When I dedicate my time to the timeslots in the Wishing Well, I can obtain more things.

First of all, I get an awareness of how I spend my time. Secondly, I get my prioritised stuff done. And if I am ahead of my schedule, this gives me the freedom to do other things. Besides, I perform most of the activities I do because I love to do them.'

Referent: 'You can find further details in 'Exercise 8: Time Planner' in Appendix I.'

Senius: 'I dedicate my first timeslot to "My Morning Rituals" (Timeslot 1), Exercise 9. I use it for morning affirmations, exercises, yoga, meditation and my Wishing Well.

'You may argue against spending so much time in the morning. It did annoy me too because I do not want to steal the time from my remaining activities. The answer, in my case, is to get up earlier in the morning.

'In case you have fixed working hours, you can still use the Time Planner. You just have fewer and probably shorter timeslots to distribute.

'As you also will notice, there are no plans for the weekends apart from Timeslot 1. This does not mean they are without activities. If there are no specific plans, I still consider what I want the day to bring me. Apart from that, I like that the weekends differ from workdays.

'It is also a good idea to be aware of the potential waste of time, like watching television, which is often a time killer. However, I do allow myself to watch a movie now and then, as well as news, in small doses. But I prefer to see documentaries and use YouTube for the same purpose.

'I also enjoy reading books. My choice of videos and books is anyway related to my fields of interest to keep myself up to date.

'In the beginning, I ended my day by writing a diary. It is short and contains only highlights, which brings me in a mood of gratefulness for the day. I prioritise my next day and end the day with affirmations for a good night's sleep.

'Later, I realised that prioritising my day at night could disturb my sleep, because I brought them with me to bed causing me to brood about how to carry them through. Now I concentrate most activities in my Wishing Well in the morning. In the night, I am still saying *thank you* for the day and my affirmations.'

Your Backpack

Your journey is by love and wisdom elected.
and you know your call is by yourself selected.
Whenever you are with an obstacle confronted
See it as an opportunity you have wanted!

You never have to feel alone on your expedition.
Your guide is behind with assistance and attention.
Your divine intuition creates your access to the light.
With faith and confidence, you bring delight.

You know from experience what is needed.
You have your tools with experience crafted.
You never give up because you know the light,
which at the end will give the persistent right.

When fears occur in its disguises, you face the darkness.
You know darkness cannot be conquered with darkness.
The evil wants to saw doubt and blow out the candle.
Therefore, reject the first thought while you can.

Source: Oracle

The Faces of Fear

Oracle: 'Fear is a powerful emotion induced by perceived danger. This primitive human emotion can be traced back to our early ancestors when we were hunters. It was a matter of survival. Fear has two responses on your body.

'The first is a physical sensation, a biochemical reaction that induces universal reactions such as increased heart and breathing rate, high adrenaline levels, increased muscle tension and sweating. The second is the reaction you attach to the sensation.

'When the danger is real, this alert mode is an efficient countermeasure for survival. However, nowadays in most situations, this is not the case. Please remember that what we observe through our senses is a subjective perception eventually translated to fear in our mind.

'Other specific fears are a result of learning experiences. As an example, if you fall from a building, you can develop fear of heights. In some cases, this fear can be transferred to a worried person observing others' fears.

'Another interesting finding is that some biochemical reactions are connected with excitement, which can lead somebody to seek dangerous situations under controlled environments in the beginning. But as the effect fades out because you get accustomed to it, some even try real danger to get the pleasant sensations; people following this mechanism are also labelled adrenaline junkies.

'In more general terms, fear is the opposite of love and nearly as powerful as love, but love will at the end always win as the Source possesses the highest frequency. It also means that you are disconnected with the Source when you are in a state of fear. Nevertheless, fear is a substantial barrier and can have many faces.

'In this context, I will differentiate them in six categories: internal fear, death, external fear and a variation of fears, worries, diseases and the most prevalent disease in the industrialised world—stress.'

Internal Fear

Oracle: 'In general terms, fear is an illusion like any other belief. In a modern context, the reaction to fear is often inadequate. When you manage to see through it, it loses its power.'

Senius: 'I have seen an example of this in a television programme about phobias. As I remember it, a phobia is an irrational fear connected with a specific situation or object that does not present a real concern. However, the person perceives it as something to fear about.

'In this case, it was a woman who was scared of snakes. In the beginning, she was looking at a snake from a far distance. Even this made her feel anxious and freeze. The psychologist managed to deactivate her fear by convincing her that it was safe to look at it at a distance.

'The psychologist gradually led her closer to the snake, although now and then, they had to go backward. But in the end, she managed to have the snake around her neck without getting into an alert mode.'

Oracle: 'This methodology is labelled systematic desensitisation and requires professional support. The primary cure is to make sufficient exposures under a controlled environment. This bombardment of vulnerabilities makes the person familiar with the situation, which gradually reduces the body's sensation and associated emotions.

'A phobia and less severe fears are dependent on individual perception and not on the real risk. From a broader perspective, it is also interesting to acknowledge that emotion is a response to sensations in the body and not to the observed object or situation. It is something that you can use proactively, which I will come back to in connection with meditation.'

Rhodopis: 'I can add that, in general, humans are very good at imagining different fear illusions that are not rooted in reality but where your body reacts as if the fear was real. A typical example is the fear of not being able to fund your family's living costs due to disease or the potential loss of your job. They may be an illusion initially, but if you don't change your focus, you will attract what you don't want in compliance with the Law of Attraction.

'Your personality control, to a great extent, is your ability to get out of the mess. As Henry Ford so wisely expressed it: "Whether you think you can or you think you can't—you're right".'

Senius: 'I used this statement in many situations, and I am convinced that it works this way. It is another way to express the Law of Attraction.'

Oracle: 'I fully agree. If you look at your convictions from the outside, you will see they are conditional truths that are valid for no one else but you. Therefore, consider your thoughts carefully, so that you only bring energy to the thoughts you desire.'

Senius: 'How does this relate to the materialism, the hamster wheel, we talked about previously?'

Oracle: 'The immediate fear that keeps you in your hamster wheel is that you are not capable of maintaining your standard of living, especially when you are young. An excessively high burn rate may be the cause, combined with what the commercial world has convinced you that you need to have.'

Senius: 'In case I choose to get out of the hamster wheel, what happens next?'

Oracle: 'You may wonder whether you can find another job that will fulfil your call. There's no need to worry about that because when you talk about something you are thrilled about, this will be evident to the receivers. This will often give you new opportunities because they may know somebody who needs someone like you. Due to your passion, they will mention you in positive phrases and thus pave the way for you.

'Besides, it does not need to be an either-or decision; it may also be a gradual change where you spend more and more time on what you want.'

Senius: 'What happens if I choose to postpone my call?'

Oracle: 'Then you may incur into another fear. The risk is that you do not manage to get there because your hamster wheel takes most of your life. You can die before your time. But when you follow your call, this risk is absent.'

Senius: 'Are there any other types of fear you want to highlight?'

Oracle: 'Yes, there are two other types of fear I want to mention. The first one is related to your dreams, which often connects to your call. Fear can prevent you from realising your dreams. But dreams do not come out of the blue.

'You have attracted them yourself, and they are mostly planted in your mind by your supporting souls from the spiritual world. Therefore, you should never ignore a dream. Instead, please pay attention and consider how it may fit into your actual situation and what it is taking from the fears that prevent you from realising your dreams.

'Most fears exist only in your brain. Discuss it with your real friends, who know you so well that they can help you look at your dream from a realistic perspective.

'The above is especially challenging when you are used to getting a regular pay check. Many dreams get killed because people do not dare to leave their regular pay check behind. Either due to little faith in their capabilities or due to the reaction from the environment. So be cautious whom you're listening to.

'The second and last fear I want to mention is your romances because when you love somebody, you make yourself vulnerable. Your greatest fear is that your choices may cause your loved one to leave you. You are scared to be at fault.'

Senius: 'Now, are you judging me?'

Oracle: 'No, I base my reasoning on my observations. But the critical message in connection with failures is that it is okay to fail as it is a vital part of self-development. So, stand by your mistakes and become wiser.

'Summa samarium, your fear can be a hidden catalyser for an infinite list of reasons preventing you from realising your call. The art is to be brave enough to acknowledge the fear and act anyway!

'As an old quote states, "Who nothing dares, nothing wins", and the gain to follow your call is many folds higher.

'But it can have personal costs. Some fear scenarios will emerge. It is up to you what you find most important—your call or the situation where you feel fear.'

Senius: 'In my case, I have chosen my call; why be satisfied with less.'

Rhodopis: 'It is a typical, logical rationale that fits your way of thinking, Senius.'

Senius: 'I agree with you. On the other hand, it does not mean that it always is comfortable. It sometimes has unpleasant consequences. Among others, my choice has the outcome that I have lost more friends on the move.

'The reason is that my endless seeking of answers for the essential questions has changed my attitudes and opinions about what is real and crucial.

'Some of my friends remained in their convictions, which I fully recognise. The gap has made the content of our friendship meaningless. The hard part is to get a constructive leave as it hurts sometimes. For me, because I feel I hurt some people as they do not necessarily understand me and they have had confidence in me.'

Death

Oracle: 'A consequence of the life cycles is that when you get into the world, you also will have to leave it at some point. More precisely, you'll leave your tools behind: your body, thoughts and feelings.

'This may generate anxiety for quite a few of you because the thought of death prevents you from living the life you want. This fear can have many causes, e.g., fear of the unknown after death or the opposite fear of the judgment of your deity, premature death, worry for other's death and the anxiety for a slow and painful death.

169

'The mentioned reasons have one thing in common: they all depend on your convictions. But let me examine them one by one.

'Fear of the unknown is natural if you do not have any faith or conviction giving you an overview of what comes after life. As a result, this fear has motivated quite a few to seek a religion where they can seek alleviation.'

Senius: 'My dad has confirmed your view with his colourful humour. Even the devil goes to the monastery when he gets old!'

Oracle: 'Hmmm. It is indeed a colourful and unique form of humour. Let me now continue with the next one, fear of judgement by your deity. It has been prevalent in the past to force people to behave and follow the laws formulated by the priesthood.

'In the past, most of the preaching occurred with a fear perspective. Today it is more diverse in the different religions and congregations. For monotheistic faiths, fear is still prevalent because in their view, you only have this one chance to live. But we will return to this topic in further detail, later in our dialogue.

'Premature death can have more reasons, but the main one is getting involved in an accident, which in theory, can happen to anyone and prevent you from living your call or life in general.'

Senius: 'Why do you say in theory?'

Oracle: 'Well, as I have emphasised earlier, there are no coincidences. The Law of Attraction works without exception. On the other hand, I do not suggest that anybody should feel any guilt because it is often unconscious. See it as another reminder to be more conscious of what you bestow your thoughts on.

'The second is fear of other's death, which can happen if you are dependent on another person in order to realise your basic needs or dreams. But never judge this dependence, because you do not know that soul's call.'

Senius: 'Why do you pinpoint this?'

Oracle: 'When you judge somebody, the fingers point mostly at yourself. There is something you do not understand because it does not comply with your subjective perception. The moment you judge, you are disconnected from the Source.

'The last one is the fear of a slow and painful death. The argumentation is the same as for premature death. Besides, this way of dying can be part of the call for that person.'

Senius: 'It might be out of place, but I have to ask if there is any objective reason to fear death.'

Oracle: 'No, fear disconnects you from the Source. Life continues after death but in a different dimension. I will address this in detail in "The Process of Death" later. But do not overinterpret the answer. It is not about doing an activity during your life and getting a reward after death.

'In fact, this attitude would reverse your development. On the other hand, you cannot prevent people from saying that martyrdom is rewarded which is something they may have inherited from their interpretation of their branch of religion, culture etc.

'Like any other leave, your bodily death means that something else can begin. In this case, it is a farewell to your beloved ones, which of course is a difficult and sad moment.

'Let me start shedding light on how you could strike a balance in your life cycle, based on your earthly perspective. If you found your call and acted it out, you have done the best you could to enrich your life and soul. If not, there are probably many other things you have done that can make you grateful.

'Besides, for your own sake, you must forgive others that may have insulted or hurt you. It does not necessarily change their situation, but if you do so you can leave with peace in your heart and soul.'

Senius: 'Why is it important to be grateful?'

Oracle: 'Because gratefulness brings the right mood in your mind and brings you in harmony with your soul.

'When you end a chapter, it also means that a new one can begin. You leave your worn-out body and mind behind, but your soul, your faithful and immortal I, will be united with your real home.

171

'There is nothing to fear. You will experience nothing but unconditional love. Nobody judges you, and while you are here, you do not even judge yourself.'

Senius: 'What exactly happens when I die?'

Oracle: 'We will come back to this later. In brief, though, you can see all your actions in life from your point of view and how it has impacted the actors who took part in them. Besides, you will see your life in a higher context with your former lives as a reference for defining your next mission, your new call.'

Senius: 'Does this mean that I will be reborn again?'

Oracle: 'If that is what you want, yes.'

Senius: 'This discussion reminds me of a pilgrim I met on my last Camino journey. He worked as a nurse in an intensive care unit in a hospital. He had the opportunity to talk to many people who could not make it, and most of their regrets were about what they could not manage to do, e.g., not realising their dreams and things they were not able to manage in their relationships.'

Oracle: 'Yes, they are widespread topics, and this is a reminder not to postpone what really matters to you.'

Rhodopis: 'Another perspective comes to my mind, related to the perception of age and death. One way of looking at age is to say that the older you are, the higher is the risk of death. Another way to look at it is that the older you are the higher is the probability that you continue to grow even older.'

Oracle: 'It is a great example of different perceptions on the same topic. Statistically, both statements are correct. The first way corresponds to a mind focusing on the negative aspect—a worried mind. The second way focuses on the positive aspect—an optimist mind.'

Senius: 'I can identify myself with the latter. I think of age in another way. If a child is 10 years old and turns 11, the change rate is 10%. If you take a person who turns 51, the change is only 2 %. In other words, the elder you are the slower is the change. That is something that comforted me as it is also the way I have experienced it when I follow the development of how people grow old.'

Rhodopis: 'I do not appreciate your juggling with figures, Senius, even if you have a good point.'

Oracle: 'Well, I understand your point, but you assumed that it is a purpose in itself to grow old. This precondition applies to only some cases. From the soul perspective, the determinant is whether further years will add more value to your call.'

Senius: 'Does it mean that it is the soul that takes that decision?'

Oracle: 'In the case that the soul concludes that there is no point in staying in the body any longer, it will make the decision, and your ego cannot do anything about it. If that is not the case, your ego can influence when death takes place as you have freewill.'

Senius: 'It sounds a little too abstract for me to understand. Can you add an example of both scenarios?'

Oracle: 'When the soul thinks its mission is completed, it will seek to go back to its origin in compliance with itself, its guide or Master depending on the matureness of the soul. When that happens, you will lose your joy of life and feel full of days and die in peace.

'If the soul finds that there are unfinished things to do, you can shorten your life through your will. In its most extreme form, you can use your will to commit suicide, or you can be so obsessed by materialism that your body erodes, or you may have an inappropriate lifestyle to mention a few.'

Senius: 'Thank you. I think I got it now. I can add that every morning I wake up and feel healthy, I am thankful.'

Oracle: 'It is a good habit and sets a great start for your day.'

Rhodopis: 'And typical of you, Senius, as you always focus on the bright side like the sundial.'

External Fear

Oracle: 'You may feel an external fear when an exterior event can impact your life, family, friends, or your possessions. An example of the first category is, among others, when the terrorists' praxis randomly chooses their victims. War is another category that can impact all of them.

'These kinds of events are outside your control. Your choice is how you address them in your context.'

Senius: 'I am a little confused. Could you be a little more specific?'

Oracle: 'First of all, you can consider the options you have and evaluate the risks for each. Say, how probable is it that you are affected by that specific event you fear? Most of them tend not to come true, and if at all, to which extent will they impact you? As you probably will realise that it is often out of proportion because most people let their feelings get away with them.

'Let me illustrate this by an example. Imagine an outbreak of a new virus that has no cure, and there is a specific risk that a certain percentage of people will die. You will see that fear can spread like rings in the water. Often there is no rational justification, but the feelings run away with people.

'Often, they forget the denominator, the probability of getting infected and the probability of dying if you attract it.'

Senius: 'Who do you mean by "the denominator and though the probability"?'

Oracle: 'My point is that perhaps only a minor part of the population may get infected because authorities are getting better at isolating the infected people. Say, less than 100 out of 100,000 people corresponding to 0.001%. And those who will die are, say, less than 0.5%.

'If you multiply these two factors, you end up with less than 5 people out of 1,000,000 people. I admit that it is unfortunate for those who are affected by the disease and their relatives, but news tends to magnify the reality to reach as many viewers as possible. What they report is inaccurate and often out of proportion.

'At the national level, politicians often use manipulation to persuade their population of their interpretation of an event. They misuse fear because it has the power to alter people's rational way of thinking as an example by preserving their safety in connection with a disaster.

'Your option is to consider how you bestow your thoughts on the situation with as little energy as possible.'

Senius: 'I am not quite sure. What is the point you're trying to make here?'

Oracle: 'Immediately, there are two reasons why I say that is your only option. First of all, you attract what you give your focus to. Therefore, keep your thoughts on your soul's desires. Secondly, what you judge, you will become yourself someday.'

Senius: 'Why?'

Oracle: 'The mission of your soul is to develop itself towards ongoing higher aims. To do this, your soul will need to experience all kinds of situations that it does not understand. Through this process, you define your call, and through this, you define who you are.'

Worries

Oracle: 'Worries are variants of fears, and as many threats, hypothetic. It is something that can happen in the future. But the issue is that they often prevent you from taking any action or they may even generate more worries.

'You may think that worries prevent you from doing things that could potentially harm you, but the wrong side of this view is that it makes it harder for you to realise that it is a negative feeling. As a result, it prevents you from living your life.

'If you believe that worries are harmful to your health, they will poison your life. As like attracts like, your health will be harmed.

'But in both cases, it is a harmful and counterproductive feeling that will reduce your quality of life. Besides, if you are worried about something, you'll tend to feel more anxiety, which initiates more worries, and it reinforces itself in a destructive circle.'

Senius: 'What is the solution?'

Oracle: 'As worries are something that can happen in the future, the short answer is to get back to the present. In the present, you are always safe.

'The second thing about it is that you probably see threats more dangerous than they are in reality. Thereby, you tend to overgeneralise single events, e.g., if your application for education results in a rejection, you generalise it to "I will never get admittance to higher education". Another bad habit is to convert rejections to your shortcomings and always expect worst-case scenarios or make negative interpretations without substantial evidence.'

Senius: 'I understand your argumentations for why worries might occur. But what are the countermeasures in challenging worries to get back to the present?'

Oracle: 'First of all, distinguish between those you can do something about and those you cannot.

'To the first category, you have to act upon them and take countermeasures. Firstly, you need to be aware of the fact that they are there. Next, let them pass through your mind without any attachment to avoid giving them more attention or energy. Instead, you can replace them with good thoughts or use some of the items from your list in 'Exercise 5: Switch Feelings' in Appendix I.

'If it is the latter category, surrender to uncertainty. It does not make sense to use energy on something entirely out of your control.

'You can spend time writing your worries down in the morning to get them out of your mind and then challenge them by giving them a reality check. But the most important thing is that you decide not to draw more energy to them by leaving them out of your mind for the rest of your day. You can repeat the exercise the next day and so on until you feel you got rid of them.'

Diseases

Oracle: 'As a starting point, your body can maintain itself. It is a pretty robust and advanced device that will serve you well during your entire lifetime if you treat it well.'

Senius: 'I have always been amazed by its ability to repair itself. I remember as a kid, how easily my wound healed and when I recovered from an infection. On the other hand, I have also noticed that quite a few people suffer from chronic diseases.'

Oracle: 'You are right. The reason is that if the body is put under pressure for a longer period without reaction to the early symptoms, it will show up. It is a very old cognition, among others stated by Hippocrates. He announced already before Christ, that diseases do not come out of the blue.

'They develop from small daily sins against nature. When too many sins have accumulated, diseases appear all of a sudden. A more contemporary way to translate his words is that if you ignore the signals of your body, it responds with diseases.'

Senius: 'When we talked about "The Cognitive Diamond" and "Beliefs", you mentioned that we could think our body to health or disease depending on our perception. Can you elaborate a little on this?'

Oracle: 'It is great you raise the question. One root cause of most diseases is that you have resistance against your present situation. You feel that your life does not develop the way you want, people are mean to you, you are overlooked at work or whatever else may make you grumpy.

'The point is, as long as you do not accept your present situation, you will be suffering. This suffering may attract other things that make you the breeding ground for further unhappiness and expose you to diseases.'

Senius: 'I guess the way out is to accept the "as is" situation?'

Oracle: 'Yes. That is the first step to accept your present circumstances. The next step is to be thankful for what you have. In this way, you move your attention to positive emotions and become a change maker for yourself.

'This way you align yourself with the Source and guide you through the recovery process. Besides you can use some of the tools we already talked about here.

'One way to look at diseases is as outcomes of different ways you stress your body. In general terms, there are two main categories.

'The first category is physical stress, which consists of many different sources: poor food, chemical residuals in drinking water, airborne pollutions like smog, viruses and bacteria and radioactive emissions, to name a few. Injuries belong to this group as well but differ in the sense that it usually happens immediately.

'The second one is mental stress, which can be imprinted from the environment, either by yourself or by a combination of the two.

'But before we delve into the two categories, I would like to add some common characteristics. The beginning of any disease is a wrong behaviour that either stems from you or is imprinted from others, e.g., pollution.

'Apart from injuries, there are some general stages before a disease occurs in both categories. The first step is that the source gradually makes the body more impure. Maybe the body can remove the toxins initially, but, after a certain time, they start accumulating, and the first mild symptoms emerge.

'In the next step, the toxins spread to the body where they find the most sensitive spots. At this point, medical care is usually required. In the third step, the disease gets worse, and in the last stage, it exacerbates and eventually contaminates other vital organs.

'When it comes to medicine, you need to be aware that it is a coin with two sides—it treats the symptoms and not the root cause. Drugs have their eligibility, but they also have side effects. In many cases, another medicine becomes necessary to reduce the side effects of the first one, with the potential risk of introducing new side effects. In this way, you may be initiating a destructive cycle.

'Therefore, you should use medicines for a limited period only. There are examples where long-term use of medicines has worsened the disease it was meant to cure; for example, sleeping pills. It is essential to diminish the use of drugs to what is strictly necessary and look for the root cause instead.

'Quite a few tend to find substitutes in nature, which medicine men have used for thousands of years. Here too, you have to be aware of what you take, because even nature has items that are unhealthy and fatal, at times. Nevertheless, always be cautious.

'Next, there is a development phase involving two groups of people: the first group, the treatment group, receives the real drug/treatment and the second group, the control group, receives a pill they think is the drug but in fact is not. But because the control group believes in the cure, some or even more recover from the disease than those who received the actual drug. This effect is labelled the *placebo effect*.

'The exciting thing is that the placebo effect works as the medicine should do, minus the side effects. In other words, if you have faith in the pill, the body can create what is needed to heal you. In more general terms, it would also be possible without a pill if you believe it will work. At the same time, you also must be willing to treat the root cause.'

Senius: 'Well, that is pretty amazing. However, not everyone gets cured, and they end up feeling guilty on top of their disease. If they fail on their own, don't you add more fuel to their disease?'

Oracle: 'If you put it this way, it seems so. But the world is not black and white. First of all, you cannot blame anyone for something they are not aware of. My point is that what you believe tends to be a self-fulfilling prophecy.

'Besides, I do not claim that you should cancel any treatment you are offered, but be cautious and take responsibility for your situation. Too many people deposit their will to their doctor when they announce their expectations are putting them in the victim role. That is never a good idea.'

Senius: 'It makes sense. But when it comes to the root cause, it may be out of the person's control, e.g., if the environment caused the disease, say, when smog causes lung cancer.'

Oracle: 'I agree that there are situations where it is out of your hands. But they are rare. Did you know that the root cause of most diseases in the western world is your lifestyle?'

Senius: 'I do, and unfortunately, this tendency has spread to other parts of the world because they are gradually adopting similar lifestyles. And I believe society is a major contributor to this development, e.g., production of substandard food products.'

Oracle: 'I agree. We also talked about this in connection with the community. My point is that you should take responsibility for your life. Even it seems like there are situations you can't change, you can always do something to improve your immune system.'

Senius: 'Can you be a little more specific on how we can improve our immune system?'

Oracle: 'As Hippocrates also stated: "Let your food be your medicine and let medicine be your food". To that, I want to add: If you're going to live longer, make your meals shorter. Furthermore, he also suggested that physical activity is necessary to stay fit.

'I think it is time to delve into the two main categories.'

Physical Stress

Oracle: 'Let me start with those that stem from the outside. One thing you can do is to consider where you choose to live. There is a tendency to move to bigger cities where the air is polluted from traffic and factories.

'From a health perspective, it is not a good idea, particularly for children who are more vulnerable when they grow up. Therefore, if you plan to have children, it is worthwhile to consider this.'

Senius: 'What about radioactive emission?'

Oracle: 'This form of pollution is even more dangerous because it is invisible. At the least, you can choose to live in a place that is at a safe distance from nuclear plants and where their wastes are stored.

'Next is radon; it can leak from the ground into your house. The radon level may be public in your area. Alternatively, you can ask somebody to measure it.

'For most remaining sources, it might be easier to make countermeasures. Mediocre food has become a big issue. I talk about fast food and highly processed food with a lot of unhealthy additives. It contains a lot of sugar and salt because they are both potent and cheap flavour enhancers.

'Moreover, they have a lot of more or less empty calories. One of the consequences is that when you eat such foods, the sugar level in your blood will increase drastically and then becomes low after a short period, and you start feeling hungry again. It is mainly an issue for poor people because it is cheap or they pay insufficient attention to their health.

'The outcome is a dramatic increase in diabetes 2, which previously affected only older adults. But nowadays, you find children below 10 years of age with diabetes 2. In addition, obesity appears to be prevalent at an alarming rate, which is related to many diseases, such as cardiovascular diseases in particular. Furthermore, the number of people affected by cancer is also increasing.'

Senius: 'I don't understand why such kinds of food are allowed to be produced if it has such a negative impact on people's health.'

Oracle: 'I agree. The industries' main arguments are that they produce what the consumer wants, and the consumer can voluntarily choose to buy it or leave it. Overall, it is important that regulations are made and strictly implemented, as previously mentioned when discussing about the community.'

Senius: 'What do you recommend?'

Oracle: 'It sounds simple because the answer is that you need to make your food from raw materials. You also avoid all other additives that the producers include for various reasons, e.g., to preserve the food. The problem is that poor people can hardly afford to buy raw materials.

Besides, it is time-consuming to prepare. For this reason, those who can afford it rarely do it.'

Senius: 'What about residuals in tapping water?'

Oracle: 'It depends on where you live. Another thing is that you only find the residuals you look for when testing the water. Besides, the limit value for a given pesticide is only valid if it is on its own. If there are more pesticides and chemicals, the limit value is less. But it is not considered at present when the tests are evaluated.

'Your choice is to buy water. In any case, I recommend you keep your immune system intact.

'Moreover, you need to be physically active for at least half an hour every day where your pulse is getting higher than slow walking. However, like anything else, you can exaggerate. For instance, running a marathon is not healthy; in the short term, it reduces your immune system.

'A rule of thumb is that too much and too little blight everything.'

Mental Stress

Oracle: 'The most critical factor is how you choose to respond to a particular impact. If your relations have been carried by love, you will probably have a brighter mind and exhibit positive behaviour, looking at possibilities and constructive outcomes.

'On the other hand, if your relations have been built on fearful relations, you will most likely have a dark mind, suspicious, worried and exhibit shy behaviour. The resilience will probably be very different in both situations.

'Let me illustrate this with a black and white example. If your resilience is high, the probability of getting sick is low. And if you get sick anyway, you will consider what you can do to be fit again.

'If your resilience is low, you may ask yourself why you got the disease and confirm yourself in your unfortunate circumstances, bringing further energy to your negative self-perception and thus, prolonging your illness.

'Of course, it does not have to be as polarised as stated in the example. On the other hand, a light mind will have a more comfortable starting point in life. However, it does not mean that one is better than the other. It depends on the soul's karma, which equals the gap the call intends to close.

'Today, the danger to be exposed to physical stress from wild animals is mostly absent for most people. However, the issue is that it does not prevent you from perceiving a situation as dangerous. Remember that what you observe and experience is only a subjective interpretation of reality but not necessarily the objective reality itself.

'However, the body may act as if it is a real danger—moving energy to the muscles to make you fit for fight or flight. Alternatively, it makes you freeze, which is rarely an appropriate reaction; I will therefore exclude it from our further discussion. The backside of the coin is that other parts of your body are suffering, e.g., your brain and guts.

'If this persists, you will develop stress. Typically, you will lose the ability to concentrate and memorise. Furthermore, food digestion becomes poor and cannot remove toxins effectively. The immune system is diminished, exposing you to diseases. Stress is the source of most diseases.'

Senius: 'What are the main reasons to stress?'

Oracle: 'You can find stress in many disguises. It can stem from expectations, either from your environment, or what you perceive of people's expectations of you, including family and loved ones or a combination of both. If it is from the environment, the trigger is often from work due to ongoing profit optimisation for private organisations and demand for higher output within a given budget for public organisations.

'If it is from your interpretation of the environment, it is often triggered by how you want to be perceived by your spouse, friends or society in general. Social media may reinforce this by drawing an unrealistic picture of how happy everyone else's lives are. However, what everyone presents is typically their interpretation of a perfect life, which is nothing but illusions and personal branding that is a far cry from the reality.'

Senius: 'Can you come up with a few examples from the areas you mentioned?'

Oracle: 'At work, the pressure may arise from the need to deliver more tasks within the set time frames. Incentive systems often reinforce such mechanisms. Managers tend to distribute their stress to the next level. At some point, it reaches your table.

'The outcome is that you may work more than is suitable for your health. Moreover, pressure may increase the number of mistakes, which in turn doubles the task making you even busier than you were. Your mood may change and perhaps get irritable and have a short fuse.

'Next, you may bring the lousy mood back home and quarrel with your spouse. Suddenly you find yourself in a spiral of bad events, and you have no base where you can find rest or sleep. And the symptoms begin to show up.

'You may want to provide your family with nice frames at home despite the debts you may have from your studies and choosing to own a flat or a house with an added mortgage to your budget. And to make it happen, you bought your home in suburbia to make it affordable. You may realise that you also need a car, which adds additional debt.

'Overall, it rocketed your monthly operation costs, and you have to work extra hours and save money on your housekeeping. You are in a hamster wheel, and you may get worried about what happens if one of you falls ill or gets fired from work. That could start a chain reaction where you push yourself beyond the limit and end up with stress.'

Senius: 'Even my situation has been different; I have had time at work as the top management hired a vice president for the organisation where I was responsible for a part of it. He was extreme and put high pressure on our organisation. I went more or less in survival mode, and I remember that I once sat in a meeting and could not remember the participants' names even if I had known them for years.

'It was terrible, and I realised that I had to do something. The solution came shortly after the management decided to fire him. Nonetheless, I felt I was caught in the situation.

'Can you provide some general solutions to get out of such traps?'

Oracle: 'Thank you for your example. It is very common in the sense that people often feel trapped as you did. In general, you have more options. The most common ones you already know: fight or flight.

'However, as it is a perception in your mind, there is also a third option, stay without a fight. Let me go through them one by one. Before you delve into one of the options, you should consider whether what you do at present complies with your call or not. It can help you make the right choice.

'Next is to consider the three options in the proper order: fight, stay without a fight and flight. Besides, the earlier you act, the higher is your probability of success as you still possess your full power. Even if that is not the case, have faith in the fact that you can still manage, although it will be a more challenging starting point.

'When you choose to fight, you can try to renegotiate to mitigate the situation. Alternatively, you may delegate some of the work to other people or remove tasks that do not bring value to what you have to deliver.

'The next thing you can do is the same situation as the stay without a fight is facing. When we talked about "Tools to Release Your Call", most of them are useable for getting out of the situation.

'The "Creation Process" teaches you that you are responsible for what you experience, and here, it is a flag telling you that you have to change your thoughts so you can create new circumstances. "Visualisation" gives you a way to imagine your new reality, which can be reinforced by "Affirmations". "Intuition" and "Dreams" are additional tools that can inspire you.

'Another magnificent tool is meditation. First of all, it can remove the chatter going on in the subconscious mind, which is counterproductive noise consisting of negative beliefs like feeling unworthy and always feeling the victim of circumstances.

'When you meditate, you will learn that your breath and pulse decrease. Furthermore, your mind gets quiet, and your body delivers all the healthy chemicals your body can provide. It has healing power. Let this significant announcement be a prelude to meditation, which is the next topic I want to bring up.

'Finally, we have the flight or escape option. Before choosing this option, it is important to reflect on the entire situation to understand how you ended here in the first place. It is a prerequisite to learn and avoid a similar situation in the future.

'If you can find another job without compromising your call and other obligations, it can be tempting to choose. Just remember that the easiest solution is not always the right one.

'On the contrary, this option might also be hard to decide if you have committed yourself to more than what you should have. You may be in a situation where you want to quit, but your operations costs are so high that you need your present pay check to survive.

'In that case, you are in the same situation as in stay without a fight at least short term. And the countermeasures are the same as presented there.'

Peace

Love is the absence of fear, which is its opposition.
Inadvertently, feelings may get you in opposition.
Negative input automatically creates a negative feeling.
Simple because like attracts like. How excruciating!

Is there a way to be released from this mechanism?
Is it possible to reconcile peace and this with realism?
Can the action-reaction pattern be detached?
I seek my peace and want to win the match.

A wise guy has the topic sincerely observed.
And has the root cause of his own observed:
An observation creates a sensation in the body.
The sensation creates reactions in the body.

The chain is observation, sensation and reaction.
Detaching the last two elements breaks the attraction.
It is a breakthrough. But how do I avoid the reaction?
If you see things as they really are, you break the attraction.

Vipassana meditation can be the tool for your release.
In the beginning, you learn your thoughts to freeze.
The second stage is patiently to observe your sensations.
However, without responding, just observations.

Source: Senius

Yoga and Meditation

Oracle: 'When we were discussing the creation process, Senius, you mentioned meditation as a tool, which I believe it is. The first exercise, "Thoughtless Presence" (a meditation exercise) was introduced so you can focus on your breathing. And you might wonder why I did not bring this tool up then; the reason is two-fold.

'First, there are a number of meditation techniques, and second, it takes a lot of effort and a significant amount of time to be proficient in the type of meditation you choose.'

Senius: 'My experience confirms your last statement. I have struggled with meditation for a long time, as mentioned in the "Adult Private Life". I now got back to it because I realised it is a discipline I need to master to fulfil my call. Besides, to me, yoga is a prelude to meditation.

'Would it be okay if I bring it up first?'

Oracle: 'It is fine. You can, however, meditate without yoga. Please explain your motives.'

Senius: 'Mainly because I have used it in meditation programmes I followed in the past, I realised that it is a good way to focus my mind for the meditation process, which is good preparation.

'Furthermore, it balances the chakras, which are the source of harmony, and improves the connection to the spiritual world. I use the term "spiritual world" because I am sometimes uncertain of what or who is on the other end. Until recently, I believed that I was in direct contact with the Source.

'But I have come to an understanding that it depends on my maturity. And the maturity complies with my level of frequency. In addition, I have learnt that yoga improves my agility and health.'

Oracle: 'I agree with your learnings. As you correctly describe, it is a way to focus your mind, which is an excellent prologue to meditation, and the health benefits are there for sure. If you ask a yogi, they do not separate yoga and meditation.

'They see yoga as a union of body, mind and spirit. But it is also mirrored in your daily life: how you act and communicate, your ability to remain centred independently on the environment, what brings you harmony, joy and so on.

'Whether you want to include yoga or not is a matter of how much time you want to dedicate to your practice. For those who are new to meditation, you may find it overwhelming to do both from the beginning. The most important thing is that you make it a daily habit.

'At present, I will focus on meditation. In general, most meditation techniques share three consistent features:

- Repetition: it can be a word, a prayer, a sound, a picture, a smell, your breath, etc.
- When a thought comes to your mind, accept that it happens, let it go and focus again on the chosen object.
- It has to be performed daily and preferable at the same time of the day.

'I will circumscribe our discussion to the type of meditation that helps you understand what you want to obtain and fits your mind.'

Oracle: 'Then what is the purpose of your meditation then?'

Senius: 'Well, I think the main purpose of my meditation practice is to support the overall purpose of my life, which is meaningfulness, peace and happiness. And I do this primarily through my call. I think meditation can support my call because it aims at the removal of suffering, which stems from negative emotions.'

Oracle: 'Hmmm. I see your point, but how can you rephrase this into a positive purpose?'

Senius: 'I want to obtain peace and harmony to see things as they really are.

'To get there, I need to find a way to detach from my negative feelings, triggered either from internal or external stimuli through my ego. I have realised that when I do not manage to control my reactions to those stimuli, consciously or subconsciously, I have no power over my feelings anymore. This state is what I beforehand called suffering, and as long as this persists, peace and harmony cannot be achieved.'

Oracle: 'I like your rephrased purpose for a start, and I agree with your observations and conclusion. The root cause is negative feelings, and they can be triggered by others or by your mind. If you recall, we also talked about this in the discussions about feelings.'

Senius: 'I am still experimenting with different methods, and for me, it is still a discipline that I want to develop further because I see meditation as a key to connect with my soul, intensify my consciousness and act as a communication channel to the spiritual world.'

Oracle: 'More than 2600 years ago, a person named Siddhartha Gautama took up an old meditation praxis. After 49 days of meditating underneath a fig tree, he attained *awakening* or *enlightenment* and he came to be known as *Buddha*, which means the *Awakened One*.

'This meditation tradition is labelled Vipassana[11], which means to see things as they really are. It can release you from suffering by actually taking control over the root causes we talked about when discussing fear.

'For example, when a person scares you, some sensations in the body such as an intensified breath and heartbeat are triggered. In Vipassana meditation, you use this self-observation technique without reacting subconsciously to them.

---

[11] There is a global non-profit organisation providing Vipassana meditation. You can find more information on their site: www.dhammaorg.

'In this way, the attack loses its power, and you do not supply the person with the energy required for fuelling the mood. Through persisting training, you can get a release from this automatic reaction and start to live a peaceful life.'

Senius: 'It sounds appealing to me. Another benefit I see is that it is not limited to any particular religion and you can practise this method irrespective of your view. I have started using this meditation method as part of my morning rituals which I perform every day.'

Oracle: 'I agree. It is an excellent way to practice meditation.'

Senius: 'You mentioned that you liked my rephrased purpose "for a start"; what did you mean by that?'

Oracle: 'Great that you noticed it. To obtain peace and harmony is a nice objective, but what happens when you achieve it?'

Senius: 'I have an idea of what you are getting at. When we talked about "Mental Health" where I saw the driver for motivation was the gap in both desires and the call. Here you highlighted a big difference between the two: desire is a craving that originated from the ego, whereas the call is a vocation to heal the soul. Nevertheless, I guess that what I previously have seen as the purpose is merely a prerequisite to obtaining enlightenment as Buddha did.'

Senius: 'Do you mean that enlightenment is an ongoing objective?'

Oracle: 'That is what I wanted you to realise. The enlightenment Buddha attained was a breakthrough for him, but it was just the starting point for a process leading to further development. It is worthwhile remembering that nothing in your world is static. If that were the case, everything would become stagnated, contradicting the Laws of the Universe.

'You stated in the beginning that enlightenment was your primary purpose. I assume it means that you have other objectives as well.'

Senius: 'Yes, I do have other purposes which are more short-term. Let me make a few examples.

'In the beginning, I concentrate on my breathing as in Vipassana, and then I let go of my mind in a thoughtless state without any expectations.

Thoughts will pop up. If it is a reminiscence of the brain's everyday chatter, I will just notice, accept it and let it pass without feeling any sort of attachment. However, after a few minutes, messages come to me from the spiritual world, which I write down immediately after the session.

'While I breathe in, I imagine a white healing light (Prana) built up in the Heart Chakra and I place the tip of my fingers there. Before I breathe out, I move my hands to my knee, as an example. Then I imagine that the energy flows into the knee. After a few breaths, the knee becomes warm. I use it to heal myself.

'In another variant, I use the same mechanism to send out energy addressed to a person I know is not well. Again, I imagine that I accumulate energy while breathing in. When I breathe out, I visualise that energy transmitted from me to that person.

'As I receive the energy from the Source, my energy level is not compromised. Furthermore, I use this second type of process to build up my energy level if I visit a sick person. This way, I ensure that I can give the person positive energy.

'When I struggle with a topic, I use a seed thought for meditation. Next, I observe what pictures and thoughts are popping up. I often get surprised by the outcomes.

'The chakras we spoke above previously can be used in different ways. In the context of meditation, I use them to scan the centres to detect any imbalances in my body, which on a physical level are often perceived as tensions. This is possible because the chakras are connected to the glands of the body, impacting both your physical health and feelings.

'However, if what I am talking about is completely new to you, I would not recommend meditating on the chakras without getting previous in-depth instructions and training. There are more pitfalls that can compromise the balance between the chakras, causing both mental and physical issues. If you want to improve the balance, you can use "The Five Tibetans" mentioned previously.'

Oracle: 'These are excellent examples. I can only recommend those who experience our dialogue to seek meditation techniques that can fit into their purpose. The main rule is to figure out what purpose meditation should fulfil and have at least an apparent reference.

'The time you have to practice before you harvest benefits from meditation varies a lot. A few obtain results after a short period, especially if they start with a simple method and perform it as a persistent daily praxis. Most people will get the benefit of their efforts after a few months.'

Senius: 'I can add that, for me, the best time for mediation is the early morning before anybody is awake.'

Oracle: 'It is an excellent time of the day if you like to get up early in the morning.

'About meditations, I would like to add one thing that you are not familiar with yet. You can meditate with others in a group, which creates a synergy raising the energy level. You should strive for harmony among the group members making love and peace.

'There is another perspective of meditation in the big picture that I want to address; it may be an additional encouragement to meditate. Since the existence of mankind, they have been disconnected from the divine Source, a process described in Genesis as The Fall.

'Meditation is a way to reconnect with the Universe and the borders dissolve into Oneness. It is something you cannot grasp rationally but only be experienced[12].'

Senius: 'I completely agree, which is why it is difficult to express this in words. I assume it is because our language is built from objects outside ourselves, while our subject or our being is interpreted inside ourselves. We miss words for the fusion of the notion. While it happened to me, I felt the divine energy and love from a new level.'

Oracle: 'Yes, it is a unique peak experience which also raises your self-awareness.'

Rhodopis: 'When we talked about "Thoughts", I understood that the key to famish the ego was to be present in the moment and be aware in

---

[12] Peak experiences discussed in the chapter about 'Faith.'

our soul's consciousness. Therefore, I see meditation as a training tool for awareness and to build a solid connection to our soul.'

Rhodopis: 'Can you elaborate something more on my perception?'

Oracle: 'Dear, Rhodopis, it is an essential insight that you are revealing, and I would like to add a little more to this. Thoughtless awareness in the present moment is the highest purpose for meditation as it opens the possibility to see things as they really are. When you master this, you can also apply this ability to your daily life.

'It will bring the unconscious chatter to an end and reduce the ego to the tool it is meant to be: something you use if you want to perform a task consciously, only.

'It may accelerate your development, and you may even surpass your call. If that happens, your original call is fulfilled, which will inspire you to renew your call.

'Let me conclude this topic by adding that there are also significant physical benefits of meditation, such as decreased blood pressure, pulse, breath frequency and metabolism, which is the opposite of what happens in your body when experiencing fear and stress. In addition, it impacts quite a few of your genes and your living age is therefore prolonged.'

Preparing the End

Life is like a flower. A seed is a start in the ring.
With sun and rain, the flower is a harbinger of spring.
It brings beauty and a pleasant smell in the summertime.
In autumn, it spreads its seeds, and it is its end of time.

The life cycle is with the ring a symbol of belonging.
And for newly married people a graceful beginning.
The flower sprouts, grow, flowers and spreads its seeds.
Humans have many more years to see where it leads.

The human consciousness may feel like a tough rival.
In the autumn, the conscience announces its arrival.
Can I look back with joy, and did I keep my word?
Did I live my call and bring light to the world?

I do not judge your life, nor do I judge my own.
I am grateful because I in my home am known.
I feel confident, happy and free in my state
that I return to my soulmates in the eternal state.

Source: Senius

The Process of Death

Oracle: 'As people grow older, they also become more aware of the fact that life does come to an end. The perception of death is mainly dependent on individual expectations. Religious persons may have troubles with their own death too, simply because they feel uncertain of the outcome of their deeds and because they believe they have only this life to live.

'The process you will experience may differ quite a lot depending on your maturity level and your connections to the spiritual realm. It correlates to your level of frequency and consciousness; something I will return to later when dealing with vibration spheres.

'From your perspective, and considering your knowledge, death is just a crossing where you feel at home. Besides you know when your time has come. Therefore, you will feel calm and peaceful and you will have the time to comfort and say goodbye to your loved ones and letting them know that you are fine.

'When it comes to young souls, your job as a relative is to help them let go of any fear. Fear translates into disconnection with the Source, thus making the process unnecessarily difficult. Besides, deceased beloved relatives will likely appear to comfort you when you are a young soul.

'It is as vivid as if some of your living relatives paid you a visit. You will feel unconditional love and compassion, prepared to let go. This also may be your first sign that the time to leave this world has nearly come.

'In case you have any unfinished business, now is the time to bring them out of your mind. Both experiences, visits from deceased ones and close of unfinished business, will help you calm down and align you with the Source, making the transition more comfortable.'

Senius: 'What can an unfinished business be?'

Oracle: 'It is often something connected to our relations. Mostly it is about talking with some relatives to forgive or be forgiven. It can also be to acknowledge what a relative has meant in the person's life or to address an important message.

'In the next phase, you are in both worlds. You may have your close relatives at your side in the physical world as well as communicate with some of your dear relatives in the spiritual realm, who are waiting for you.

'When you die, you can see the relatives who were there with you from above your deathbed. Their grief can be so overwhelming that you will try telling them that everything is fine. But you realise that you cannot get through to them. You suddenly feel a drag, a pull you can still resist if you want to.'

Senius: 'Why should I want this?'

Oracle: 'Some souls find it hard to let go of their bodies because they have largely identified themselves with them, especially young souls, who are struggling in this passage.

'In the last phase, you send a message of your death to your ancestors and other relatives who have been influential in your life. In the physical world, it happens through a dream where you appear with a bright light around you to impress love and compassion. If you receive the message while awake, you often will feel it as a physical sensation in your body, which will be hard to overlook.

'When you are contacted and told that your relative has died and compare the time of death with your physical sensation, you will realise that there is a match in time.'

Senius: 'The last phase reminds me of my paternal grandfather. I saw him in my dream and felt that he was blessing me. I didn't make the connection for years after his death, where I read an article about what you are explaining, although I do not recall where I read it.

'When my maternal grandmother died, I had severe stomach pain in the morning. Shortly after, the phone rang, and I was informed that she had died. The evening before, we were dining together. She was happy. No one knew that it would be our last gathering together.

'What happens after death?'

Oracle: 'It varies according to one's maturity level. In the present case, death is quite harmonic making the transition easier.

'You see a bright light at the end of the tunnel from a distance. Further into the tunnel, it gets darker, but you can still see the light. As you beam through, it becomes lighter and lighter.

'While beaming through, you will see your life as a movie from two perspectives. As an observer and as a witness to how your actions impacted the engaged actors in your life. We also addressed this topic while speaking about death in connection with fear.

'When you are through the tunnel, the events that follow depend on your matureness.

'Let me consider the youngest soul first. He or she meets a relative the soul knows with confidence. The relative will comfort you and hand you over to someone who brings you to your destination. Remember, the youngest souls do not have any guide during their first incarnations.

'The next group of souls meets their respective guides, who help the souls acclimate to the spiritual realm. The guide then brings the soul to the cluster of souls he belongs, to join his soulmates. It is an excellent experience for all members. For the most experienced souls, they find their destination on their own. But the reunion with the soulmates is still a great event.'

Senius: 'What kind of destination is it?'

Oracle: 'Each soul belongs to a group of soulmates, as mentioned before. They live in their enclave, which is hard to describe from an incarnated perspective. Simply put, it is a distinct energy formation.

'For example, you, the referent and a tiny handful of other soulmates belong to my enclave. You are also classmates. It means that you can assist each other in preparation for your next incarnation.'

Senius: 'Hold on. When I asked you previously, you said that I could incarnate when I wanted to do so, isn't it?'

Oracle: 'You are right, and my former answer still holds true. However, I know that when you have consolidated your knowledge from your last incarnation with the former ones, you will ask to incarnate again.'

Senius: 'How do you know that?'

Oracle: 'It is pretty straightforward. When you return and accumulate your experiences from your present and past lives, you will realise that some experiences are still missing.'

Senius: 'So, is my destiny predictable?'

Oracle: 'No, not in the sense you think of. But my answer is based on my experience the most likely outcome. However, you are welcome to surprise me. That would make me happy.'

The Transition

My dear relatives are here for the last time.
I am peaceful and see my eternal friends in a line.
They reach out for me, and I feel an attraction.
I become lighter and can see their reaction.

Beneath me, some relatives try to pull me back.
The doctor shakes his head, and my body is like a sack.
I see their tears and grief and feel sorry for their act.
I try to say I am fine, but they do not seem to react.

The drag becomes more vital, and I feel like leaving.
I am lifted, and new inspirations are revealing.
I am in a tube and discern light in the far distance.
Meanwhile, I see my life without any resistance.

In the end, my guide is waiting with anticipation.
I am surrounded by light, love and compassion.
I feel blissful, and we flow together to my union.
It is time for an anticipatory soulmates reunion.

It is like a father who brings back his son
And the time melts away like snow in the sun
Without notice, it is time for preparation.
I have to build a new call as aspiration.

Source: Senius

Preparations to Birth

Oracle: 'Whenever birth takes place, many preparations go on in the spiritual as well as the physical world. There are three stages, as described below. The soul prepares a framework, which contains the major learning the soul wants to experience—its call. In the physical world, a woman gets pregnant, the baby starts growing and the soul merges with the baby and becomes a person.'

Transition Phase

Oracle: 'While souls are in transit in the spiritual realm, they have to go through a process where they look at their last incarnation and compare it with the purpose and design of their latest incarnation. The second step is to do a synthesis with the experiences of their past lives. With this offset, they exchange views with their soulmates who operate similar tasks. The outcomes are enriching for all the souls in the group.

'Each soul prepares a framework for the next step while working in their class. Please note that the souls follow their own path, so the reciprocal stimulation and support lasts until the soul has fully prepared its framework. There are exceptions though, which I will come to later.'

Senius: 'What is your role in the process?'

Oracle: 'It is the same wherever a soul is, which also includes you. I primarily inspire and encourage you to leave your comfort zone to boost your progress. You see, every incarnation is about developing new ways to overcome the issues you individually have decided to experience.

'I also teach you in some of your everyday challenges, and you also play the problems from different perspectives to get a higher understanding of how it works while being in the spiritual world.'

Senius: 'But what does it bring us since we lose our memory when we incarnate?'

Oracle: 'Here, you can check out different scenarios to understand how it works in theory. But to understand it in reality, you have to experience it on your own body in the physical world. And yes, you lose your memory when you incarnate, but you can access the memory from your soul as you become more mature.

'Until then, many ideas come to your mind from here. It is up to you whether to react upon them or not.'

Senius: 'What happens when the soul has prepared the framework?'

Oracle: 'After several iterations, a soul comes to a point where its work is sufficiently mature. Then the soul is ready to be shown different future scenarios. These scenarios fit the learning areas wanted by the individual soul. Therefore, there is always a match between the different scenarios and the framework prepared by the soul.'

Senius: 'How is this presentation orchestrated?'

Oracle: 'Try to imagine a room similar to this one. It just requires a far stronger energy field as it has connections to different places and people. You can watch each scenario on an imaginary wall with an integrated virtual screen. In principle, it operates like our present communication, but far more advanced.

'What you perceive is actually happening in real-time in the physical world, and at the same time, you operate the screen with your thoughts: you can scroll back and forth in time. You can enter the screen to feel how it is to be in the mind of that person or any other person in his or her intimate environment.'

Senius: 'Wow! I am overwhelmed. How is it possible?'

Oracle: 'Well, the dimension here is out of time and space. Everything here is a manipulation of energy. The benefit is that you can get a very vivid sense of the person's life even if his or her dimension is beyond your imagination ability.'

Senius: 'Do I choose freely the scenario I want to join?'

Oracle: 'You do. But the scenarios you watch comply with your desires, which are translated into energy with different frequencies. Your stakeholders deliver the scenarios you can choose from. The contributors assist you in selecting the best scenario to bring you in a position where you have the best opportunities to obtain the learning set in your framework.'

Senius: 'How are these scenarios generated?'

Oracle: 'The scenarios you watch come from different sources: your framework which is modulated by those who follow your development, and a transmission device, which matches the available material bodies with the needs of different souls.'

Senius: 'I must admit that this is beyond my understanding.'

Oracle: 'I completely understand your reaction. Note that it is also a highly advanced manipulation of energy, which differs from what you know from your physical world. Besides, it is less important, as long as you acknowledge that the environment around you has a pledge to honour your framework with love and compassion.'

Senius: 'Thank you for comforting me. I have confidence in you and trust you do what you can to support whatever is best for me, considering my knowledge and experiences. Until now, you introduced me to your role, my soulmates and the framework. Who follows my development?'

Oracle: 'I am not allowed to reveal this to you. But, in general, it is souls that support your development, and as you mature, they recruit you for other purposes. Besides, the followers can change when your development requires it. I cannot be more specific even if I know that you want to know more.'

Senius: 'Okay, thank you. Are bodies and souls interconnected?'

Oracle: 'Sure. You can see the transmission device I mentioned as a logistics programme that balances and optimises demand (souls) with supply (bodies).'

Senius: 'Are there any conflicts between souls and bodies?'

Oracle: 'Never. Simply because souls do not have the same pool of choices, they do not choose simultaneously. Souls choose their bodies in a prioritised order. A body disappears from the pool after being chosen.'

Senius: 'If I look back at my own life, there have been certain significant turning points that had an enormous impact on the direction my life has taken.

'Isn't my next incarnation rather predictable, since I may have seen all the scenarios all of these decision points before incarnating?'

Oracle: 'No. When you incarnate into a specific scenario, you can experience what you have scheduled in your call. However, you have not seen the full life story in all details, and you do not know all possible outcomes. Besides, your access to what you have watched depends on your maturity/ability to recall what you have seen. Don't forget that you also have free will, which may impact the outcomes.

'Besides, there are other facets. The scenarios require collaboration with other souls. It means that parts of your situation fit into other soul's scenarios.'

Senius: 'Can you give me an example?'

Oracle: 'A marriage or partnership is a common agreement among two souls with complementary characters which makes it possible to create synergies along with their own learning experiences. For example, soulmates may choose this set-up for a couple of lives in some cases. That is an example where a couple brings what they are supposed to do: They are more together than separate.'

Senius: 'Can you be a little bit more specific?'

Oracle: 'Sure. Let's say the first person is visionary and tends to stray away from reality, whereas the second person is rational and well-grounded. Despite the differences, if they learn how to use this gap constructively, they will both observe a positive outcome. The first person will have more realistic visions and support to make them a reality.

'On the other hand, the second person will have an opportunity to grow to a higher level of understanding of new possibilities. They will both experience the mutual joy of living.

'In this case, it is beneficial that they have the same maturity level. In many cases, it is advantageous if they are soulmates. If the gap is too significant, they will tear each other apart, and if they do not realise it early on, they will separate sooner or later.'

Senius: 'It sounds great. But when we incarnate we lose our consciousness. How is it possible for the two souls to recognise each other and live another earthly life as soulmates?'

Oracle: 'Before the incarnation takes place, the soul makes agreements with the souls who will play a significant role in their life. They agree on a "memory trigger" that can have many different expressions.'

Senius: 'Can you give some examples?'

Oracle: 'A very common example is when you meet somebody with whom you click right away, and you feel like you have known each other without remembering it. It is often a soulmate.

'Another significant example is the mutual choice of a life companion. The trigger is often a special glance or a way of behaving. In fact, a couple can pair up for more incarnations to optimise their development.

'Most couples are of different gender, but some incarnate with the same gender. The spiritual realm is above this perspective. It is a matter of what the souls want to act out, and the spiritual development which is immaterial, is independent of body gender.'

Rhodopis: 'Your statement will provoke quite a few humans!'

Oracle: 'I understand your concern. How humans judge is a matter of upbringing, culture trait, religion and so on. However, my purpose is not to please anybody's prejudgements, but to teach you how to see things as they are. The only adaptation I do is adjusting my teaching to the level of your maturity so you can harvest as much as possible.

'You can also feel resistance to somebody without even knowing the person. It is still a soul who crossed your way but has the role to challenge you in your development areas. Even if they might annoy you, bear in mind that their role allows you to grow.

'This can also be seen in family members who are there for you to grow and vice versa. Therefore, see them as your teachers, especially when you feel they annoy you. "Memory triggers" can also be more subtle; it can be a phrase from a song, a particular gesture or an item.'

Senius: 'What about the body I invade? Is it a victim of my choice?'

Oracle: 'No, not really. A body and a soul become a person as already described in 1. Gen. 2:7:"Then the Lord God formed a man from the dust of the ground and breathed into his nostrils the breath of life, and the man became a living being".

'It is a perfectly mutual common destiny. Based on the above, there are roughly three primary categories of souls you will meet in the incarnation: soulmates, challengers and guides. I mention them in the plural.

'You will meet some of them in connection with a specific focus area, others for a short period of time and finally a few for your entire lifetime. The last category includes your partner and your real friends.'

Senius: 'Do I also meet you as a person in the physical world?'

Oracle: 'It is possible, but rare. Most souls will meet guides in connection with issues within their area of responsibility. I mention these categories to make your mind aware, so you know how to deal with them. All of them are a blessing if you understand how to use them for your development.

'There is also somebody taking care of you in the spiritual world. We may call them supporters.'

The Supporters

Oracle: 'When I spoke about those who signed off your framework—they are also your supporters who care for your development during your incarnation.'

Senius: 'Where do you fit in? Are you my messenger?'

Oracle: 'I am just your immediate guide and do all I can to facilitate your development to the extent you allow me. But as I mentioned before, the connections you make here and your level of consciousness both impact your abilities.

'Even though I'm not allowed to inform you about your relations here, I can give you a direction. I am your intermediate contact and responsible for this dialogue. Another strong relationship is your Master who is interested in you. Although I cannot disclose the name, I can tell you that the area of your Master is love and wisdom.'

Senius: 'What do you mean by "allow you"?'

Oracle: 'As the old saying goes, "when the pupil is ready, the teacher shows up". This saying still holds true. If you want to connect, you have to use your superconscious mind, the soul. But most of the time you are in your ego—your lower thoughts and feelings.

'At this low-frequency level, you are disconnected. Another metaphor, you have to tune in to the right frequency on the radio to find the right channel and to receive information from your supporters, including your Master and me.'

Senius: 'How do I do that?'

Oracle: 'You do this by asking questions and seeing what happens. But in more general terms, it means that you have to raise your frequency level. You can feel the connection through a higher energy level.

'In your case, the frequency is that of love and wisdom corresponding to the energy you derive from your connections. In addition, you get bright ideas, which correspond to what you are seeking. Many of those ideas come from us. Another channel is through your dreams. The highest energy level can bring you revelations, as in the case of Buddha and any other prophet you can think of.'

Senius: 'Does this mean that we have the same capability as Moses?'

Oracle: 'In principle, you are born with the same potential and it depends on the call you intend to solve. But most people do not even look for that option because they have been told that their holy books are nothing but the ultimate truth. However, none of the present religions would be here in their present form without the past.

'The issue is that most religions claim that they have the patent on the truth, and that is the end of the story. This naive self-understanding prevents any further development and makes them inconvertible with each other, which has caused huge clefts and been of the sacrifice of endless conflicts. Ultimately, it became the reason for killing many people in the name of God! A contradictory way to preach love and mercy.'

Senius: 'Does each soul have a dedicated group of supporters?'

Oracle: 'Well, it depends on the soul's maturity level. A simplified but more tangible model explaining how it works in a Christian context is to see God as the centre, surrounded by concentric vibration spheres. The closer you are to the centre, the more mature are the members of that vibration sphere. In other words, the closer you are to the centre, the Source, the higher is your frequency level.

'If we look at the Earth, there is a growing population. The majority are very young souls who have to choose their destiny. They do not have a dedicated group of supporters.

'Their primary guidance is their conscience, logical reasoning and the environment of their incarnation. They are in the outer vibration sphere.

'In the second outer vibration sphere, a soul has its first assignment as a guide. The guide is one of your close relations, typically a family member from an earlier incarnation. It is a more mature soul who can help you balance your nature to create more harmony.'

Senius: 'Is this where I belong since I can talk with you, and do you belong to the same vibration sphere?'

Oracle: 'You can consider this later. Concerning the vibration spheres, mine is one level closer to the Source than yours. If you remember the beginning of our meeting, the referent could recognise you and Rhodopis but had only intuitive feelings for me. This is because I am at a higher frequency level.

'Let me introduce you to the next vibration sphere. In this group, an aspirant angel is assigned to you as a guide with the mutual interest of accelerating your development.'

Senius: 'What does the guide do exactly?'

Oracle: 'The guide mainly urges you to fulfil your call and supports you with dreams, hunches, great ideas and prevents you from being harmed. But because you have free will, it is up to you to act upon what you receive.

'In the fourth vibration sphere, the guides are angels sending you unconditional love. These guides communicate primarily through emotions. If you are in doubt, you have to focus on how you feel. Depending on the character of your call, a Master can have an interest in your development.

'Between the fifth and the next vibration spheres, you have more mature angels, maybe including archangels.'

Senius: 'Why do you say "maybe including archangels"?'

Oracle: 'My knowledge goes no further than my level in the hierarchy.'

Senius: 'Have you got any idea of where the Master belongs to?'

Oracle: 'No, I could make a qualified guess, but I'd better let it go for the time being, as it does not have practical relevance for any of us. However, what I can say about the next vibration spheres is that their members hold extraordinary power. They guide members with high commitments and responsibilities attached to their work in the spiritual realm.'

Senius: 'So, God does not follow each soul?'

Oracle: 'God is the *Source*, a term I prefer to use. As a concept, God has too many different associations that belong to old religions and is therefore misleading. The Source does follow each soul through its universal consciousness, which pervades everything and everywhere.

'However, the Source has delegated the spiritual domain to its servants to bring support to guides and incarnated souls. Development also goes on in the spiritual world in different vibration spheres. Everybody here has a call too.

'I have the pleasure to support you. By following you, I am also reliving my challenges, which is part of my call.'

Senius: 'You said that a Master has become interested in me. Can you tell me why?'

Oracle: 'Yes, overall. The group that follows you is dynamic. They have different interests and come and go, and new members can join depending on how you decide to develop. Simply put, you have attracted those who find interest in what you intend to realise right now.

'It also works the other way around. The more supporters you attract to your group, the more support will be transmitted to you. If you stay focused, it will be far easier to realise your intentions. It is an example of how your connections are dependent on your level of maturity, as mentioned previously.'

Senius: 'Is staying focused an issue, as you stated?'

Oracle: 'Yes, indeed. There is an ongoing conflict between your ego and your soul. Just like most people, you get distracted by the environment and your ego. When you are occupied with practical tasks, you are working on the conscious mind level, which is on a lower frequency level.

'And when you are accustomed to working at that level, you tend to get restless when you take a break. Your lower frequency level generates restlessness as compared with your soul or superconscious mind. It has been a typical trait in your environment and you share it with most people in general.

'At present, you have created frames for your incarnation that make it easier for you to focus on your soul's frequency level. However, you still get distracted. An excellent countermeasure for you is to do what Buddha did—meditate, a praxis you already included in your daily routines. But keep in mind that you have to be more persistent.

'It increases your focus and opens your connection to the spiritual realm. In other words, it helps you identify yourself with your true self, your soul. When you come to the point where your ego is under the soul's control, your development will accelerate exponentially, and you will become a blessing for your spiritual relations in the physical world.'

Senius: 'I wonder whether the battle between my ego and my soul also has supporters in the spiritual realm?'

Oracle: 'In short, yes. And if you consider it, you also know this from the Bible, for instance, Revelation 12:7-9:"Then war broke out in heaven. Michael and his angels fought against the dragon, and the dragon and his angels fought back. But he was not strong enough, and they lost their place in heaven. The great dragon was hurled down—the ancient serpent called the Devil or Satan—who is leading the whole world astray. He and his angels were hurled to the Earth".

'And as we haven't come to the end of this time, it is still an ongoing battle. If you remember what we said about Genesis, there is a battle between your soul and your ego, which also happens in the spiritual realm and your physical world. From a Christian perspective, your salvation will be fulfilled in the best way through your purpose in life, your call.'

Senius: 'So I can also be contacted from the dark forces from the spiritual world?'

Oracle: 'Yes, you can. Don't you remember how Satan tempted Jesus in Matthew 4:1-11 or Job?'

Senius: 'Yes, I know them. But my question is more about how to avoid attracting the tempter?'

Oracle: 'As long as you stick to your call, you are safe. And the way you know it is that you will feel unconditional love. For those who haven't found their call yet, it is a little harder because there is a risk that they can mix love with desires, e.g., attraction to another person who resides in the lower feeling, whereas unconditional love is a person from the higher feelings.

'If you are in doubt, you can ask the following question: Is the love I feel altruistic or it is the feeling that stems from one of my desires?

'If you raise this question honestly, you will be able to remove any doubt. But it also means that when you declare death over somebody or even does it in the name of your God, you are in deep water. You can be quite certain that it does not come from unconditional love—what God is, independent of whatever you call your God in any religion.'

Preparations in the Physical World

Oracle: 'The motivations for getting pregnant vary, and some would even claim it was an accident. However, whatever the motivation, it is never a coincidence; the persons involved can be more or less conscious of their call. There is always a symbiosis between the parents and the child/children.

'Let me start with an example of a match between parents, and especially their youngest child, Wolfgang Amadeus Mozart[13](1756 – 1791). His dad, Leopold Mozart, was a musician too. He started to teach his son to play the harpsichord when he was 5 years old. And he played magnificently.

'At six, he composed his first pieces of music, which his dad wrote down. He also played the violin, and soon he superseded his father's capabilities at a very young age.

'I want to highlight this example because the only way this is possible is because Mozart brought skills with him from former lives. What a soul has learnt in a previous life is carried forth in future lives in the soul. In this case, the father's interest triggered a fantastic speed in the development of Mozart's latent competencies. If he had started from scratch, this would not have been possible.

'Every soul brings talents from earlier lives with them. It also explains why some feel attracted to a specific profession where they can make extraordinary progress.'

Senius: 'In my case, I haven't had that feeling. When I chose to go for my dad's shipyard, it was not because I really felt for it, but it was more of an obligation.'

Oracle: 'I understand your perception. That happened because you followed the expectations from your surroundings instead of following

---

[13] Source: Article from Wikipedia about Wolfgang Amadeus Mozart.

your call. However, you did not end up there. Your metier was more in the areas of development, project management and human resources. In all these cases, you were able to satisfy your endless curiosity.'

Senius: 'I see your point. Now, another question. Why are there so many dysfunctional families?'

Oracle: 'It is a matter of what each soul intends to experience in this life. All members play a role in the family puzzle. They are each other's precondition. As we spoke about previously, it is a match of development areas that correspond to their respective karma.'

Senius: 'But in some cases, the child's possibility for a normal life is very poor. Does it make any sense?'

Oracle: 'It always does. However, it can be hard to understand from the outside as long as you do not know what the person's call is. What you may consider as a tough destiny will mostly be just perfect for what that soul intends to experience.'

Senius: 'Can you illustrate a situation that can make it more concrete?'

Oracle: 'Let us imagine a child who is born disabled without the ability to use his legs. Most people will feel pity for that child. Let us assume that this child's call is to learn to receive support from others and feel their compassion.

'Besides, the child may want to experience intellectual skills which would compensate for its missing mobility. For example, Stephen Hawking[14], his achievements have been extraordinary.

'In my example, the child's call is complementary to its parents. They get the opportunity to learn to override their own needs for the benefit of the child. It can be a way for the parents to learn to replace selfishness with sacrifice without seeing it as a burden but as their own call.

'Besides, it can bring a lot of joy about what is possible in the presence of motivation. Furthermore, it is also a great way to experience strong family relations.'

---

[14] Stephen William Hawking 1942-2018 was an English theoretical physicist, cosmologist and author assigned to the University of Cambridge at the time of his death.

A Great Question

Is there a purpose of life, or is it just random relativism?
Some have tried to bridge faith with Darwinism.
Believers and atheists have it passionately discussed.
Many have to their respective points of view rushed.

The development of beliefs you can find in this illustration.
The community was an answer to the tribe's conservation.
Like other species, the members found in the group protection.
Homo sapiens were hunters, but alone without preservation.

The detailed language gave them additional indomitability.
They shared their experience and raised their agility.
Their tribe grew further, and they became a superior voice
and attracted other minor tribes as a better choice.

With their imagination, they made abstract conceptualisations.
Immediately it brought the tribe new, strong prescriptions.
The common tale gave the tribe additional growth options.
It helps them to be in their often dangerous situations.

Here the cornerstone for our very early religions is possessed.
Since they have developed to those who many today have confessed.
However, the tale does not end but continues, so beware.
The question is in which direction you your journey prepare.

One thing is given; we have an inherent urge to create granted.
Simultaneously we have a heartfelt need a meaning of life wanted.
I have tracked down my own path and will it to you so on leak.
We are different, and our path is tailor-made. So, don't be weak!

Go for your path without letting you stop by others censure.
Your sand any other path you can as the fruit of a tree assure.
A healthy tree bears healthy fruits and will you enrich without delay
A weak tree bears bad fruits and will make you insidiously decay.

In the same way, I know when I to my soul connect:
Happiness, blissfulness, and peace in my mind I select.
Your illusions turn into cognitions, and a key is formed.
When you are at the gate of heaven, you will be informed.

Source: Senius

The New World

Oracle: 'To put our prehistory into proportions, I would like to remind you of a few key facts. The Universe is approximately 13.77 billion years old[15] and the Earth is 4.54 billion years[16]. Depending on how we define our ancestors, there have been humans for approximately 200,000 years[17] or only 0.0002 billion years. Civilisations have existed for less than 6,000 years.

'What stands out to me is that humans have been around on Earth for a minimal period. During this short period of time, humans have assigned their faith to religions that are less than 4,000 years old[18], which is just 2% of the number of years homo sapiens have been living on Earth.

'There have been more primitive religions beforehand, which have influenced the beliefs we have today and were, in fact, prerequisites for them.

'Another way to put it is that the development went on very slowly in the beginning. This also suggests that the progress in our souls has been correspondingly slow.

---

[15] Source: https://www.space.com/universe-age-14-billion-years-old

[16] Source:
https://www.nationalgeographic.org/topics/resource-library-age-earth/?q=&page=1&per_page=25

[17] Source:
https://www.universetoday.com/38125/how-long-have-humans-been-on-earth/

[18] Source: https://www.history.com/topics/religion/judaism

'In the first development phase, the human being is happy when he feels recognised for what he did. It is a joy that is in the ego in its lower thoughts and feelings. The development is about survival.

'The next phase is where humans start to recognise that there are things more prominent than the ego within themselves, their soul, which make them experience suffering. In this phase, primitive religions have their prevalence. Here the "new" religions fit in too.

'In the last phase, humans give up concupiscence to focus on higher thoughts and feelings, which gives the soul the lead in the incarnation. When we spoke about roles, I mentioned that your development depends on your perspective, circles or spirals. I want to bring this into a higher context.

'Try to imagine that one life is just one dot on a piece of paper. When you have lived several lives, you can start seeing a line or a tangent that later turns into a circle. As long as you solely are in the ego, the circle will remain in its form as a circle.

'In the beginning, souls find joy in the recognition and admiration for the lower thoughts and feelings. You reside in your ego.

'It later turns into a craving transforming into suffering, which leads to the next stage. You start realising that there is something more prominent than the ego, your soul. When you start realising that there must be something higher than your ego, a new perspective starts emerging. It will create a small slope on the circle.

'From this perspective, you realise that your ego is nothing but a tool for the soul through which you can learn your call to get the best out of life. This development leads to renouncing your desires and releasing higher thoughts and feelings. The slope progressively increases until the circle is turned into a spiral where the diameter gets smaller and the gradient gets steeper. Your development rises exponentially.'

Senius: 'Let me try to translate it into a language I understand. If I present your explanation in a coordinate system, x would be the number of incarnations and y would be your spiritual development. In the beginning, x will grow with one unit for each incarnation, while y will be zero as the new soul will stay solely in the ego for quite a few incarnations, the circle you mentioned in the beginning.'

Oracle: 'Yes, that is correct.'

Senius: 'When a being realises that there is something bigger than the ego, the value of y starts to grow, and that is when the circle is turned into an emerging spiral.'

Oracle: 'Yes, that is correctly interpreted.'

Senius: 'In reality, there is a third dimension, z. It starts with awareness for something higher, which opens for recognition of the soul. This awareness later turns into a certain degree of identification with the soul, and finally, you realise that you are the soul.'

Oracle: 'It is another way to explain it. The z dimension is the degree you act on your soul level. When you reach a point where you are your soul most of your time, you will not have to incarnate anymore. In that case, you will not find it attractive to reincarnate and you will be assigned to other spiritual missions.'

Rhodopis: 'It is probably a nice description if you are a mathematician and think the way you do, Senius. I perceive it differently and prefer to feel it. It is very blissful to be in the soul state. I feel I get lifted, and my struggles become bearable and easier to solve.'

Oracle: 'It is a great point, Rhodopis. Unconditional love is the strongest force and is linked to your state of being consciously, your soul.'

Rhodopis: 'Thank you. In reference to the former perspective, 200,000 years is a short period which explains why there are very few mature souls on Earth.'

Oracle: 'It is an accurate analysis, Rhodopis. In addition, it means that development before this period has been quite extensive, which is also confirmed in the evolution of the Universe and the Earth.'

Senius: 'It makes great sense. Now I understand why the development between each reincarnation is not linear. It also explains why most people choose to join religions that are a few thousand years old. Besides, it generates positive perspectives for our future despite all the threats the world is facing right now.'

Senius: 'How many people are there in the development groups you mentioned?'

Oracle: 'If you look at the world today, you can imagine that there are most people in the first category, which also explains why there are many national leaders who prioritise their own needs first and get the majority of votes for them for this very reason. This explains the prevalent nationalism.

'The second group has a few numbers in the range of one out of a few millions of the world population. Nonetheless, they are not equally represented in politics or religious governance because they are modest and humble. That is not what the majority values. The last group is extremely rare.

'This discussion makes me think that mature souls could soon reach a critical mass that can lead to radical changes. The question is when will they find the time to mature to rock the boat again. It may create a new common understanding built on the present religions, just as they were built on the former primitive beliefs!

'But let me start from the beginning and let us see what the new world could bring through new and less coloured glasses.'

A Creation Story

Once upon a time before the time of the Universe,
in a human sense incomprehensible in reverse,
the unknowable was in its timeless and dimensionless phase,
and everything there is, was everything there was in that case.

And everything there is, is me, who always has been and will be.
I have a persistent urge to create and let life be.
In my state, thought and action follow like steps on a ladder.
With a Big Bang, I transformed energy into matter.

The transformation scattered new elements around.
Multiple elements in the outer space are now to be found
The space between them makes them disclosed.
All with infinite emptiness enclosed.

The elements move around as in a race.
The time has simultaneously been raised.
The elements create a mosaic as crystals of sand.
Time, space and relativity go hand in hand.

Source: Oracle

The Beginning of the Universe

Senius: 'I find the beginning of Genesis in the Bible a wonderful description of the creation of the Universe. The description was created by Judaism and shared by Christianity and with some modifications, was adapted by Islam.'

Oracle: 'Yes, it is a very poetic description that fits into what a patriarch like Moses could comprehend with his background, culture and time of living. I have been in contact with my Master who will join us in a moment to give you a complementary description considering your present knowledge.'

Referent: 'Suddenly, a form materialises in front of us. I feel intense love and compassion and also awe, and the character is without any doubt the Master who starts to communicate with us right away.'

Master: 'Dear souls, your guide asked me to present a more complementary view that fits into your present understanding. In addition, you should know that in this context, I represent the voice of what you so far have labelled "God", "Source" or as stated in John 14:10:"Don't you believe that I am in the Father, and that the Father is in me? The words I say to you I do not speak on my own authority. Rather, it is the Father, living in me, who is doing his work".

'Genesis can now be reformulated as follows: Once upon a time very long ago, in a human sense eternal times ago, the Universe was in its timeless and dimensionless state. And all there was, was all there was. And all there was, is me, who is and who always have been and who always will be.

'I have a persisting urge to create and experience. Therefore, I decided once again to create a Universe, where I can live out my dreams, which you are part of too.

'In my state, the distance from thought to action is non-existent, and the reaction comes promptly in the form of a sudden transformation of energy into matter. The change implies a division of the Universe. Now you find multiple elements just like there is space between the elements, making it possible to distinguish one aspect of matter from the other, and an infinite emptiness surrounds everything.

'The immediate consequence of the expansion is that an element can now be in one place and later in another, and time has though also been brought into your world. Time, space and relativity go hand in hand.

'I experience it differently in my state, and it is beyond your ability to comprehend and perhaps of no significance to you. Anyway, you should know that I have thoroughly enjoyed the diverse development processes that emerged before your creation.'

Referent: 'The tale leaves a moment of total silence until Senius takes the courage to ask a question.'

Senius: 'Thank you for your overwhelming speech. May I ask you some questions?'

Master: 'Yes, please go ahead.'

Senius: 'Our worldly understanding suggests that when there is full harmony, the world is static, but in the presence of an imbalance, development follows. Does this also apply to your state?'

Master: 'Yes. It was a desire to experience being in every physical facet. The only difference is that the creation of the Universe took place immediately. In your world, there is a time delay to leave you time to reconsider your desires.'

Senius: 'There is something I am not sure if I had comprehended it correctly. In the Bible, God is portrayed as a male person with human characteristics. In this group, God is portrayed as the Source, which actually covers the entire spiritual realm.

'Do you have anything to add to this?'

Master: 'Let me start with the Bible first. Moses was a patriarch and could not imagine God anything but male. As you have realised, this attribute does not make sense in this place. As stated in Genesis 1:26-27:"Then God said, 'Let us make mankind in our image, in our likeness, so that they may rule over the fish in the sea and the birds in the sky, over the livestock and all the wild animals, and over all the creatures that move along the ground".

'So, God created humankind in his own image, in the image of God he created them; male and female he created them.

'That was how Moses was able to perceive it. And the soul is indeed without gender. But the rest of Moses's interpretation goes the other way around: Moses interpreted God with human attributes.

'God is love, but control and punishment are the opposite of love and do not come from God, which Moses expected with his background.

'In your current state, you might see God as the Source. Souls in the spiritual realm are manifested, and they can, in principle, stay as long as they want in this state of being. Compared to the human understanding of time, it is eternal.

'When they mature and are free from desires, they can voluntarily choose to return to me, which is the state of Unmanifested being, which is what God is. And I have a leg in both the Unmanifested and the Manifested world whenever I am needed there.'

Senius: 'It is a lot to digest. So, the relationship we have with God also must be different. Isn't it?'

Master: 'Let me tell you how it works in the eyes of God—I have created the surroundings for you; it is your responsibility to fill out these frames. And it has been so from the very beginning. I am the observer who neither judges nor interferes.

'You are created in our image—you can create whatever you want. Therefore, take responsibility for your creation!

'But know that you are not on your own. As you have realised, you have access to souls in the spiritual realm who are attracted to your field of interests. The Law of Attraction works here as well.'

Senius: 'Allow me to express my surprise, because that is not what any monotheistic religion preaches.'

Master: 'I understand your surprise. However, I have no desires or needs. But you have, and so do your ancestors. Initially, humans were closer to God, as described in Genesis.

'But you became attracted to materialism, pulling you away from the Source, as you labelled your god. At a certain point in time, you invented prophets to be your middlemen, replacing your own direct contact with God. These prophets unintentionally drew you further away from God, while your ego took over your soul in the driving seat.

'The duality you perceive between your soul and ego makes you think that somebody has to do something for you as you do in your daily transactions. This also applies to a patriarch who expects that his minions would succumb and in return get protection against external enemies, which complies with the perception of the tribes at the time.

'In the next stage, you made buildings around your sanctuary with a lot of precious art, including gold and jewels. Nothing was too expensive for the house of your God. To finance all this, you were very creative in the ways you collected money.

'Your ancestors imagined a God that reflected their sense of self, so they created one in their image. Ergo a God who is worshipped, honoured and jealous, punishes, among others, which true human characteristics.

'But Jesus told you something else in Luke 17:20-21:"Once, on being asked by the Pharisees when the kingdom of God would come, Jesus replied, 'The coming of the kingdom of God is not something that can be observed, nor will people say, here it is, or there it is, because the Kingdom of God is in your midst".'

The point I want to make is that God is love, compassion and freedom. What you have created is the opposite—fear, self-sufficiency and bondage. But each one of you has the potential to turn around and follow your call.'

Senius: 'I have one last question: How do we avoid all the conflicts that prevent us from overcoming the common issues the entire world faces?'

Master: 'It will last until you realise that there is no "them" and "us". All souls have the same origin and ultimately return to the same destination when they are ready for it. As mentioned previously, the only way to obtain this is to have an altruistic view, which requires that far more people than now are more mature.

'In this context, maturity means higher and broader consciousness which can be accelerated through your connections in the spiritual realm. It is not a linear progression, but an exponential one. I know all this overwhelms you, but do not let it stop you; somebody has to start the process, and you can do that from the beginning to the end.

'I will conclude by stating that most of your readers will be surprised as you are, at the least. You were born with the free will to choose on your own. If this will have any purpose, you will also have a chance to learn from your mistakes, which can take many lives to master it.

'Alternatively, as your monotheistic religions preach, you have only one life. In this case, I will claim that your free will is not free, because if you fail to live up to the laws as the priests interpret them, you are lost forever. But as always, it is up to you what you want to believe.

'With these words, I want to leave you with your guide. I wish you a good journey ahead until we meet again, which will happen before you know it.'

The Master disappears the same way he arrived. When he said goodbye, his blessing came with great compassion.

Oracle: 'Do you have any reflections you want to share, Senius?'

Senius: 'Yes, indeed. On the one hand, I feel sad that we have moved so far away from the Source. On the other hand, this explains all the violence and wars I saw in "The Picture Bible" and why most religions are extremely intolerant of each other's standpoint. It is really tragicomic because we are all connected to the same Source.

'The last topic reminds me of the two Caminos I walked with. What really stood out for me was the cohesion I perceived with and among the pilgrims. Wherever they came from, they were friendly, open-minded, helpful and present in the moment.

'There was mutual acceptance across all boundaries which under normal circumstances separates people. It is a far stronger bond than I observed at home, which seems to impact both the state of mind and behaviour. It gave me a feeling of oneness with them and with our true origin.'

Oracle: 'It is a great experience with which quite a few pilgrims can identify themselves, although they may express it differently according to their personal preferences. I can add that experiences like the Camino have a certain energy concentration due to the fact that so many pilgrims hike the route every year and consider the reason why they are there.

'In general, we are all connected to the Source and interconnected with each other. A derived consequence is what you do affects the whole. However, it also means that you have the power to create your own reality.'

Senius: 'The Master's speech was so impressive that it was hard for me to formulate my questions. However, I realise I missed one.

'Who did Moses, Jesus and Muhammed talk with, because there seem to be more layers in the spiritual world? Between that world and God, am I still missing an appropriate designation for this notion or concept?'

Oracle: 'Your question is only of academic interest. My point is that they all perceived that they were in contact with God. Concerning the notion of God, you got a designation, the Unmanifested.

'What we have designated as the soul is the pool of souls where we all belong. So, I have to correct my understanding as well.'

Rhodopis: 'I noticed that ultimately the soul is not immortal. I wonder what the link is between the soul and the Unmanifested?'

Oracle: 'Thank you for your reflection, Rhodopis. Your question reveals a new insight. As the Master stated, the soul is Manifested. I realise that as long as the soul is an independent unit, it will be mortal. When it merges with the Unmanifested, it is dissolved and its essence merges into the Unmanifested.'

Senius: 'If this is the case, is the soul just a shell with an immortal essence?'

Oracle: 'It is a great derivation Senius. Some bricks fell in place for me. The essence you talk about is its consciousness. Seen from a physical perspective, people often perceive consciousness as part of the physical body which dies with the body.

But as you can understand from the Master, that is not the case. The soul leaves the body to take its place in the spiritual realm. The reincarnation process continues until the soul has no desires anymore. Ultimately, the soul dissolves, while the immortal consciousness merges with the Unmanifested.'

Referent: 'The guide becomes silent for a moment, looks very thoughtful and seems to forget where he is.'

Oracle suddenly continues: 'The clue is that consciousness sustains matter and keeps interacting with itself as an intrinsic feedforward-feedback mechanism. In this way, it continues developing itself.'

Senius: 'Sorry, you lost me there.'

Rhodopis: 'Me too.'

Referent: 'The responses from Senius and Rhodopis seem to make Oracle present again.'

Oracle: 'I apologise. What I just said was another insight that was just revealed to me. It was actually not meant for you.'

Senius: 'Please do not leave us without an explanation of what you have realised.'

Oracle: 'Very well. I will give it a try. As mentioned previously, the way we experience is through attributes. They are defined and realised by their opposite or antithesis, as stated about feelings.

'You can visualise this as a stick with two ends and something in between that makes it possible to distinguish between the attribute you observe, e.g., short or long. In this way, each end defines the other end. Between the two, you can have a scale to obtain a standard reference.

'Another way to put it is that when you observe something, your perception of what happens depends on your background and experiences. In general, you have three aspects as mentioned when we talked about beliefs: a subject, an object and your subjective reference that colours what you see. In other words, the outcome is subjective experiences that are later stored in your soul.

'That means that the soul observes your ego on the one hand, and on the other hand, the consciousness of your soul can tap into the fraction of the generic consciousness where it belongs. I realise that I use this generic consciousness as a channel through which I can follow and connect to you.

'But if it should have any relevance to you, it would be this: When you want to tap into the fraction of the generic consciousness you have to go inside, which is what you do when you meditate.'

Senius: 'It sounds impressive to me. But what did you mean by "an intrinsic feedforward-feedback mechanism" which continues developing itself?'

Oracle: 'Well, when you find a cause to a phenomenon, it will raise new questions, and consciousness can apparently create and reflect itself as an independent and separate unit. Another way to put it is that consciousness is the cause of its own existence. This is what I meant by intrinsic.

'Try to imagine that this mechanism works at all levels. It goes even crossing the border between the Unmanifested and the Manifested. While you can tap into your tiny fraction of the consciousness, the Unmanifested has access to all of it.

'It means that development expands dramatically. In its essence, I believe that is why the Unmanifested initiated the Universe.'

Senius: 'Wow! Have you just revealed the purpose of the Universe and explained that the Unmanifested consists of all consciousness?'

Oracle: 'Well, it is all very new to me, and I should probably have kept it for myself, and I do not dare to comment on your conclusion, Senius, which may be too premature.'

Senius: 'On the contrary, if that was the case, consciousness must be part of what has existed at all times, including prior to the Big Bang, right?'

Oracle: 'As I said before, it is outside my knowledge, and I do not have further comments.'

Rhodopis: 'What do you mean by "development expands dramatically"?'

Oracle: 'The Master said that the development of consciousness is not a linear progression but an exponential one, which I just explained to you. In other words, my interpretation is that every single soul collects its subjective experiences and these experiences all end up accumulating into consciousness. Imagine that goes for all souls through all times.

'Then the development of consciousness grows at an exponential speed. That is great news, which may overcome the murky description you mentioned when you talked about the "Key Challenges the World Is Facing", Rhodopis.

'I know you would like to learn more, but we are getting to the border of my knowledge. Besides we have gotten too far away from what is of practical relevance for your call.'

Senius: 'If that's the case, I will raise another topic. I am wondering whether our prehistory can bring more light over who we are and what has led to the perception of what Moses demonstrated, which was typical for his time of living, e.g., his patriarchal view.'

Oracle: 'It might be a good idea. I will give you a compressed summary with the most common features of the ancient past, even though there were deviations of course, which are less relevant in this context.'

Prior History

Oracle: 'Try to imagine how it was when your ancestors were hunters. They roamed around in places where they could find food and shelter. They only had a few belongings allowing them to move frequently.

231

'They lived in tribes to protect themselves from predators and competing tribes. Life as hunters was dangerous. When they got hurt, it could have fatal consequences. The focus of life was survival.

'The roles between men and women were very well-defined. Men were hunters and protectors of the tribe. In contrast, women took care of the children until a certain age and were responsible for the food preparation and construction of the temporary camps.

'Men were generally outgoing, aggressive and valued courage and strength especially, which also determined their place in the hierarchy.

'Women were valued for their practical skills and ability to cope with the other women in collaboration. But they were also rivals when it came to favours of the higher-ranking men.

'This perception of the team members is the foundation for the development of the patriarchal view. In its essence, the patriarch protected his minions in exchange for loyalty. Even if men and women were dependent on each other, men were considered superior.

'Humans have additional exceptional characteristics that make them unique as compared to other species. First, they have a complex language, thus making it possible to share knowledge and experiences, accumulate them and hand them over to the next generation. Besides, it also made it possible to create larger groups with the ability to specialise in various social functions.

'Second, the ability to imagine and create abstract ideas gave them many superior benefits, such as strategic planning to conquer other competing species. In addition, it could be used to construct abstract ideas about their tribe.

'Third, as compared to animals, human brains are not fully developed at birth. The benefit of this is that humans can adapt to various environments. The downside, however, is that it takes many years for a child to become independent.

'The group size matters. Even with the above characteristics, the group has a finite size. To overcome this barrier, they combined the characteristics by creating familiar tales. As a result, they did not need to know each other personally, which created a sense of common belonging. The group could grow further.

'Religions in the early days used these abilities in different ways.

'The last thing worth mentioning is that humans are conscious, which makes reflection a possibility. A derived effect is that humans are aware that death is inevitable. Therefore, it was significant to use their imagination to assign power to different objects to increase their courage while hunting and conquering enemies.

'In parallel, the tales were further developed into myths and rituals, including stringent rules of order. Consequently, lawlessness was punished, either by death or exclusion, which often had the same outcome.

'At a certain point in time, some tribes became social communities where a higher specialisation emerged. Among others, some started to become craftsmen and others began to save seeds, and early agriculture emerged.

'Farmers and villagers developed possessions and eventually the need for the exchange of goods, which became a significant practise in people's behaviour and life. Simultaneously, the need for long-term planning became necessary to manage both supply and demand over an entire year.

'Hunters continued sharing their belongings within their tribe while still respecting the hierarchy. They were forced to move to more and more deserted places.'

Senius: 'Was the development of towns driven by specialisation and trade?'

Oracle: 'Exactly. It expanded further with the development of infrastructure, including but not limited to along the rivers and the open sea. Access to water became an essential source of creativity, growth and wealth. In this way, people became more open-minded to other cultures.

'On the other hand, it was also used to loot weaker neighbours. Thus, the primitive "them and us" view has long existed and remains to this day.'

Senius: 'How did their myths and rituals fit into the social order?'

Oracle: 'Great that you got me back to the core issue. As the societies grew and developed differently, the original myths and rituals drifted away. They were gradually adapted to remain meaningful.

'I mentioned them in plural because while you were spreading all around the Earth, these tales were creatively readjusted. Moreover, as society became more mature, the search for meaning in life began.

'At a certain point in time, you introduce gods in your stories and started representing them. Often, they were pictured in two ways: in a very huge size to illustrate their greatness in a temple or on a minor scale, which could be used in processions in connection with special annual events.

'In early religions, Gods were often in plural with a different area of responsibility, which reflected the needs of the design of their society, e.g., hunters, farmers, villagers, warriors and so on.'

Senius: 'Since so many developments in various areas happened simultaneously, didn't it cause some sort of confusion among the different societies?'

Oracle: 'It did to a certain extent. There were different rites of passages where group members were "welcomed" or "purified" for a specific purpose, typically in connection with dangerous hunting, wars or more social events like religious parties. There were quite a few ceremonies in the different societies and simultaneously you can trace many standard features among them.

'On the other hand, when different forms of religion existed side-by-side, issues about what was "holy" and "pure" existed, even in the early stages of history.

'For example, some groups of societies did not consume pork because it was either considered "holy" or "impure". In some Syrian cities, pigs were sacrificed and eaten afterwards, and in the rest of the year, the same action was considered a taboo.'

Senius: 'How was the governance of the early religions?'

Oracle: 'It is another interesting perspective. In the beginning, it was a matter of survival. As the tribes turned into communities and eventually nations, they needed a structured responsibility.

'For example, in the Inka kingdom, the organisation was very simple but effective. A person could be responsible for, let's say, 10 people. He reported to another person who had to report for an equivalent number of persons and had the corresponding responsibility and so on until you reach the leading team, headed by its master. If somebody failed, they were punished, which also applied to those in the higher ranks.

'In other parts of the world, it was more sophisticated, but less flattering reasons came into play like personal pride and vanity.

'Thus, religious governance soon turned into power, control, strict rules and punishment which was built on fear. It was reinforced by the fact that those days people were spread over large distances and transportation was slow and inefficient. Communication had to be simple, easy to understand and easy to control.

'Simply put, it is that if there was no God, humans would be the masters who will decide what is right or wrong, thus giving the individual the right to be the smith of his/her own fortune and thought. This freedom was not welcomed by the patriarchs ruling their minions.

'Besides, many despots demonised people with other beliefs, a strategy still used in the propaganda of various regimes nowadays.'

Senius: 'With our beliefs, what is the essence of our early religions?'

Oracle: 'I am glad you ask the question because it is the main reason why I accepted your proposal to address the topic. It has fertilised the human soul to be ready to attract a new religious setting.

'The main points of interest to our discussion on the early religions are as follows:

- Their way of living paved the way for the patriarchal society.
- To be able to survive in their often-dangerous environment, they assigned power to different objects to increase their courage.
- As size matters, they created tales/myths, making it possible for their tribe to grow without needing to know each other personally and create a sense of belonging and of unity.
- It was not required that they believed in the myths. It was sufficient

that the rites were completed in a prescribed way and complied with the rules.

- The leaders created the early religions through an ongoing adaption of myths and rituals to fit into their current living situations.
- The myths and rituals were transformed into supernatural gods with a different area of responsibility.
- This development has paved the way for the religions you know today.'

Senius: 'Your last statement makes me think of a paradox: Each religion preaches that their religion is nothing but the truth, and they cannot be the truth altogether. Can you shed some light on this paradox?'

Oracle: 'Sure. At the beginning of our conversation, you mentioned the story of the three men who wore differently coloured glasses, right?'

Senius: 'Yes, my letter to the pastor.'

Oracle: 'If you see the outcome for each participant, they perceived the wall in the same colour as the glasses they wear. Everyone claims that their colour is the truth because that is what they experience. On the other hand, it means that every religion contributed significantly in creating the different societies that, among others, dictate how you should treat each other in the community.

'Hence, they still have their eligibility because of their purpose— bringing order and giving basic common living rules. The unfortunate thing is when you conclude that everybody else is wrong, to the extent of forcefully converting them to your religion.

'As you stated, you need to see the event first of all from the outside and without coloured glasses. Let me take the outsider's perspective first. When you see it from the outside, you at least can understand that they cannot be the truth altogether, but acknowledge that they are parallel perceptions created during the creators' culture, time of living and capabilities.

'As you realised this perspective is harder to reveal without coloured glasses. What you first need to acknowledge is that these parallel perceptions apparently cannot be correct forever because they change and adapt. The next step is to be brave enough to look at new perspectives that contradict the beliefs you have inherited and to go out of your comfort zone. That is what you are doing, Senius, as part of your call.'

Senius: 'Yes, I realised that my glasses are coloured too. At the same time, I believe that it is possible to make the colour less intense. Can you bring my perspective further?'

Oracle: 'Everything will be revealed to you when you are ready. For now, I can only tell you that when your soul consciousness grows, you will pass a critical point where you get access to the Source and see the bright light. That is the ultimate perspective that I too, am striving to obtain. And when it happens, you will no longer want to incarnate again.'

Senius: 'When I look at history, I find many similarities between the different religions, which at their core have the same ingredients: obey your God, follow the prescribed rules and practice them in your daily lives. Despite the differences, they are all built on the same foundation, love, with different interpretations. Nevertheless, many people have been killed in the name of God.

'I often wondered how those who possessed the power could interpret their holy scriptures to their own benefit. I believe the message is simple: Be loyal to the governance and in return get protection from external enemies. Apparently, their covenants are valid for members only.'

Oracle: 'You are right, unfortunately. Even if they have a lot in common in their essence, they turned out to be exclusive and cannot embrace the spiritual truth that everyone is connected to, have the same origin and ultimately ends up in the same place. It is just a matter of maturity of the incarnated souls.'

Senius: 'I also wonder why fundamentalism still exists, particularly in the western world where Enlightenment has taken place. Can you elaborate on this?'

Oracle: 'As I mentioned before, any religion is in its essence built on love. If somebody's standpoint contravenes with this, they have been taken over by their egos and lost their way.'

Senius: 'It reminds me of my confirmation, where I had to confirm my faith, and the priest gave each of us a saying. Mine was an African saying: There is no path to a fruitless tree.'

Oracle: 'You had a bright priest.'

Senius: 'He was. However, I do not understand how extreme fundamentalists like the Islamic State can get supporters and even members. Can you explain?'

Oracle: 'Well, in many ways, you have been living in that part of the world where harmony prevails as compared to places where the IS developed. In the latter part of the world, people are generally poor and can hardly get their most basic needs covered. For the same reasons, they have low education. Their faith is strong as perhaps the only way to survive in such difficult environments.

'Unfortunately, this makes some of them easy victims for somebody who can supply their basic needs in exchange for fighting the non-believers to their interpretation of Islam.

'They perceive their situation as unrighteous when compared to countries of the western world that are living in abundance despite their immoral way of living (as they perceive it). This has led to outrage and eventually turned into hate, which is the opposite of love. It is extremely unfortunate because it will only prolong the time to spiritual development.

'The western world has been through the same development. Let me just remind you of your crusades which were also brutal.'

Senius: 'Will it never come to an end?'

Oracle: 'It will when the remaining Islamic community takes active responsibility for their members across borders. A starting point could be to assist the countries in stabilising their legal government, e.g., through humanitarian support and eventually together with the global community. But the Islamic world has to take the lead.

'There is another focal point that I feel is worth underlining. All religions reflect the development of mankind, from the very primitive religions to the ones you know today. God, the Source or whatever name you use, is and will remain constant.

'It also means that they all may lead to a higher awareness of the divine. When this happens, fear will start to subside and lead you to new insights. When enough souls reach that level, the present religions will be transformed.'

Rhodopis: 'It sounds great. On the other hand, I presume that the established religions will fight against this outcome. Just as today where most of the rivalries are between different religions. And at the end of the day, it is about organisational power, which no organisation would give away voluntarily.'

Senius: 'I agree, Rhodopis. The ultimate consequence would be that the present religions one by one are dissolved over time.'

The Source of Faith

All our religions are in history drafted,
and with contemporary understanding crafted.
Their meaning is not entirely misplaced
when you one of them in your hearth has placed.
They have our ancestors wanted
and them many sufferings haunted
We have them for that respected,
While we our own thoughts rejected.

If you with a religion let you fulfil,
your thoughts in prison you fill.
It does not your thirst at length quench,
but locks your soul to the last trench.
If you, your God want to please
you have your soul to release
There your deity is glowing
And get your thoughts flowing.

May you, your cup with these thoughts seal
which your soul with great joy can feel.
Then you can your freedom enjoy
without being chained to others joy.
Your call of life is given you for good
with certainty in the grove of God.

Then you are in a state you can rate
on solid rocks of your faith.

Source: Oracle

The Ultimate Dream

Oracle: 'We have now been through different perspectives. Does this raise additional questions?'

Senius: 'When we spoke about gaps in perceptions, I mentioned that as long as egoism, nationalism, diverse religions and other excluding preferences rule the world, peace is just an illusion. I have to find my path at least at my level instead of focusing on the big picture, spreading my own development to my environment. I think this is the point where we are now.

'The main issue in my call is to find a way to merge my dad and my grandparent's views, i.e., freethinking and religious faith. Through our discussion, it is hard for me to find room for the classical religions in their present state.'

Senius: 'How is it possible to get out of the trap of being locked in old religious forms of belief, without losing the values our nations were built upon?'

Oracle: 'Well, that is actually what your call embraces; therefore, it is your responsibility to figure that out. But let me give you a clue though.

'The religions humans adapted to originated from convictions. These can be seen as an accumulated sum of development steps from the early religions up to when your present faiths emerged. It was what we discussed when dealing with the prior history of mankind.

'Each of the early religions has been adapted to the prevalent culture that their founder has inherited. Besides, they are influenced by the founders' upbringing.

'My point is that "God" has no needs, as you heard from the Master. Religions are instead all about your own needs because they were all created to comfort you and not the other way around.

'To come to the second part of your question, you can still keep your culture to maintain and develop your values. The only difference is that you would not have a superior authority that may overrule you unless you build something to replace it.'

Senius: 'I see your point. On the other hand, if we lose the guiding star, don't we risk ending up in chaos?'

Oracle: 'You get your answers as you ask for them. I assume that what you mean is that if everybody follows their call, you will end with chaos. But that is exactly the beauty of it. Calls can be combined in endless numbers of ways.

'Your respective calls support you in executing them. Many calls are complementary and are therefore one another's prerequisite.'

Rhodopis: 'Dear, Senius, you may consider it from a different perspective. What kind of demand do you want to be fulfilled in a spiritual fellowship?'

Oracle: 'It is a great question, Rhodopis.'

Senius: 'Do you mind shedding further light on this?'

Oracle: 'You already know that the best thing you can do is to fulfil your call. In the process, you also do what is best for your community because every call is about love for the Source and your neighbour.

'Besides, you will still need faith to carry out your call as well as support from the spiritual realm—your supporters. Hence the absence of traditional religions doesn't mean keeping your faith or spiritual insights aside; in fact, it is the other way around. Beliefs have been our ancestors' way to express their faith.

'The unfortunate thing is that the ruling members have misused their role to keep their power due to their egos. This organisation complies with the concept of the survival of the fittest.'

Senius: 'It is getting clearer now. Religions are an attempt to embrace the spiritual realm in a language/way people are capable of comprehending, given their time of living.'

Oracle: 'Exactly, and for that reason, the monotheistic religions had to be built on the patriarchal perspective, which was the prevalent frame of understanding at the time.

'But let me return to my original purpose of bringing up your call. Imagine what it would be like if everyone else also followed their calls. Then everyone would be on their paths leading to the development of higher consciousness.

'Can you imagine the impact it would have on your world?'

Senius: 'Yes, it sounds like a dream to me. Love is embedded in everybody's call which means that we would all take care of each other. This would ultimately make organised religions superfluous, although people would still feel the need for some spiritual guidance. On top of it, the need for possessions and control for security will fade out, thus enabling individuals to look at each other not with fear but with love and compassion.'

Oracle: 'Any religion you can recall has the same foundation—love, although their praxis often demonstrates something else. It is also ironic how most religious leaders, including the followers, focus on the differences instead of what they have in common.

'It is aptly described in Matthew 22:34-40, The Greatest Commandment: "Hearing that Jesus had silenced the Sadducees, the Pharisees got together. One of them, an expert in the law, tested him with this question: 'Teacher, which is the greatest commandment in the Law?'

Jesus replied: 'Love the Lord your God with all your heart and with all your soul and with all your mind. This is the first and greatest commandment. And the second is like this: Love your neighbour like yourself. All the Law and the Prophets hang on these two commandments".

'Irrespective of your religion, the verses above describe what love is about. "God", the Unmanifested, is love. And if you follow your call you will, without exceptions, be following these two commandments. The essence of the first commandment is that by sacrificing your ego you devote your creator your service, which is your call.

'And if you do so, you will also love your neighbour as if he or she was yourself. Therefore, they are like one.'

Senius: 'But that is only what I see when I dream that "everyone follows their call". Why doesn't it come through?'

Oracle: 'There are many reasons. Let me mention some of them. You are at different development levels, which also mean that your ability to understand will differ.

'The majority of souls are more or less in their ego, and they cannot understand other souls when they operate at the soul level. And they do not like those they do not understand. This contributes to the consolidation of a "them and us" image, which inevitably creates tensions.

'Furthermore, when they see a developed soul's behaviour, their own lower state of spiritual development is exhibited, which they do not like either. You can say that it hits them twice.'

Rhodopis: 'There are other smaller religious groups using religion as a way to legitimise a conquest of other people, and it doesn't really matter to them if by doing so they act in disrespect of their faith. These particular cases are built on fear. Therefore, these dynamics have nothing to do with religion. It is about souls who have lost their way and turned to terrorism or terror organisations such as the Islamic State.

'As a result, other global citizens who live in a well-informed society and are more peaceful may react with anger or hate towards these lost souls. However, as expressed in the Law of Attraction, the reaction will only attract more of what they do not want.

'A more matured soul can shake their heads or show compassion towards them because they understand the destiny these souls have chosen.

'In general, everybody is responsible for how they perceive and react to a given situation. Violence against your neighbour is an example of hardening your heart as a reaction to outside circumstances, e.g., because your neighbour reacts in a way that differs from your expectations. A choice that only darkens the mind and attracts additional suffering is caused by your ego.'

Senius: 'But why is it necessary with all that evil?'

Oracle: 'Evil is an interpretation you ascribe to their actions. We talked about duality and how opposites define attributes. If you do not know what evil is, you neither know what good is.

'Another way of saying it is that it is the souls who choose a stony road to awareness and let this be a reminder for you. You can always know whether you are on track or not by looking at the fruits of your actions. The ego brings you short-term fruits, and the soul brings you long-term fruits.

'Besides, there is always a match between the victim and the violent actor as the Law of Attraction also confirms. At the end of the day, it is about your ability to set your expectations, which are created in your mind.'

Senius: 'It is a little depressing when I look into my surroundings and not least the news.'

Rhodopis: 'Dear, Senius, I understand your reaction. I can add that terror organisations proclaim and spread their teaching which they have committed themselves to. As Oracle has pointed out, you can judge them from their fruits. By our definition, the Islamic State does not follow a call.

'On the other hand, they may have a role in demonstrating that religions are exclusive and have fought one another since the time of dawn in human history.'

Senius: 'Will it ever end?'

Oracle: 'It is up to you and nobody else. Guidance can be described as in "Alfa" at the beginning of this book, which explains how this development will take place. At some point in time, you will reach a consciousness level where it will no longer be necessary.

'You will instead seek the truth, which will be revealed to you. My immediate evaluation is that this is not just around the corner.'

Senius: 'Why not?'

Oracle: 'Imagine the consequence. Your purpose in entering the world is to let your soul feel and understand whatever it still needs to learn. However, at some point in the future, you do not need to return to the physical world.

'On the other hand, if you have come to that point of development, you do not want to return to Earth. But as most of you are young souls, the need will persist. However, if you continue misusing the resources of the planet, your chances to incarnate might decrease significantly.'

Senius: 'Excuse me, but I feel you with your last comments you turn the dream into a nightmare. So, what is your point?'

Oracle: 'Well, you asked why you do not see your dream in the real world. And I apologise for spoiling your dream. Nothing is given beforehand, and I do not have access to that far distance of time.

'But if you look at the last century, as a global community, we have been very destructive. The increasing consumption is slowly preparing your grave unless you do not start implementing severe countermeasures immediately, as Rhodopis stated.

'But to give you your dream back, you just have to take responsibility for your actions. It is part of your call. Be an excellent example as illustrated with the snowball example, and let it roll down the mountain.

'As we discussed earlier, the movement has to start in the society and progress all the way up. If you are persistent, you will attract enough people to help you reach the critical point where you impact the collective consciousness. Then things will begin to accelerate. So, in order to realise your dream, just go for your call, all of you!'

Senius: 'Thank you. Your last statement has made me feel at ease again.'

Rhodopis: 'On the world level, the UN is the only global organisation that would have a mandate. They formulated "Sustainable Development Goals", which we discussed previously.

'The UN needs to be reformed and should apply stricter requirements to the individuals holding important positions in the organisation. The foremost prerequisite to a position holder is to have an altruistic view superseding national interests.'

Senius: 'Isn't that a demanding criterion and hard to implement, which suggests that nations should hand their sovereignty over to the UN?'

Oracle: 'You are entirely right, but it would be a lengthy process. The first step is to agree that it is necessary to put in practice holistic solutions for all global citizens. Besides, the UN needs to address the root causes of the most urgent global issues, as discussed previously.'

Rhodopis: 'In addition to these, nations need to be demilitarised to a certain level, and nuclear weapons should be abandoned and undoubtedly transformed for peaceful purposes. Try to imagine what that would mean!

'The massive amount of resources spent on destructive devices would be used to stabilise societies and remove poverty.'

Senius: 'Although it is a very idealistic dream, I believe the gap with reality is extremely significant because it involves dealing with huge businesses employing many lobbyists. Just see how many weapons there are in the USA alone. It is astonishing!'

Rhodopis: 'I understand your pessimism. However, the first step is to talk about it, and the next step is to make a plan and carry it through.'

Oracle: 'I understand your pessimism too. But when you can dream it, you can also make it. All that you have created constructively started with a dream.'

Collective Consciousness

Senius: 'I realise that our discussion is moving from consciousness from an individual level to a collective perspective. Is collective consciousness a different concept?'

Oracle: 'Yes, it is. It has more layers of meaning. First, it is a sociological concept regarding shared values, beliefs and knowledge in a human tribe or group which ties its members together, gives them identity and sets frames for their behaviour. In addition, it fosters patriotism and nationalism, which demonstrates how complex the original human tribes have become.

'Furthermore, it is the reason why you are blinded by your own culture until you meet people from other cultures who behave differently, which makes you realise that culture is a human construct dependent on where you were born.

'Having said that, culture has its own benefits too. For example, if your culture believes that education is a valued asset for your country, educational institutions, such as schools and universities, are prioritised.

'On top of the students' professional skills, they also get skilled in analysing an issue from different perspectives and in thinking out of the box. Consequently, most students become more open-minded and look at religions with a more nuanced view.'

Senius: 'Another way of putting it is that the rainbow perspective replaces the old black-white thinking.'

Oracle: 'Precisely. In our context, collective consciousness is also when you focus on a common ritual to make a desire come through. It is an ancient concept used by the American Indians to ask for rain through a rain dance, for example.

'When more people gather around a shared desire, the effect can be potent. For this reason, prayer should not be underestimated.'

Senius: 'So does prayer work?'

Oracle: 'It does work independently of which religion you confess to. It is another way to use the Law of Attraction. It is one of the primary reasons why people are confirmed in their own faith.

'Therefore, it is an unfortunate moment when different religions conquer each other. Since they use the same tool, prayer, to realise their desires, they should agree upon shared aspirations, which would amplify the strength and effect of prayers.'

Senius: 'If that's how it works, why isn't this the rule instead of the exception?'

Rhodopis: 'A religious community is like any other organisation. It is similar to an organic being which wants to survive and preferably grow too. Anything that may challenge its dominance will activate its immune system, causing a fighting reaction.'

Senius: 'I can apply this mechanism to my former workplace, a huge private enterprise. Now and then, you have to reorganise the organisation to remove the unwanted fats. Each part of the organisation tries to get its significant areas prioritised. Survival of the fittest is always at play because competition is not only with external rivals but also between internal departments.'

Oracle: 'It just emphasises that as long as the "them and us" view is prevalent, competition is inevitable and will result in sub-optimisation, which is often disguised as a derived goal to support the organisation's overall purpose. As long as the majority works at the ego level, this is pretty much the outcome.'

Senius: 'Concerning praying, why does it work independently on the religion you confess to?'

Oracle: 'The mechanism is pretty simple. If you do not have faith in yourself but have confidence in your God, you will succeed anyway, because your common prayer will materialise through the Law of Attraction. The only difference is that you use the concept of God in various names as a vehicle.

'In other words, your desire will come true if your faith is strong enough as a group, with or without any God. It is a matter of confidence or self-confidence, respectively.

'Collective consciousness exists on different levels. At the top level, it covers the entire world and the different religions as already mentioned, as well as continents, superpowers, nations, communities, etc.

'Many will try to navigate you into a specific view fitting their interests, for example, heads of religious organisations, states, interest organisations, etc.'

Senius: 'Can you mention another example to illustrate this mechanism?'

Oracle: 'The financial market is a good example. Stocks and bonds do not follow the real economy; they follow the expectations the market has for their potential. The market consists of those who take part in the business. If the majority is expecting a positive development, prices go up, and vice versa.'

Senius: 'I've noticed, at times, that the market reacts exactly to a person's statement. How can this be?'

Oracle: 'You are right, and I acknowledge that there are exceptions from the main rule. The reason is that a few people in the financial market have a reputation for being able to predict changes or have a robust mandate in the market. People trust them, and this makes their prophecy self-fulfilling.

'Likewise, you can find leaders who are capable of leading many people, but it is a two-edged skill, for example, World War II, where a demagogue like Hitler managed to deceive his people, while Churchill managed to implement countermeasures under complicated circumstances.'

Rhodopis: 'Social media also contributes to influencers who suddenly set a new agenda impacting collective consciousness.'

Senius: 'I agree. From the examples above, I see that it is sometimes possible to impact collective consciousness. As previously discussed, one of the key challenges our world is facing is pollution, which has been generated over the last one and a half centuries. In addition, due to the increasing living standard in populous countries, pollution is ever increasing. Moreover, the population is also growing. All these factors are alarming and call for a sense of urgency.

'Is there any way we can use collective consciousness to turn this potential nightmare into a dream?'

Oracle: 'A very constructive question. And the answer is yes, there is always a way out. That said, with what you just summed up, it is apparent that the more time you spend on discussing without action, the bigger countermeasures are required. But as you can see from the above examples, it is possible a person can turn a critical situation into effective action.

'Humans have, through history, been marvellous at inventing solutions when things got extreme. Most importantly, timing plays a critical role.

'A recent event exemplifies this in the climate area. Suddenly a schoolchild became a spokesperson for the issue of climate change. Even though her role divided people, she had the opportunity to talk to the UN and the World Economic Forum Annual Meetings Davos 2020, which is remarkable. But the task is at your desk.'

Senius: 'How do I distance myself from the collective beliefs I am subjected to in my society?'

Oracle: 'Well, in this case, it is pretty obvious. Do what you can to support the collective belief with positive thoughts and inspired actions. Generally, in most cases, you are unconscious about the collective beliefs unless you have another outlook based on other cultures.

'In the latter case, you have a choice where you also have to take consequences into account. Tolerance for diversity can be quite different in various cultures.'

Senius: 'How do I choose a belief that best suits me?'

Oracle: 'You have your call as a reference. If the options you have are evenly related to your call, choose the one with the highest frequency level that corresponds to the highest level of consciousness.'

The Big Events of Life

Senius: 'I understood that God does not need to be worshipped, but I have a need to do so, and I believe I talk on behalf of many people. What can I and those who share this need do?'

Oracle: 'You can agree to create what you need through your imagination. Let me illustrate this by an example.

'You can still use some of your holy places to accommodate this need, but there should be a different approach.

'When it comes to prayer, the essential purpose is to show gratitude for your call and the gifts you receive. But you should definitely not revert to the old worship of God where you have somebody to interpret on your behalf. It would reverse your development to the old situation.'

Senius: 'What about all the big events of life which we still practice today as important rites of passage?'

Oracle: 'You will still be able to practice them. However, you would need to rewrite the content. Let me outline some examples from your Christian background.

'Baptism will get a new perspective. For instance, it can be transformed into a speech where the parents show gratitude for the task they got to help their child find his or her call. The pastor's statement will correspondingly inspire them to do so in the name of the holy unconditional love.

'The godparent's role is to support the child in achieving this and take over when necessary.

'Confirmation is transformed correspondingly. Due to the guidance, the confirmand has received from the people he is surrounded by, the call is already known to everybody. He just has to confirm the responsibility to act out the call. That will accelerate his development.

'Partnerships, including marriages, will be about a different reason than it is for most of you today. What the couple agrees upon in the first place is to help each other to live out their call. Aligning expectations before engaging in a partnership improves the ability to create harmony in the relationship.

'Many engage in partnership for unhealthy reasons. For example, if you do this to make your partner happy or you don't know your call, you may then want to try to change each other, which quickly becomes an attack on your personal integrity and your call.

'In a partnership, you are solely responsible for your call. You may think it sounds selfish, but remember it is the reason why you are born into this world. However, with complementary characters, you can help each other with your respective development.

'Finally, you have funerals. Death also gets another meaning. Indeed, saying goodbye to your beloved family member or a friend is always the hardest. But the difference is that you now know that the member you just lost has a bright future ahead, surrounded by soulmates and others whose only interest is to help and support. The loss you suffer is foremost your own.'

Senius: 'I am uplifted by your perspectives. I would love living like this.'

Oracle: 'So what is holding you back? You are the master of your life.'

Senius: 'I think I am starting to understand what you are aiming at, but the majority of people do not share the same opinion you are presenting.'

Senius: 'Can you tell us something more about this?'

Oracle: 'You are right that the majority does not think this way, but there is actually more than you think. The best thing you can do is to follow your call and stand by it. Then, you will automatically attract the right people, right circumstances and so on.'

Senius: 'Thank you. Everything you say sounds great, but if I look at my actual incarnation, I am grounded again. I wonder why I feel caught?'

Oracle: 'You can have this feeling only if you do not follow your call.'

Senius: 'What do I have to do?'

Oracle: 'You can either stay by your beliefs or stand by your call and do whatever it takes despite the consequences. As I mentioned earlier, without exception, your call will always be your best choice as that is your soul's desire and the purpose of your incarnation.'

The Ten Commandments in a Contemporary View

Oracle: 'In a historical perspective, the commandments have been conveyed to the Jewish people through Moses as the first monotheistic religion. As mentioned earlier, the interpretation has been coloured by his understanding. The Commandments have also been used as a guideline for Christians, like Jesus in the Sermon on the Mount in Matthew 5-7 refers to more of them.

'Besides, he underlines: "Do not think that I have come to abolish the Law or the Prophets; I have not come to abolish them but to fulfil them", Matthew 5:17. In other words, he follows the same spirit of the age.

'Once more, I have asked the Master to join us to interpret the Ten Commandments in a contemporary view.'

Referent: 'The Master returns as he did his entrance the last time, and I get filled with the same feelings as the last time, awe, love and compassion.'

Master: 'Dear souls, it is nice to meet you again. In general, the Ten Commandments should be viewed from the perspective of love as it is expressed in 1 John 4.18: "There is no fear in love. But perfect love drives out fear because fear has to do with punishment. The one who fears is not made perfect in love".

'For this reason, I will replace "shall not" with "should not" because I do not judge or punish you. But if you want what is best for you, your call, you will remain compliant with the Ten Commandments.'

1. I am the Lord your God; you should not have strange Gods before me.

Master: 'It is still valid as there is only one God, which is me. Since I am the Unmanifested, it makes no sense to make any picture of me or worship it as stated in Exodos 20.5. I am certainly not a jealous God, nor do I judge you, but the description Moses made of me complies with the spirit of the age.

'If you follow your call, the mission of your soul, then you also have a clean conscience and perform the deeds I mentioned in the Sermon on the Mount.

'Another way to express it is that your soul is connected to me as a drop is to an ocean. When you are in harmony with your soul, you are also in harmony with me.'

2. You should not take the name of the Lord your God in vain.

Master: 'I am love, and that is my being. It is also reflected in your soul. Therefore, be likewise. You can do so when you conduct your call conscientious and be that lighthouse you decidedly are, as written in Matthew 5:14: "You are the light of the world. A town built on a hill cannot be hidden".

'Additionally, you should never swear, as written in Matthew 5:33-37: "Again, you have heard that it was said to the people long ago, 'Do not break your oath, but fulfil to the Lord the vows you have made.' But I tell you, do not swear an oath at all: either by heaven, for it is God's throne; or by the Earth, for it is his footstool; or by Jerusalem, for it is the city of the Great King. And do not swear by your head, for you cannot make even one hair white or black. All you need to say is simply 'Yes' or 'No'; anything beyond this comes from the evil one".'

Senius: 'I can acknowledge this based on previous experience. When I look back, I promised fidelity to something that was right for me at the time, but as my insights grew, it lost its value. I have learnt this by the hearth. I am, therefore, reluctant to make promises.'

Oracle: 'It is a wise decision, Senius.'

Master: 'Yes, it is one of your challenges. However, it becomes easier gradually as you over time and little by little develop your consciousness.'

3. Remember to keep holy the Lord's day.

Master: 'At that time, the Sabbath was a sign between you and me, as written in Exodus 31:13:"Say to the Israelites, You must observe my Sabbaths. This will be a sign between me and you for the generations to come, so you may know that I am the Lord, who makes you holy".

'Again, you should see it to the best of your own: To give your body time for restitution and to make room for getting in contact with your soul, your true self. Like many other things, you have over-interpreted it in the spirit of the age and made it to a deed to do nothing! This has never been the intention.

'You find an example in Matthew 12:1-8:"At that time, Jesus went through the grain fields on the Sabbath. His disciples were hungry and began to pick some heads of grain and ate them. When the Pharisees saw this, they said to him, Look! Your disciples are doing what is unlawful on the Sabbath.'

'He answered, 'Haven't you read what David did when he and his companions were hungry? He entered the house of God, and he and his companions ate the consecrated bread—which was not lawful for them to do but only for the priests. Or haven't you read in the Law that the priests on Sabbath duty in the temple desecrate the Sabbath and yet are innocent?

'I tell you that something greater than the temple is here. If you had known what these words mean, I desire mercy, not sacrifice, you would not have condemned the innocent. For the Son of Man is Lord of the Sabbath".'

4.   Honour your father and your mother.

Master: 'When you chose your circumstances and became incarnated, you came into the life of your parents. That is the frame you accepted to let your soul have the best opportunities to explore and gain the experiences it needs to become more whole. Therefore, you should be grateful to your parents.

'At the time of the commandment, parents were also seen as my substitute. If you did not obey your parents, it was considered as dishonour, which causes misery. Unfortunately, some of you became too jealous and punished your children, which created fear in them. An unintentional outcome was that these kids were insecure about their parents' love, and in some cases, turned their feelings into anxiety and mistrust.'

Oracle: 'The guideline for everybody is, as already mentioned, that any deed should be inspired from the perspective of love.'

Master: 'As stated several times, a call is always built on love and do not intend to harm anyone.'

5. You should not kill.

Master: 'From this commandment and going forward, your fellow human beings are your responsibility. In the past, many people have been killed in my name. My name has been misinterpreted and misused.'

Oracle: 'Holy outrage is nothing but an act of self-righteous.'

Master: 'The commandment is broader than to kill somebody, as mentioned in Matthew 5:21-22:"You have heard that it was said to the people long ago, You shall not murder, and anyone who murders will be subject to judgment. But I tell you that anyone who is angry with a brother or sister will be subject to judgment. Again, anyone who says to a brother or sister, Raca, is answerable to the court. And anyone who says, You fool! will be in danger of the fire of hell".

'This kind of behaviour will darken your mind and is incompatible with your call.'

6. You should not commit adultery.

Master: 'This commandment has a lot of attention in your minds and requires a more profound interpretation.

'As you have said previously, partnership is an opportunity to live out the call of each partner and harvest many of the fruits of love. It is also an opportunity to have children, a great gift and a big common task.

'First of all, the institution of partnership is a recognition that there is a mutual commitment to be something more than you would be on your own, and this commitment is based on love.

'Furthermore, if you choose to have children, the partnership is also intended as a loving and stable foundation for their upbringing. Most of the children's attributes are founded during this period, where they are most vulnerable and need help to become whole individuals. Therefore, you should nurture and maintain your partnership as a starting point.

'Unfortunately, many have entered into partnership for different reasons, as mentioned earlier. This increases the risk of a dysfunctional family. In case there are children, it is of cause the parent's responsibility to take care of them even if it means sacrificing their own needs.

'Nonetheless, the cleft can grow so deep that a separation might be necessary at some point, not least for the children's sake. But it is painful for everybody, and it leaves scars on the soul. Therefore, it is highly recommendable to be aware of what your call needs. When you decide to be part of a marriage, align your expectations with your partner.'

Senius: 'It is meaningful to me even though it is different from my own experience. When I look back on my choice of partner, I was not aware of my call.'

Senius: 'Does it mean that I may have been lucky because my choice did not end in a divorce?'

Master: 'I understand you can experience it that way. However, as you also know, there are no coincidences. Besides, it is more nuanced. Let me illustrate it with the picture your grandfather used in his speech at your wedding. You were like a raw diamond, which needed to be grinded.

'Each time the diamond touches the grindstone, you hear a scream. But after each grinding the diamond becomes more transparent and beautiful. So, even though it hurts when it happens, it is necessary.

'In this way, you have adapted to each other within your unconscious call, and your initial infatuation has almost unnoticeably turned into a more enduring love.

'It is, fortunately, a common practical path. As soon as more of you become aware of your call, more will also choose partnership for genuine reasons, replacing ego motives with your soul's call. In return, their partnership will remain happy, and the need for separation will diminish.

'In your case, you also have a mutual understanding to give each other space to live your individual interests and balance them with joint experiences, which reinforces your relationship.'

Oracle: 'I can also add that you have had another advantage because you implicitly always have been conscious about your personal integrity, which has been a great support for you. Moreover, you have had clear expectations from each other, e.g., a clear split between your area of responsibility in your fellowship.'

Senius: 'Thank you for your answers. But what about people who separate and enter into another partnership?'

Master: 'Dear, Senius, as stated in Matthew 5:32: "But I tell you that anyone who divorces his wife, except for sexual immorality, makes her the victim of adultery, and anyone who marries a divorced woman commits adultery". This not only emphasises the seriousness of associating oneself with another partnership but also demonstrates the morality in those days.

'If you see it in a contemporary light, you need to understand what went wrong in your first partnership. If you are not aware of the reason, there is a significant risk that the next partnership will lead to the same circumstances. In that case, it is better, for your own sake, to refrain from a new partnership. As said, I do not judge anybody, but I wish you the best, which remains your call.'

7. You should not steal.

Master: 'The commandment is meant to protect your fellow human being's property and other possessions. The one who steals will lead a miserable life. Stealing is not only a loss to the owner, but also works regressively for the thief's development. Instead, be good and kind to the poor, so that their distress does not translate into the temptation to steal for survival.'

8. You should not bear false witness against your neighbour.

Master: 'When you speak, you should be earnest, and if you follow your call, which is about love, you will always be on the right side. This does not only apply to when in court but also whenever somebody asks for your advice.

'When you hear negative gossip about your fellow human beings, you should refrain from adding fuel to the fire. Therefore, do not let the gossip spread any further. On the contrary, if you hear positive comments about someone, you should let the person know. Because your talk should be for joy and good only.'

9. You should not covert your neighbour's wife.

Master: 'Separation is one thing, entering into a new marriage is another and the third thing, the worst of all, is to covet your neighbour's wife, as stated in Matthew 5:28: "But I tell you that anyone who looks at a woman lustfully has already committed adultery with her in his heart".

'It expresses the same old morality, and Islam asks the women to cover their female attributes in order to avoid tempting the men. I do not judge you; however, for your own good, you should strangle such thoughts before it manifests because it is mostly a desire from your ego.'

10. You should not covert your neighbour's goods.

Master: 'It is a common statement among people to say that thoughts are duty-free. But as you have discussed previously, this is not the case. The Law of Attraction has an impact even though you do not bring the thought to life. As Pro. 4.23 states: "Guard your heart above all else, for it determines the course of your life".

'For this reason, do not covet your neighbour's goods. For where your treasure is, there your heart will also be.

'Let me end this list with a wish for you: May you find the courage to overcome your reservations. As always may love and compassion be your compass in life. Thank you and goodbye.'

Referent: 'The Master disappears in the same way as he arrived and leaves some emptiness within me.'

Oracle: 'Are there any closing remarks or questions?'

Senius: 'Thank you. I have obtained what I aimed for. I am grateful that you have met my request.'

Rhodopis: 'Thank you. This session is worthy for me too.'

Referent: 'I am very happy that I could be a part of this extraordinary event. Thank you!'

Oracle: 'Let me end this session with a closing question for you. Are you ready to leave?'

Senius: 'Thank you for accommodating my request for this meeting. I feel readier than ever.'

Rhodopis: 'I got an input for my next call and feel ready to formulate it.'

Referent: 'I feel grateful to have had this opportunity and am thrilled to bring it to life in my book.'

Oracle: 'Very well. Let us return to our respective calls. Be blessed in your call.'

Referent: May this also go for you, dear reader: May you find your call or have a desire to find it so you can bring happiness to yourself and your surroundings. Be the change you want to see in the world.

'As I started with a question at the beginning of this journey, let me end with another one: Why go for less than your specific call?

'It is the best outcome for you and the world.'

Thank you!

The Best Version of You

You have now witnessed a full life cycle,
and learnt that incarnation is a recycle.
May it bring your life to a revision
so your will fill it with nutrition.

The Universe is one immense energy field.
Everything is interconnected to yield.
You are though connected to the Source.
Use this knowledge as your resource.

You know that the power is available for you.
With faith, the power is all yours.
You possess all the tools you need.
Let humanity reap your seed.

Let you become the best version of you.
Throw the barriers away from youth.
It is time to let your life flowers bloom.
Let your call bring light to you soon.

Don't change yourself to win the world.
Stay right with light from the spiritual world.
Be the change you want to see in the world.
Be your call to the best you can,
for you and the world.

Source: Oracle

Synthesis

Referent: 'Dear Reader, we have now been through a journey from "Alfa" to "Omega". "Alfa" is illustrated through a stylised diamond, characterised by its beautiful brightness, yet hard and cold at the same time. During your life's course, you may have undergone a development symbolised by a stylised heart, which is soft and vulnerable but also warm and emphatic.

'The introduction raises an important question: *What is the most decisive life issue you need to figure out?* My answer is short and precise: it is to know why you are here. It is to find your specific call and get the experiences your soul has decided to experience in order to be more mature.

'In the back mirror, this becomes obvious. You will understand that you need to be physically present to gain the experiences you need, and when you find your call, you will also realise that you are an eternal soul, while your body, thoughts, feelings and mind are nothing but tools.

'However, there are many steps before getting there. To get a clearer overview of the process, you are invited into the beyond. The access is the *Rainbow Portal* leading to the spiritual world where you meet the initial actors: Senius, Rhodopis, Oracle and the Referent.

'The story has a few fundamental premises linked to Senius' convictions and based upon his experiences: Life is meaningful when there is a purpose. We are here to gain experiences that are accumulated both individually and on a larger scale in the spiritual world.

'Everything in the physical world has a life cycle. Our body is a mortal tool, but our soul is immortal and returns to its home after physical death. Here it prepares for its next incarnation. In this way, each soul incarnates numerous times.

'The story starts in the "Melting Pot", which reveals that reincarnation is a concept that existed long before humans developed their religions, which were developed over a significant period of time. However, it has gradually changed to fit the needs of our societies during the development of our consciousness.

'We learnt that we have to build our own life puzzle from the bottom up without the big picture. It makes Senius feel frustrated because he is used to having the drawing to build the house before the actual building process. Without the drawing, a number of detours can occur, which Senius believes is a loss of valuable time. But in the process, we learn and things learnt become a meaningful part of our journey.

'If somebody presents their interpretation of the big picture, you may get locked in their view. It can be acceptable if it complies with your call. For Senius, it is a trap and beyond his call. He needs to turn his focus within him and open the door to the spiritual world.

'We learn that our ability to fulfil our call mainly depends on two factors: who we are connected to and our level of consciousness. Besides, there is a balance between the challenges embedded in our call and capabilities. Nobody is just freewheeling. Therefore, see obstacles as opportunities to grow.

'Creating a family is a mutual decision for all its members, new-born babies included, because coincidences do not exist. A coincidence is defined as an event where we miss the insight into its creation.

'In "A New Transition", we get a sneak peek into the preparation for incarnation, and we learn how a baby and a soul merge to form an individual human being. We get an understanding of the correlation between Senius and his family. Most references for our outlook are founded in early childhood. Since we have chosen the frames ourselves, there is nobody to blame. One should see parents, possible siblings and close relations as teachers.

'We also get to learn about another universal law, *karma*, which is older than religion. It is a neutral, non-judgemental law. Morale and ethics are a human creation.

'It is time to delve into "The life of Senius in Brief". Once we know that we have a call, the experience of Senius can be an inspiration to find ours. In Senius' case, we learn how quite a few of his beliefs have been created through his family relations and his position in the group of siblings. Among others, he learnt that he has broken the pattern of his family.

'During his work life, he participated in different development programmes, of which two of them particularly stand out. In one of the project management programmes, he learnt how birth order influences personality traits. In the second programme, he receives a personal drawing.

'It is seminal, even though he first realises this after coming back home. In fact, he first realises the meaning of the lighthouse picture. The meaning of the remaining drawings crystallises many years later.

'Generally, his work life has all been about development, which propagated to his personal life, since it pushed him to have an eye for development in all areas. In his first job, he had a manager who he did not choose. It was a bad experience at first, but in the back mirror, he realises that this was an opportunity to move to other job positions. The experience was an eye-opener and confirmed that an obstacle is an opportunity.

'Senius tried more than once to find a purpose in life. Working life itself was not sufficient to close the gap, for example, between his grandparents' Christian faith and his father's view, which has created a strong dissonance in his life. This once again shows that when we do not have the full picture, we can hardly avoid detours. The point, however, is to never give up. If we are persistent, we will find our way. Keep on seeking.

'At some point in time, his wife triggers Senius to pick up the thread again. Here we see an example of a trigger that was agreed upon before the incarnation. The little story about the men with the coloured glasses is a reminder that we might need to seek inspiration for our call outside our relations.

'In "A Perspective in the Back Mirror", Senius suggests looking into his family and close relations from an outside perspective.

'In "Gaps in Perceptions", Senius starts to reflect on the former input and realises the meaning of the Rainbow Portal. He also sees how his parents impacted the way he brought up his own children.

'He sees the danger of becoming a "workaholic" and of forgetting the original purpose of work, letting the work become a purpose in itself. This may lead to a hamster wheel for mainly two reasons. First, we often want more than we need at once, making us run into debts and thereby increasing the demand for monthly payments.

'As a result, we work so hard in order to make ends meet. When we get back home, we feel burned out and don't have much to offer our family.

'Second, good and service providers are extremely good at creating products or services that may not be necessary. Even if they are mere illusions, their agenda is effective because they spend a significant amount of time and money on marketing. These goods, however, are mainly surrogates. You cannot buy your call with cash.

'Senius experiences another eye-opener in connection with coaching as the focus persons have brought many solutions to their issues he wouldn't have thought of.

'While Senius got the inspiration to his first book on Gran Canarias, we get an example of how his connections convey messages as a mix of input from his spiritual connections and his ability to visualise the outcome by seeing himself writing his first book.

'In "Personal Character", Senius derives a number of his characteristics based upon the identified gaps. It is critical to be aware of personal attributes that do not fit into our call. It is essential to be aware of it as early as possible as, because the longer we wait, the harder it is to change. This could be attributed to the fact that there is a direct chain from thoughts to actions.

'But there is always a way out, even if we do not know how that part of our personality originated. Senius' example of confidence illustrates this.

'On "The Life Journey", we talk about Senius and reflect upon the most critical areas of his life, which is also meant as an inspiration for us.

'Senius prioritises his call and its underlying preconditions—health and personal resources. The next priority is his family where wealth comes into play to create security and freedom. The third priority is his close friends. But in reality, priorities constantly shift depending on the current situation.

'Senius sums up his call using a picture: the rainbow portal, the lighthouse, the bird and the sundial. Only the lighthouse was recognised to be the call until about 5 years ago. He was aware of the most important puzzle piece, the rainbow portal, only recently. The puzzle pieces fit, though not necessarily come in a logical order.

'Another characteristic attribute to a call is that it always creates meaningfulness and contributes to the world's whole. The gift by serving your call is that being something for others creates the true feeling of happiness, far more profound than any possession can offer you. The more mature a soul is, the higher is the impact on the surroundings.

'Health is an essential prerequisite for Senius' ability to perform his call. He distinguishes between physical health, diet, fasting and mental health.

'Physical health is mainly maintained by walking and some high-intensity training. Besides, yoga also contributes to health, which is part of Senius' daily morning rituals.

'When it comes to diet, the rules of thumb are eating as natural as possible and avoiding over-processed food and fast food. Intermediate fasting is a great supplement to give the body more time for internal repair.

'Mental health is maintained through yoga, meditation, hiking alone, writing and discussion with close friends. Wealth is a balance of creating security and freedom, and it is essential to avoid being devoured by work.

'Senius sees the family from the role of a parent. Senius has children born in two different generations, which gives him a possibility to reflect on how they were raised. The first two were very similar to how he and his wife were raised.

'Their parental attitude was relatively impulsive, while the last one has had more mature and advisedly frames. The last kid's childhood ended far earlier than her elder siblings, but to some extent, it also has something to do with the external structure, which has changed a lot due to technological advancements.

'In both cases, they have tried to give them bright and loving frames. It seems like all of them have a prosperous life.

'When it comes to friends, it is essential to distinguish between close friends and the rest. Close friends are those who you can count on also during unfortunate times. You do not necessarily meet often, but you know they are there whenever needed and vice versa.

'In "The Community", we look at situations around the world in a helicopter view. One key issue is pollution, which is mainly driven by two factors: the growth of living standards in populous countries and growth in the world population. This creates an untenable state and increases the risk for a severe pandemic. The more the people and the more we move around, the higher the risk of transmitting diseases.

'Another potential risk is the storage of nuclear bombs. These bombs are sufficient to destroy every human being.

'A lot of the food we eat is of low quality and are not ethical or healthy. A lot of additives harm our bodies. On top of this, pollution contaminates food as well. As a consumer, there are certain things we can do or contribute, as Senius describes in "Diet".

'It is a hard nut to crunch because producers, remedial industries and healthcare system have all been built upon this set-up. It is a huge task to do it right. But it is up to us whether human beings should be a parenthesis in the Earth's history.

'At a personal level, the best thing you can do concerning the community is to be an excellent example for your surroundings. In this way, you can generate a snowball effect.

'More extreme approaches are as example, minimalism. Even though it is not an option for most of us, it can still be an inspiration to reduce consumption and pollution.

'In "Foundations", it can be acknowledged that we incarnate with an empty memory. It is as if we bought a computer. It just contains a steering system that corresponds to our autonomy system. The programs we install on the computer is parallel to the behaviour we copy from our family, which gradually becomes the reference we create to interpret the world.

'Fortunately, we have chosen the family ourselves. Therefore, there is nobody to blame and no victims. Instead, all members are each other's teachers.

'In "The Cognitive Diamond", we learn how the feeling of human connection is between the outside world and our ego, consisting of a body interrelating with thoughts and feelings expressed through behaviour. It goes hand in hand with classical wisdom. Many of us remain with this perception our entire life.

'If we want to aim for more, we need to realise that there is more than we can comprehend with our five senses. It is a step into another realm, the spiritual realm, which actually sets the physical world's frames. Our connection is the superconscious mind, true self, soul, etc. But as we're talking about faith, perception and belief, it makes good sense to use the word soul.

'We learn that the soul has three different domains. A divine domain withholds divine love and compassion, where the potential for enlightenment and unity lies. The second domain is our individual area where our former incarnations are stored, recording present life, karma and present call. The last domain is the communication centre connecting the soul with the spiritual world and the ego.

'The soul can communicate through feelings, thoughts and body. The key here is how we open the door to the communication channel of the soul. All of us have a longing that our ego cannot fulfil.

'As stated in Matthew 7.7-8:"Ask and it will be given to you; seek and you will find; knock and the door will be opened to you. For everyone who asks receives; the one who seeks finds; and to the one who knocks, the door will be opened".

'The point is that we need to have faith to get access to the spiritual realm. It cannot be reached through our senses, but it can be experienced.

'Furthermore, our soul is connected with the body through seven energy centres that control our different body areas, called *chakras*. My main take away is that it can help us to identify issues and heal them.

'In "Beliefs", we realise that it is not about what is right or wrong, but about the different experiences that generate different beliefs. The experiment with the three cups illustrates that, at a certain point, we will experience that other people have references different from ours. In the experiment, it is easy to understand that two opposite outcomes are possible.

'But in the real world, we usually only know our own part of the experiment, and the people close to us tend to have the same perception as we have. The conclusion is to be open-minded and maybe become wiser.

'In general, you can divide beliefs into negative and positive, give you headwind and tailwind, respectively. The earlier we realise our beliefs, the easier it is to replace the negative ones and nurture the positive ones. Whether a belief is positive or negative depends mainly on our call, which is based upon our former lives through our karma. But we also have a free will that can impact the outcome of our incarnation.

'Faith is an intrinsic conviction in correlation with your soul, while a belief is an extrinsic frame of understanding. But as we learn, the distinction may overlap as Senius had experienced two different types of faith. The first one is the naive faith he inherited from his grandparents, which is actually imprinted from the outside and later a more mature faith built from his own experiences.

'Furthermore, it is seminal that the latter type of faith can only be experienced when you believe it is possible.

'Likewise, we learn that mature faith includes peak experiences wherein the last doubt can vaporise. In the case of Saul (later renamed Paulus), the knowledge he obtained on his way to Damascus became the reason for his conversion to Christianity.

'Many people have concluded that peak experiences are for prophets only, and therefore, do not look for such opportunities themselves. As we learn through Senius' peak experiences, it is an opportunity for everybody. However, you have to believe it is possible. The examples of peak experiences you learn about in this book are on top of the former description of Paulus' experience in chronologic order:

- The scenery with the rainbow portal taking place in the "Introduction".
- The vision Senius receives in Gran Canarias about his first book in "Gaps in Perceptions".
- The out of body experience while meditating.
- The bright staircase during the Sunday service in the church, in "Faith".
- The Big Bang experience in "Dreams".

'In other words, peak experiences can occur in many different ways.

'Values are to a high extent above the personal level, e.g., through religion and culture. Here, our place of birth also comes into play. However, this has also been part of our choice when we chose our family before incarnating.

'We learn all the values Senius adopted: faith, unconditional love, curiosity, trust, responsibility and hard work. On a national level, freedom of speech, humour, social responsibility, humbleness and individual independence.

'In "Roles", we learn that all of us play many different roles in different contexts, e.g., as a husband, father, colleague, and so on. Several models exist to describe different stereotypes. On the one hand, using roles might be beneficial to give insight into significant attributes, but on the other hand, they ignore individual divergences.

'An example of attribute is the introvert or extrovert character. Due to the birth order in his family, Senius has developed something in between, ambivert, which is a result of an individual divergence coming into play out of the role scheme.

'Another layer of roles is the business role, which is about objective setting and the more mature altruistic role built on principles and independent of outcomes.

'It is time to discuss what tools we can use to release our call.

'The "Creation Process" reminds us that while pursuing our call it is pivotal to remember that we are subjects to the Law of Attraction, impersonal and universal, which works whether you believe in it or not. We can realise our call by being aware of this law and using it deliberately. In fact, most of us are unaware of this law because we live in our ego—we are absorbed in our daily routines.

'Getting our thoughts under control, for example through meditation, can help us be more aware.

'Visualisation is another helpful tool towards awareness. It is about focusing on what we want and associating our desires with the feelings we would have once our wish is fulfilled. The aim is to keep our feelings positive and use our thoughts constructively. It requires a lot of praxis, especially to become independent of other's impact on our mood.

'In "Coincidences in The Big Picture", it may seem as events with no particular purpose initially, because we are unconscious about their connection to what we are aiming at. However, as soon as we pay attention to them, they start to become meaningful. Then they become more frequent and we realise that they are connected to our call. It is another utilisation of the Law of Attraction, i.e., like attracts like.

'Affirmation is another supporting tool that uses realisation of a future event by formulating it in the present tense and sustaining it with positive feelings. Many affirmations start with "I am", e.g., "I am one with my Creator" or "I am love".

'Praxis is again the way to success. A good exercise is to state your affirmations out loud in front of a mirror and try to overcome your resistance. It is worth it!

'"Birth Order" can give us insight into many generic attributes of one's disposition and behavioural patterns. It goes for grandparents, parents and siblings—Senius' descriptions are examples of how you can look into your family to find out more about yourself.

'Many of our "Thoughts" and "Belief" are rooted in and derived from our childhood. It is, therefore, necessary to look at our childhood to unlock the conditioned thoughts that do not fit into our call and escape the pattern.

'If we elevate our perspective to the soul level, we can open our awareness and tap into the Source's understanding, which pervades everything and everywhere. It will ultimately bring us insights on a divine level. It is also the ultimate test of your faith, simply because it can only happen after you truly believe it is possible.

'Then, "Feelings" are a vital component of our compass. Whenever a negative thought appears, it should be a wake-up call, because it means that there is something we need to pay attention to. We should not frame this negative feeling as 'good' or 'bad,' rather as a potential area of development.

'The earlier the better, because it is easier to redirect the energy at the beginning before it grows stronger. In that case, it can eventually be neutralised by an affirmation. A helpful tool, in this case, is to switch feelings, i.e., making a list stating all the areas of strength we have and all those that give us positive feelings.

'Intuition is probably one of the oldest tools available to us since ancient times. It seems like many of us have lost this capability in the name of fact-based knowledge. Fortunately, it seems to be experiencing some sort of renaissance. It is above logical thinking, and fear might influence it to a point where it leads some to argue that intuition does not exist.

'Because it is an essential tool, it is important to practise and learn how to separate the input from thoughts, feelings and body sensations from the ego. We can recognise the difference because inputs from the soul send us altruistic thoughts, feelings that are a blessing and sensations in the body that all make us feel lighter.

'Dreams are another tool that can give you significant input to something you are struggling with, consciously and unconsciously. Whenever you have a dream and remember it, try to relate it to your current situation. It can also be a daydream, which normally is related to something you just have in mind. Sometimes both types of dreams can be related.

'Then, "The Wishing Well" is an essential tool that is comparable to a laboratory of experimentation. It is where Senius prepares his day and brings the Law of Attraction to life. He sets annual goals and breaks them down into smaller steps. Moreover, at the beginning of the day, he also considers how he can do better today than the previous day.

'Senius is living a life with the freedom to decide how to spend each day. In order to prevent time from slipping away through his fingers, he made a 'Time Planner' with eight timeslots of two hours each. In "The Wishing Well", he decides how to spend the day.

'Then, "The Faces of Fear" describes seven different kinds of fear. Generally, fear is a conviction as any other belief. If we are facing real danger, it is appropriate, but in many cases, it is not. It can be illustrated by a person who has a phobia. It is real for the person who perceives it, but it is not a real risk for an outside viewer.

'Fear can also be a significant barrier in making the move towards our dream job because we have built a lot of obstacles along the way, which in most cases are conditional. Therefore, this delay us from living our call and in some cases, never execute it at all.

'In "Dead", another kind of fear is introduced with many different faces: fear of the unknown, fear of your deity or premature death, fear of slow and painful death and so on. The best thing to do is to build a serene relationship with death. In this way, we do not attract unforeseeable negative events and can rest in peace.

'When the time is ripe to leave, it is beneficial to be grateful and close any open issues that may hinder peace in our hearts and soul.

'The "External Fear" is fear caused by an outside source with potential consequences on our lives, family, friends or possessions, such as terrorism, wars and pandemics. In most cases, fear is exaggerated, because our feelings amplify it and often out of proportion to the actual risks.

'The media often magnifies it too, because bad news translates into more viewers and extra newspapers sold. The best countermeasure is to practically evaluate the causative factor of fear and accordingly spend as little time and energy as possible on it and keep the focus on your call.

'In "Worries", the fear of possible undesired future events. As it is counterproductive, the best remedy is to focus on the present moment. Alternatively, you may switch feelings as mentioned previously.

'The "Diseases" appear when we stress our body too much over an excessive period of time. Most diseases primarily result from resistance against your present circumstances and lifestyle. Stress can either be physical or mental.

'The key message is that as soon as your body signals that something hurts or you sense discomfort, it is a red flag calling for attention and action. As Hippocrates stated before Christ, illness does not come out of the blue; it develops from small daily sins against nature.

'If you do not act on the signals, you will have to accept the diseases as they come and may not get the chance to reinstate your health as it was before the disease. So why not take care of the symptoms in the first place?

'The "Physical Stress" is mainly rooted in the environment, primarily through pollution of the air that we breathe, radioactive radiation and mediocre food. The formation of bigger cities is a significant source for many respiratory diseases, particularly for children. Mediocre food causes many diseases, which could be avoided by stricter rules, although the producers claim they produce what the consumers request.

'However, the ground reality is quite different, suggesting that the bar for ethical practices should be raised. The free-market forces have failed the community as they mainly focus on monetary profits than on their consumers' health.

'The "Mental Stress" is the largest single source of diseases. Our resilience to handle stress depends on our general state of mind. The more positive we are, the higher the resilience and vice versa. The baseline is mostly developed in our childhood.

'However, anyone can reach a point where the total load becomes unbearable. The consequences vary, e.g., we spend more and more time on administrating our tasks. We lose the overview, make errors and our capabilities start to diminish. It affects our mood, and if we do not intervene or seek help, a breakdown is inevitable.

'The way out of the trap is to pull the break before it is too late and ask questions like: Does what I do fit with my call? Should I choose to fight, stay without fight or flight and is my job more important than my health?

'Based on our answers to these questions, it is possible for us to find a suitable way out.

'"Yoga and Meditation" are other essential tools to control our thoughts and connect with our inner self, which are preconditions for inner peace and harmony. They are the door to the spiritual world and all the connections we have established there, giving us access to true wisdom and have the ability to release us from our coincidental reactions.

'For Senius, yoga is a prelude to meditation, which he uses to focus his mind. A beneficial side effect is that it keeps the body flexible.

'Senius has found what he needs in Vipassana meditation, an ancient kind of meditation, which was also practised by Buddha. It has two stages. First, focus on the breath. Whenever a thought appears, you have to return the focus to the breath.

'Second is a self-observation technique, wherein you observe your thoughts and feelings as an outsider without reacting to them. You learn to disconnect your automatic reactions to the body sensations through the process, which ultimately make you free.

'Senius uses other kinds of meditations for various purposes, such as seeking messages from the spiritual world, healing the body, sending energy to friends who need help to heal themselves, preparing for visiting sick people and removing imbalances in the chakras.

'When life comes to an end, many of us struggle with the process, but the Law of Attraction also works in "The Process of Dead". Therefore, to get the best leave, we have to imagine how that would be for us. Senius describes his expectations as making it very harmonic and peaceful.

'After leaving our mortal body, we beam through to the spiritual world and simultaneously see our life from two perspectives—how we have experienced it ourselves and how it has impacted the actors we interacted with during the incarnation.

'After a reunion with soulmates and guide, a new cycle starts or reincarnation. The learnings from former lives are consolidated, and each soul has to prepare a new framework that defines the gaps and derive wanted learnings for a new incarnation.

'To complete the analysis of a life cycle, we look into "Preparation to Birth". It has three stages: defining the call, preparation of birth and birth itself; the remaining two stages take place in the physical world.

'In "The Transition Phase", the call has matured, and the soul is ready to see different scenarios that match the soul's needs and also those of the other actors in the scenarios. The soul chooses a scenario with guidance from its connections. The next step is to make agreements with other souls who play a significant role in the scenario. As we lose our soul memory while incarnating, we agree on triggers beforehand that will help us recall who these helpful connections are.

'In "The Supporters", we learn that our connections depend on our maturity, which correspond to different vibration spheres. They influence our framework and help us during our incarnations. To access these resources, we need to be aware and deliberately seek the connections by raising our frequency and energy level.

'It can be through meditation, intuition, dreams, ideas, writing and so on. Whenever you raise your frequency level, you will feel a sense of bliss.

'There are different development levels, and the higher the development level, the easier it becomes to get access to support. However, even mature souls can get distracted. Therefore, it is essential to keep practising and stay focused. Meditation is an essential tool to obtain this.

'Then, "Preparations in the Physical World" takes place likewise. An incarnation starts with a woman getting pregnant. There is always a symbiosis between parents and child/children. As Mozart indicated that talents can be transferred from former lives.

'In "The New World", we explore the preconditions for giving birth to human life, the creation of the universe and the earth. Suddenly it can be realised that humans have only lived in a very short period in this evolution. Furthermore, the religions most of us confess to were created just within a few thousand years.

'This development can be explained through three factors: the number of incarnations, the development level and the relative time you are in your soul while incarnated. Their combination describes why development was slower in the beginning and gradually becomes faster. Due to the mix of the souls' maturity, it is difficult for most of us to observe the development potential.

'In one way, it might be time to rock the boat again. To get an idea of this, it is worthwhile to go back to how our history has developed taking as reference the Christian narration of it.

'Further, "The Beginning of the Universe" in the Bible is a very poetic description. We learn that God has a persistent urge to create, and this created the universe. It also becomes apparent that many of God's attributes reflect the beliefs that Moses, the patriarch who describes the story, had due to his time of living. In other words, Moses gave God very human attributes.

'Then, "The Fall" is a metaphor that explains how we still stumble, because doubts, blame and pride distract us from our call; the serpent saw doubt in Eva, then a lie that put the blame on God to create suspicion and finally to make Eva proud. These attacks remain toxic for our abilities to realise our desires and call.

'God has prepared the frames for us. It is up to us to fill out the frames through our call. Therefore, take responsibility for your creations and actions because nobody but you can.

'An emissary from the Source, the Master, enters the scene to convey a complementary description taking the present participants knowledge into account. The Master ends his lecture by stating that the will is only free if it allows you to make mistakes to learn and improve. Therefore, it only makes sense if you can do this as often as you need to become wiser. And it takes many lives to get there.

'Senius reflects on the input he received, which makes him recall the cohesion he experienced at the Camino that gave him a feeling of Oneness, an implicit understanding that all of us are connected. It also means that we have a responsibility for the whole.

'History have shown us features that gave human beings supremacy over other living beings: Detailed language and ability to imagine; our brain is not fully developed at births, which gives us a superior ability to adapt to very different environments compared to any other species and increasing tribe size through tales.

'We see how the tales develop into more sophisticated myths and rites, which were ongoing adapted to our changed circumstances. At a particular time, gods were imagined and this paved the way to the religions we know today.

'In "The Ultimate Dream", we learn that religions assume that God has needs, but God has none. It is merely a projection of our human needs into the figure of God around which our religions have been created. It also means that we cannot just throw our religions away without replacing them with something that can fulfil the needs religions have been addressing.

'In the big picture, all religions are built on the foundation of love, just as our call is. But in order to have the ability to understand and experience what love is, we also need to know the opposite of love—fear, because it

281

is with the opposite that we can define most of the attributes of the two polarities.

'If we want to make the world a better place, all we need to do is to carry out our call. In this way, we also contribute with our puzzle piece to the whole picture—Oneness. Besides, we potentially attract other souls who can make us reach a critical point where the development begins to accelerate. It is a bottom-up process.

'When we look at the current state of the world, we are inclined to be pessimistic. However, if we can imagine the good things, we can also make them come true. But we have to believe that we can get there.

'Then, "Collective consciousness" becomes relevant in this context. It is a sociological concept about shared values and beliefs. It also describes how more people can manifest a shared desire, for instance, the way prayer works in a religious community.

'We might then wonder why different religions do not come together and make common prayers to make themselves and their communities more powerful. The reason is that a religious community works like any other organisation. There is still a "them" and "us" theme, which drives competition and makes it difficult for them to cooperate and work towards a common goal.

'It can be challenging to influence a collective consciousness, although possible, for example, the financial market and social media. This suggests that it is possible to influence the beliefs and the behaviour of many people.

'To cover the needs that are maintained by the religious communities, "The Big Events of Life" can be redefined to comply with what we have acknowledged. The Christian Ten Commandments are used to show how this could be realised.

'Baptism can be transformed to be about the child's call. As a confirmand, the child confirms his call. As he knows what it is about, it is a huge step forward in development.

'Partnership gets a definite purpose: to support each other to achieve our calls.

'Finally, the funeral becomes a more meaningful leave. The loss we suffer is most our own as we now know that our relative has a bright future ahead.

The Master interprets The Ten Commandments in a renewed view:

1. I am the Lord your God: you should not have strange Gods before me.
   The commandment holds still. We learn that God is the Unmanifested, which is why we should not make any picture of God. When you are in harmony with your soul, you are in harmony with God.
2. You should not take the name of the Lord your God in vain.
   God is love. Be likewise through your call.
3. Remember to keep holy the Lord's day.
   The purpose is to give our body time for restitution and make room for getting in contact with our soul to realise our call.
4. Honour your father and your mother.
   Our parents are our chosen base and deserve our gratitude.
5. You should not kill.
   The commandment goes beyond killing. Any attempt to harm our neighbour will darken our mind.
6. You should not commit adultery.
   This command fills a lot because many of us choose partnership for ego reasons, which have resulted in many separations. In general, marriage should be about mutual respect and realising our calls.
7. You should not steal.
   An act that conflicts with our call and brings us misery.
8. You should not bear false witness against your neighbour.
   Wherever we are, our speech should be honest.
9. You should not covert your neighbour's wife.
   It is as bad as committing adultery; therefore, strangle the thought before it gets manifested.
10. You should not covert your neighbour's goods.

'Thoughts are not duty-free. Where our thoughts are, our heart is.

'Simply put, if you follow your call, you will also comply with the Ten Commandments.'

Omega

Dear Almighty Creator!
I am grateful because you have created the frames
for me and let me choose this magnificent place on Earth
in your gorgeous Universe. I am grateful because I have found my
call and realised that my soul is my faithful mate on the ship of hope.
Therefore, my soul has the rudder that steers me into your harbour.
I am grateful because I have apprehended that we are one.
Therefore, I can live in freedom and when that
time comes, I can die with boldness.
I know we shall reunite
in your holy love
Amen.

Source: Oracle

Appendix I: Exercises

Exercise 1: Your Personal Drawing

This exercise aims to derive symbols with a short text that can visualise the individual's call and make it easy to memorise.

There are three types of actors to run the exercise:

Focus person:	You
Facilitator:	One of your friends takes responsibility to facilitate the process.
Contributors:	Your remaining friends.

You need about 3 to 5 people who know you well and are willing to openly share their observations and list them as positive attributes or areas of development.

Having a flip over, black or whiteboard, pens/chalk, table and chairs for all participants would be helpful. Everyone should be able to see what is written on the board. The benefit of the flip over is that the focus person (you) can bring home the resulting drawing. As it is a creative process where all, except the focus person, should be able to draw, using a PC is not recommended.

Roles

Focus person: To do: Listen.

Ask clarifying questions at the end of the session to avoid interrupting the process.

Respond to questions from the facilitator.

                       Not to do: Defend yourself when people talk about potential improvements.

Respond when they explain their drawings.

Respond to proposals to solutions.

Facilitator: Set the scene and inform the participants about their roles and how you want to run the session. See my proposal as inspiration.

Lead the session and ensure that all contributors contribute effectively.

Before you leave an attribute, ask if somebody did not contribute. Make sure that everybody feels good.

Before switching the topic, conclude the essence of the topic.

To set a pleasant atmosphere, start with a positive attribute.

Any attribute can be positive or negative, depending on how the focus person uses it. For instance, a positive trait can be further nurtured, but it can also go a bit overboard. Correspondingly, a negative attribute can be turned into a positive trait.

Check whether something is needed to balance the quality of the attribute you are dealing with.

If you feel that somebody is too modest, challenge the input.

When the input fades out, you can consolidate the symbols with a short text ending with a picture, as in my example.

Let the focus person comment on the outcome and probably ask clarifying questions.

Contributors: Actively engage and provide input.

Input from others may generate other information.

Ensure to write it down to avoid interrupting the speaker. Let her/him finalise before you bring in yours.

Lastly, the outcome could be so exciting that you want to run the session with another focus person; you just have to agree on what role each of you have for the next session.

Exercise 2: Prolonged Fasting

Prolonged fasting can be used to cleanse the body from toxins, repair defect cells by creating new stem cells, build muscles and for losing weight.

The first thing you have to consider is why you want to fast. Most people do this primarily for gaining health benefits or losing weight. Nonetheless, I want to emphasise that my priority is health benefits, and my experience is limited to this topic only.

When you have an idea of 'the why,' you can consider whether your current health condition allows you to go through a prolonged fasting period. If in doubt, I recommend you consult your doctor.

The below-detailed description is only meant for inspiration. You will have to find your own ways or methods that fit your actual needs.

Planning Phase

The way you carry through the Planning Phase is an essential precondition to achieve a successful outcome from fasting. I used YouTube primarily for my research. I did develop my own plan along the way because everything was new to me.

It turned out to be cumbersome because the KETO diet I have chosen was entirely new for me. I recommend you do the food plan for the Preparation Phase during the Planning Phase, including considerations about supplements if any.

Whether you want to look into the potential obstacles and countermeasures is a matter of personal preference in this phase or the next. I recommend doing it in this phase if you have any health issues.

Importantly, it is also a good idea to decide on how many days you want to fast.

Preparation Phase

A week before the planned fasting, I change my food habits to prepare my body for burning fat instead of glucose. Besides, I want to avoid eating meat as it takes too long to digest. Hence, I follow a KETO diet week plan for vegetarians.

However, I allow myself to eat some fish. As I am on intermediate fasting already, I have to prepare for only two meals a day; in my case, lunch and dinner. I also decide to have a snack during the afternoon, whenever I feel for it, something I do not indulge in during my intermediate fasting. But here it is a matter of filling all depots in the body.

Furthermore, and most importantly, I drink a lot of water to stay well hydrated.

I usually do not eat any supplements. But to ensure my body is fit for the fasting period, I take a pill, which contains all the vitamins and minerals the body needs in connection with my lunch each day. I continue drinking water with half a lemon first thing in the morning.

In the evening, I add a spoonful of fire cider (see My Recipes in Appendix II) and a little Himalayan salt right before I go to bed. However, I skip my kombucha because it contains residual sugar from the fermentation process. It is appropriate to eat some raw vegetables to get enzymes which is good for digestion.

I allow myself a cup of coffee or tea twice a day. The remaining day I drink tap water to ensure my water balance is sufficient. If your tap water has many additives, you should choose bottled water instead.

Day 1	
Lunch	Two carrots as starter. On one side of the plate, arrange some iceberg salad with chopped cucumber and add sliced avocado, trimmed with small sliced tomatoes. On the other half of the plate, add an omelette (2 – 3 eggs) fried with, for example, mushrooms, onions and tomato. Fold the omelette once so it fits the plate.
Dinner	Put the Portobello mushrooms in a preheated oven at 200°C for approximately 10 minutes. Meanwhile, toast onions in a pan and some tomatoes. Add basil pesto and mix it all. Discard water from the Portobello and empty the mixture into the Portobello. Top it with cheddar cheese and put in the oven for another 5 minutes. Toast raw cauliflower in the former pan to warm it up. Arrange on a plate.
Day 2	
Lunch	Carrots as starter. Cod roe on iceberg salad with avocado, raw broccoli, walnuts, almonds and pumpkin seeds.
Afternoon	Paleo crispbread (see Appendix II for further information) with camembert.
Dinner	Bake veggie balls with different root crops in the oven. Both can be bought as frozen products. Alternatively, make them based on your preferences, which always gives the best results. Be aware of the carbohydrate content, which in total should be below 20 – 30g per day (it is to some extent individual how much you can eat without leaving the ketones state).
Day 3	
Lunch	Paleo crispbread with camembert as starter. A large avocado salad (diced avocados), tomato, iceberg salad and a little olive oil.
Afternoon	Carrot sticks with humus. Few walnuts and almonds.
Dinner	Omelette with low carb vegetables and trout.
Day 4	
Lunch	For starters, carrot sticks with hummus, a few walnuts and almonds.

	Zucchini cut into two halves. Top up with cottage cheese mix (see Appendix II, My Recipes)
Dinner	Steaks made of turnip-rooted celery about 1 cm thick roasted in olive oil and butter with roasted Brussels sprouts in cream sauce.
Day 5	
Lunch	Turnip root celery as a substitute for rye bread with cottage cheese mix.
Dinner	Mixed salad with different green salads, brie cubes, walnuts, blueberries, pumpkin seeds with a pesto dressing.
Day 6	
Lunch	For starters, carrot sticks with hummus. Salad with a layer of chilli dressing covered by sliced, smoked salmon garnished with shrimps.
Dinner	Mixed salad with guacamole covered by prawns and topped with caviar.
Day 7	
Lunch	Paleo crispbread with brie as starters. Turnip root celery with brie accompanied by blanched broccoli.
Dinner	Salmon with Brussels sprouts in cream sauce accompanied by blanched broccoli (to get all leftovers used).

Fasting Phase

The last meal before fasting, the dinner, is at 6 pm on a Friday. The description of the day corresponds to 24 hours.

I continue with all my regular exercises. During the fasting, I drink tap water, and every now and then, I add a little Himalayan salt to maintain my electrolyte balance, approx. 1 teaspoonful a day.

Energy Level, State of Mind and Hunger level are evaluated on a scale from 1 to 10, where 1 is very low, 5 neutral and 10 excellent for the first two factors and excruciating for the last one.

Day #	Energy Level (EL) & State of Mind (SoM)	Hunger level	Rest pulse
1	EL is good; score: 9 SoM: I feel motivated, and the mood is fine. Since noon I struggled with a light headache, probably because I skipped my coffee; score: 8	To my surprise, the craving for food is nearly absent; score: 6 Water consumption: 2.5l	55
2	EL is slightly lesser than yesterday; score: 8 SoM: I feel fine and the headache has evaporated; score: 8	Same as yesterday	55
3	El is low; score: 3 SoM: My mood is ok, but affected by the low EL; score: 6 Strangely, my rest pulse is raising	My craving is a little higher than yesterday; score: 7 Water consumption: 3l	61
4	El is improving; score: 6 SoM: I feel better today; score: 7 I am beginning to miss enjoying a nice meal with my wife	Same as yesterday, although it is merely a mental issue than a physical problem Water consumption:2.5l	62
5	El is slightly increasing; score: 7 SoM: I feel better, mainly because I decided that this would be my last day, which ends at 6 pm; score: 8	Unchanged Water consumption: 2.5l	59

Note 1: 55 is my normal resting pulse.

Refeeding Phase

Day 1: I expect that this phase will last for 2 days as there is a rule of thumb that says that you need 1 day per 3 days fasting. The fast ends at 6 pm. I long for Greek yoghurt with chia seeds, oatmeal and blueberry as toppings, for starters.

However, it has to be a small portion as the digestive system is in dormancy. An hour later, I eat a few avocados with shrimps and a dressing. It tastes fantastic and lovely to feel full again.

Day 2: I skip my intermediate fasting until I have gained more weight. I already have gained 0.5 kilos since yesterday, which was surprising. For breakfast, I eat yoghurt as yesterday but replaced chia seeds with bananas.

For lunch, I made a smoothie made of parsley, cilantro, cucumber, orange and a spoonful of flaxseed oil and MCT oil. Two pieces of rye bread with a mix of great grans. The bread is labelled 1000 grains bread. It is so delicious with avocado toppings and salt and pepper. I drink my Kombucha tea for lunch.

I have beans, grilled bell pepper, parsley, cilantro, almond flakes, olive oil and thin slices of parmesan cheese for dinner. I realised that I am already eating as usual. In other words, the fast has ended successfully without any severe issues.

Exercise 3: Thoughtless Presence

The purpose of using 'Thoughtless Presence' is to learn the art of clearing your mind from thoughts in a state of being.

General Introduction to Meditation Exercises

It is essential to create suitable frames and habits from the beginning. Select a place where you can be alone and undisturbed. I have a small home office that I use for meditation.

Posture

Experiment with a posture that makes you feel comfortable and you can maintain throughout the session.

The most straightforward posture on a chair is the Egyptian posture. Use a chair with a backrest and keep your spine upright. Place your feet flat on the floor with some space in between and parallel with your shoulders.

Place your hands on your knees. Bend your chin slightly towards your chest while you look straight forward. Your breath must flow without any resistance.

I am used to meditating; I prefer sitting on the floor with my spine straight and legs crossed. If I meditate for a longer period of time, I use a substratum, a Zabuton, a large cushion to make my posture more comfortable; it protects the bones on the ankles. In addition, I sit on a meditation seat cushion, a Zafu. The elevation from the floor makes the posture more comfortable.

For more hard-core meditators, lotus postures of increasing complexity can be used: quarter, half or full lotus where you can sit directly on the floor.

You can also choose to do some exercises to improve your flexibility, which I do every day.

You can find more information on these topics on YouTube, e.g., search on 'prepare for lotus pose.'

Sight

Choose whether you prefer to do the exercise with your eyes open or closed. If you want to keep your eyes open, you should not select nor focus on anything particular. Just choose a point in the middle of nowhere.

I prefer meditating with eyes closed to deliberately reduce stimuli as much as possible for longer sessions, e.g., more than 30 minutes. I may then perform the session with my eyes partly open.

If meditation is new to you, I recommend you start with 5 to 10 minutes. It is better to have a shorter meditation where you can manage to keep focus.

Log

I recommend you make a log so you can track your progress. I write my records on the computer, but you can also use a notebook. It is a simple process: each day starts with a date and a heading describing the activity.

For example, 'Exercise 1: Thoughtless Presence.' Beneath I would write what comes to my mind immediately after the training, such as experiences, obstacles and things to remember before the next exercise in a non-structured text. Furthermore, I recommend you consolidate your learnings when you think you are done with the training.

If you need more days, just extend the period. It is better to invest the time required to master it to build your development on solid ground.

The Exercise

Before you start, decide how much time you want to spend e.g., between 5-10 minutes. You can always extend the exercise later. The most important thing is that you exercise regularly and preferably at the same time.

Be persistent, so that it becomes a daily routine/habit. Besides, I recommend you use a stopwatch, e.g., on your phone to concentrate on your exercise.

With your preferred posture, take a few deep breaths to calm your mind. Then focus on your breathing, and let its pace be as natural as can be. Whenever a thought pops up, let it go without any feeling of attachment and without any further thought.

Just accept the occurrence and return your focus to your breath. You should keep your mind clear from any thoughts or distractions for the whole session.

When you have finalised your exercise, make your notes in your log.

Exercise 4: Visualisation

The purpose of visualisation is to imagine an outcome of a desire and attach as many senses to it to reinforce the realisation.

A Minor Introduction Example

Try to imagine taking an apple from a bowl. Look at it carefully and enjoy its reddish colour. Bring the apple towards your mouth and enjoy the smell. Take a bite of the apple and feel the fresh and acidic relish and feel the sensations in your body.

What happened to you? Did your mouth run into the water?

Postscript: If you do not like apples, choose something else that you like and do your own imagination exercise.

I want you to realise that whether you actually perform the action in reality or just imagining it, the physical reaction is the same.

In the same manner, this convergence is used in visualisation to bring your desires into reality. If you can imagine it, you can attract it. The imagination plane is where the real stuff is created, and the physical outcome results from this action.

Before you start with the next exercise, find yourself a cosy place where you can sit in a comfortable chair and are undisturbed. If you know a better alternative that works for you to get in the right mood, go for it.

Besides, it is also recommended that you add as many details as possible and associate them with the feelings they create. Just use my example as an inspiration for designing your creative case.

Finally, I have chosen a tangible example because, as my experience suggested, it is more comfortable in the beginning.

When you feel ready for it, I will recommend switching to areas that support your call, mostly intangible.

Visualisation example

Desire: A new car

Imagine that you already have your favourite car with all the accessories you appreciate and in your desired colour. Your brand-new vehicle is outside your doorstep, and you are ready to take your first drive. You feel delighted and can hardly wait to get the car started.

You pick up the key full of anticipation and look into the mirror in front of you with a big smile and say: 'I did it.'

You walk outside and see the wonder in front of you. It is precisely as you have expected. The beautiful weather reinforces your impression, and you see the beautiful reflections of the sun in the shiny varnish. When you reach the car, you notice the pleasant smell of a new car.

You open the door with a push on your key and hear the click in the door and open it. The smell of the new car becomes more intense. You enter the vehicle, recognise the comfortable seat and get astonished by how the well-designed interior thrills your well-being. You close the thick door and hear a click.

The door fits so well that you notice a sound similar to when you close the door to your fridge. It gives you the impression of high quality. You see your hands on the steering wheel and notice all their well-known appearance such as the colour, your fingers, veins and so on. You are thrilled and turn the key in on-position.

The engine starts, and it sounds like music in your ears. You look in the back mirror, and the door mirror is treated with an antireflection film. You move the gear to drive and push the speeder gently and start to move. You feel relieved, filled with joy and gratitude.

Even if you have driven the same route many times, now everything looks brighter and you feel just so happy. You could drive forever. However, you decide to return home, where you drive your car into the garage.

You enter your home, place the key in its usual place, look in the mirror once again and say: 'How lucky I am.'

When you open your eyes, you will be surprised at how authentic your experience is. Well, you have succeeded in visualisation: You think and feel it as if you already have the car.

Rules of Thumb

Based on the above, a few rules of thumb can be derived:

- Choose your desire with care and dedication.
- Be trustful. Faith moves mountains; have confidence that the process will deliver the desired end result.
- Close your eyes and visualise that you already have the desired end result.
- Focus on the fantastic feelings the exercise raised.
- Add as many details to your visualisation as possible.
- Add movement into it.
- Allow yourself to feel that you already have reached the desired end result.
- Appreciate what you already have and enjoy it.
- Continue your day with the certainty that the Universe will solve the 'how.'

When you create your focus area, you must notice and be mindful of the feelings it creates in your mind, because it is the feelings your thoughts create that will determine your success. The sense of love, joy and abundance are closely related to the achievement of your goal.

When you formulate your desire, remember to use the present tense. It has to be now and not in the future. A statement like, 'I will own this car someday,' creates nothing but just a desire.

The above example only works if you trust it is possible. If deep down you believe that you will never get to your dream car or maybe even envy those who can, it is an impossible mission. You can only attract what you truly radiate. The next two exercises can help you raise your favourable feelings.

As stated in the beginning, your true desires support your call, which mostly is intangible. Therefore, I recommend you make a sanity check of your desire before you start creating it.

You can do this by asking questions like:

- How do I feel when I project myself into the future where this desire comes true?
- What are the consequences?
- Do the consequences comply with my call?
- Does it help people to live better?
- Is this desire based on understanding, compassion and love?

Exercise 5: Affirmation Examples

The purpose of the affirmation examples is to inspire you to create your own affirmations.

Below you will find the affirmations that are part of my Wishing Well, which you can use as inspiration. They are a blend of the best ones that I have picked up and developed over many years. Altogether, they support my call and my 'Valued Life Areas.'

I use only some of them from time to time, depending on my actual focus area. Besides, it is a mix of nurturing 'as is' states and for others 'to be' states. Furthermore, I adapt the list whenever new perspectives come into play.

Please also note that when the cleft between what you perceive 'as is' and what you feel is an unrealistic want 'to be,' you risk making it counterproductive. Therefore, start with something closer to your present state of feeling.

The Big View Affirmations

- I am one with my Creator.
- I feel internal peace and joy.
- The Universe is magnificent and omnipotent.
- The Universe delivers me abundance in all areas of my life.

I Am My First Task Affirmations

- I fill my heart with love until I am love.
- I honour and respect my temple.
- I have perfect thoughts and feelings.
- I love the one I am.

My Every Day Affirmations

- I start my day with gratitude.
- I create my day beforehand.
- I focus on my dreams.
- I have more time than I need.

Health Affirmations

- My body is the product of my thoughts and feelings.
- My perfect and harmonic thoughts create a healthy body.
- Physical exercises are loving actions that help my body and stimulate my mind.
- Ageing is a belief in the brain. As a countermeasure, I visualise myself as young and perfect.
- Laughter is my medicine.
- Everything incurable.

Wealth Affirmations

- I am rich and live in abundance.
- I am a happy contributor.
- Money comes easily and frequently.
- I can buy what I want.

Family Affirmations

- My wife is my love and partner under all circumstances.
- My family is my treasure that I protect and nurture.
- My home is my castle.
- I contribute to strong family bonds.

Relation Affirmations—Friends

- My friends are my joy.
- I meet everyone with openness and love.
- Every friend is an enrichment.
- I am there for my friends.

Exercise 6: Switch Feelings

Whenever you get a negative feeling, an alarm bell should ring immediately. The earlier, the better because it is easier to get out of the negative state before it amplifies. You can achieve this by making a list of past events where you have had positive feelings.

When you have an incident where you are exposed to a negative feeling, take a deep breath and switch your thinking to one of the events you have listed to get out of the negative attitude.

Below are a few examples for inspiration: When you:

- fell in love
- got your first child
- passed your exam
- were surprised and grateful
- experienced a funny incident—laughs are great—and it influences others, too were happy

The more specific you are, the better. Therefore, the last three needs to be further specified. Who knows how long your list can be! It is a fun and useful exercise, which in itself can make you feel grateful for what you already have achieved and had the privilege to experience them.

Exercise 7: The Wishing Well

The purpose is to create a time-coherent set of goals and breaking them down into manageable desires with a daily follow-up.

Goals for the Year

To start 'The Wishing Well,' I set up some goals for the year. Setting up goals is a way of daring to think big and out of the box—be generous to yourself. In the end, it is not about who you are but who you want to become.

To give you some inspiration, I will mention a few different goals from my personal Wishing Well:

- Become an insightful guide—be a bright lighthouse to the world.
- Share my journey with those who are ready to receive it.
- Be in a healthy balance between my body and soul.
- Learn Spanish at an elementary conversation level.

Next step is to inspire and explain to yourself why you will receive it.

1) Become an insightful guide

Why I want it:

Most of my life, I have been searching for my purpose in life, and I have found it through my call. Now it is time to have the courage to bring it to the highest possible level:

- Be my true identity, my soul.
- Be completely conscious and take superiority over the mind.
- Be a messenger with guidance from the spiritual world.
- Be prepared for the meeting with my origin.

Why I will get it:

- By being my true identity, I will get rid of the mind's lust.
- When the mind is conquered, I can obtain complete consciousness without the disturbance from the mind.
- Thereby, the channel to the spiritual world is open to enlighten and purify the mind.
- I believe there is a light hidden in all of us. We just need to desire it and let our connections in the spiritual world guide us.
- When our inside falls into place, the outside mirrors the same as well.
- When my days come to an end, I will walk into the sunset with joy and get up in a new sunrise with the joy of expectation.

2) Share my journey with those who are ready to receive it

Why I want it:

- While I am heading towards my primary goal, I will make notes about my experiences and share them with others who share a similar longing as mine.

- Through this act, I prove that it is possible for everyone who wants to live their call.
- Share the joy by doing it. Bring light into the world and be rewarded by inner peace and happiness, which exceeds any description.

Why I will get it:

- The world is screaming for rescue without knowing where to look because the mind fools them—the tool has taken over—and they have become passengers in their own vehicle of life.
- I will be one among many lighthouses that will show a possible escape from the darkness for those who have the will or learns ways to strengthen their willpower.
- The world is in a state of change where my contribution is to make it a better place.

3) Be in a healthy balance between my body and my soul

Why I want it:

- A healthy body is a precondition for doing what I intend to realise.
- The time I have in front of me is the most valuable of all.
- Therefore, I want to live long without feeling old.
- I see myself with continuously better and more vibrant health. My body cells constantly get replaced with healthy cells, making my body perfect.

Why I will get it:

- I have healthy thoughts, and I support them with words and inspired actions.

- During my month-long hikes, I have learnt that my well-trained body is a prerequisite for a comfortable journey.
- From now on, I will support my physical and mental development with the inspiration I receive through my spiritual guidance.

4) Learn Spanish at an elementary conversation level

Why I want it:

- My wife and I often travel to Hispanic speaking countries.
- I will return to Camino in Spain; it is a great gift.
- It is an excellent brain gymnastic and helps to keep the brain sharp.
- If I am persistent with my learning, it will enable me to access new friendships and have the ability to read a lot of great books.

Why I will get it:

- I attended a Spanish course for intermediate learners.
- I use a language application, Duolingo, regularly.

For all my desires, I have an affirmation that will materialise my desired outcomes: When desires are advisedly vocalised, they are fulfilled.

In my case, I get the first two goals covered by writing. The third goal is partly covered by Timeslot 1 in the morning and partly through the diet I consume and my general activity levels.

The last goal is covered by attending a Spanish course and the use of Duolingo.

I go through the above goals every day to see if there is anything I need to do to bring them closer.

After a while, I realised that I need to focus on something that is more short-term. What can I do to improve today? To address this issue, I have introduced a new task in my Wishing Well.

Short-Term Desires

Many of us have the same routines every morning, a process we are often unaware of. That means that we run our programs without really being present. If you want to improve your life quality, you need to stop the autopilot and focus upon a particular question or affirmation for the entire day.

Let me inspire you with some affirmations and questions:

- 'I am worthy.'
  - Most people feel they have a degree of unworthiness, often attracting more of what they do not want. Remove 'not' from your vocabulary. Instead, think about how you are worthy and how you are a gift to the world—be generous to yourself and the world around you.
- 'What habits do I have that I want to improve?'
  - For example, do I criticise others, make excuses, feel sorry for myself, am I too humble or too overwhelming?
- 'I am love'
  - The Source is love. As you are connected to the Source, you are love too. However, to attract love, you have to believe it and feel it before it reveals itself to you. You can reinforce this affirmation with another one: 'I manifest kindness and joy, all day long.'
- 'How can I remain constructive despite the challenges I might face?'
  - See any obstacle as an opportunity to grow.
- 'I am grateful'
  - To be grateful is one of the strongest magnets to attract whatever you desire. When you feel gratitude, it is because you have received something valuable that lifts you up. Believe you have already received whatever you want and be grateful as if you have received it and feel it.

- 'What can I do to spread joy around me?'
  - A smile is the shortest distance between two people. Make compliments, be kind and helpful to others.
- 'Today I will focus on seeing all the good things around me'
  - If a negative thought pops up, how can it be converted into a good thing?
  - The trick is to train the brain to see all the good and positive things around you.
- 'What can I do to bring more light into the world today?'
  - Look for situations where you can contribute to make it a better day for anybody. Visualise how you can attract somebody where your competencies can be an asset.

In my experience, it is better to focus on one affirmation/question per day. I have learnt that it makes more sense to focus on one topic for more days if you want to change a habit.

When you stumble, which is likely to happen, take a deep breath and smile and state to yourself, 'It is the old me' and then neutralise it with an affirmation like: 'The more I practice, the easier it becomes to show my true self, which is love.'

Another practical thing is to be aware of your attitude, which is what you radiate. I recommend you to look in front of you on the street, and whenever you make eye contact, have a little smile on your lips; however, this should be adapted to what is considered appropriate in your culture.

Exercise 8: Time Planner

This planning tool aims to structure your day and ensuring that you focus on activities that bring value to your call.

I have chosen to divide my day into a timeslot of 2 hours to make it simple. However, this does not mean that every activity takes precisely 2 hours nor does it mean that every day is the same. This is just an overall guideline to help me focus on things that are important to me.

For example, I could decide that one or more days I will dedicate to a specific purpose like writing, exploring a new idea or going on a vacation.

Like many of us, I have chosen to make a calendar with the same pattern: a five-day work week and a two-day weekend to experience and do different things during the week.

The key point is that you form a planning tool that fits well into what brings the best into your life.

Time Planner

Timeslot		Monday	Tuesday	Wednesday	Thursday	Friday	Saturday	Sunday
Start	End							
0:00	1:00	Sleep	Sleep	Sleep	Sleep	Sleep	Sleep	Sleep
1:00	2:00							
2:00	3:00							
3:00	4:00							
4:00	5:00							
5:00	6:00							
6:00	6:30	Timeslot 1	Timeslot 1	Timeslot 1	Timeslot 1	Timeslot 1	Timeslot 1	Timeslot 1
6:30	7:00							
7:00	7:30							
7:30	8:00							
8:00	8:30	Timeslot 2	Timeslot 2	Timeslot 2	Timeslot 2	Timeslot 2		
8:30	9:00							
9:00	9:30							
9:30	10:00							
10:00	10:30	Timeslot 3	Timeslot 3	Timeslot 3	Timeslot 3	Timeslot 3		
10:30	11:00							
11:00	11:30							
11:30	12:00							
12:00	12:30	Lunch & Siesta	Lunch & Siesta	Lunch & Siesta	Lunch & Siesta	Lunch & Siesta		
12:30	13:00							
13:00	13:30	Timeslot 4	Timeslot 3	Timeslot 3	Timeslot 3	Timeslot 3		
13:30	14:00							
14:00	14:30							
14:30	15:00							
15:00	15:30	Timeslot 5	Timeslot 4	Timeslot 4	Timeslot 4	Timeslot 4		
15:30	16:00							
16:00	16:30							
16:30	17:00							
17:00	17:30	Dinner	Dinner	Dinner	Dinner	Dinner		
17:30	18:00							
18:00	18:30	Timeslot 6	Timeslot 5	Timeslot 5	Timeslot 5	Timeslot 5		
18:30	19:00							
19:00	19:30							
19:30	20:00							
20:00	20:30	Timeslot 7	Timeslot 7	Timeslot 7	Timeslot 7	Timeslot 7		
20:30	21:00							
21:00	21:30							
21:30	22:00							
22:00	22:30	Timeslot 8	Timeslot 8	Timeslot 8	Timeslot 8	Timeslot 8		
22:30	23:00							
23:00	23:30							
23:30	0:00							

Exercise 9: My Morning Routines (Timeslot 1)

The purpose of the first timeslot is to implement my intentions for the day.

My morning routines are a snapshot of the present exercises I follow and are ongoing adapted. However, you can also use it for inspiration. Overall, I keep this routine within the scheduled 2 hours.

Topic	Description
Morning Affirmations	I am grateful for the new day. My soul and I are one, making me a lighthouse for those who seek my support.
Morning Cap	I drink a glass of water with half a lemon to clean my body.
Bathroom	My standard routines
High Intensity Training	As fast as I can, 1 minute each with two hand weights. 1. squat with hands along the sides of my body. 2. squat and lift the weights above my head, and 3. lower my hands back along the body and start with '1' again. It is vital to keep a smooth and constant pace. I do the exercise three times. After each minute, I take a break until the pulse has deceased and I can breathe normally.
Training of Strength	The exercises I use consist of isometric compression of the muscles in about 10 s for the different groups of muscles. I perform approximately 20 compressions with a Bullworker
Yoga	I use 'The Five Tibetans' and different kinds of 'asanas' that work for me. The main point is to balance the chakras, and other yoga postures will probably do as well.
Breathing	1. Posture: I stand up and spread my legs with approximately the same distance as that between my shoulders, then place my hands on each side of the waistline. 2. I breathe in slowly through my nose (as much as possible); I feel how the body expands accordingly. 3. I contract my belly as much as I can and breathe out slowly. 4. I make a small break before the next breath in. I repeat the exercise three times

Exercise Meditation	I sit on a carpet on the floor. I use the half-lotus posture but work on being able to sit in a full-lotus posture. I spend 20 min on this, but when I feel I need to meditate for a longer period, I use the Zabuton cushion and the Zafu seat cushion with crossed legs.
The Wish Well	Follow-up on the previous day. Go through desires and derived tasks. Match tasks with today's timeslots. Visualise the day ahead.

Appendix II: My Recipes

Black Bread with Cottage Cheese Mix

Ingredients for 2 persons

4 tbs. cottage cheese with top

2 tbs. flax oil

1 spoon freeze-dried wheatgrass powder

2 pcs. black rye bread, alternatively use crispbread (avoid using white bread)

Some chives

Please notice that when you buy flax oil, it has to be stored in a fridge in the store. It can also be used at home to preserve unsaturated fatty acids, primarily omega 3.

Accessories

A bowl

A stick blender

Hints

If you like cottage cheese, you do not need to add wheatgrass. I use it primarily because I am not fond of the taste of cottage cheese. However, note that adding wheatgrass can be beneficial because it contains many different types of proteins.

Instructions

Take the bowl and fill in the cottage cheese and flax oil. Mix the two ingredients with the stick blender.

Use the spoon to stir the ingredients into a homogeneous mixture. Distribute the mixture on the bread.

Top the mixture with chopped chives.

Kombucha Tea

Ingredients

5g green tea (approx. 1 tsp) per litre of water

40g White sugar per litre of water

5l Tap water

Accessories

1 pot(minimum)

1 teapot (minimum), preferably with a built-in filter or a separate tea filter

1 glass container for storing the brew[19]

1 glass bottle × 5 to store the fermented kombucha

A funnel and a shift to bottle the brew

A weighing or measuring cup

Thermometer

Paper napkins

Accessories for the first brew

Tea that has been through the fermentation process (approx. 10% of the total batch) 1 SCOBY (Symbiotic Culture of Bacteria and Yeast)

---

[19] I have presumed that you produce 4 l Kombucha. The fifth bottle is used to store Kombucha for the next brew while cleaning the container for yeast in the ongoing production.

Hints

For the first batch, you need 1 SCOBY and tea that has been through the fermentation process. You may find someone who can supply you with both or search on the internet. Please note that the fermented liquid has to come from the fermented kombucha process and not any other fermentation culture.

I use far less sugar than the standard kombucha recipe because I prefer less sweet. Note that, however, there should be sufficient sugar to enable a proper fermentation. To make the kombucha fresher, I use green tea with lemon and ginger.

Alternatively, you can use black tea; I prefer green tea. Nonetheless, this is something you can experiment with until you find your personal favourite tea or a combination of more teas.

I write my experiences down in an online log, which I find it extremely useful, especially in the beginning, as it becomes a shorter process the more you experience. I now only add the changes I make, making it possible to optimise the taste I prefer.

Instructions

Fill the pot with 2l of water.

Add the sugar for the entire batch and let it boil. Let it cool down to 85°C.

In the meantime, add the tea into the filter.

Pour the mixture into a teapot (the temperature will decrease to the preferred temperature, 80°C). Let the mix rest for at least 15 min but no more than 30 min.

Meanwhile, clean the bottles.

Remove the filter.

Pour the mixture back into the pot. Wait until the temperature is approximately 45°C or put the pot in a water bath in the sink.

Add the remaining cold tap water.

The temperature has to be above 20°C but below 32°C. I usually end at 28°C. Pour the fermented tea into the glass container.

Add the mixture and the SCOBY. Top up, so the glass container is full.

Close the glass container with a paper napkin (so the gas from the fermentation process can escape and prevent dirt and flies from getting in).

Place the glass container in a dry, dark and ventilated area with a temperature above 20°C but below 30°C. The higher the temperature, the shorter the time needed for the fermentation process to end. The new SCOBY prefers an utterly calm environment. So, try not to move the glass container frequently during the fermentation process.

You can start tasting the brew after 6 days either using a straw as a pipette or a tap, if available. The taste should be sweet-sour. The longer you wait, the sourer it becomes. Besides, I have noticed that the fragrance of the brew becomes distinct when it is ready.

With my room temperature, it fits with an interval of exactly 1 week. If you let it brew longer, it will be less sweet. At times, I have extended the brewing period to 3 weeks, which brings the taste to the one I prefer.

When it is ready, fill four bottles, using the funnel and sift to catch impurities (mainly yeast, which is drinkable but does not look nice). Tab another bottle but leave some behind that contains a lot of yeast. Remove the new and the old SCOBY.

Clean them in lukewarm water to remove the yeast and store them on a plate. Clean the glass container, fill the fermented tea from the last bottle, and add the new SCOBY for the next brew. Make the next tea ready to fill in the glass container, and your next brew is prepared in another week's time.

After some weeks, I store the old one in a SCOBY hotel for later use or give some to my friends. You have to use some of your fermented tea for the SCOBY hotel.

Please be aware that a mini-SCOBY may occur in the bottles and yeast as the fermentation process continues in the bottles. I leave the bottles as is for at least 1 week. However, it can easily be stored for many months.

The day before I want to drink the kombucha, I store the bottle in the fridge. The generated CO_2 will be absorbed and make the kombucha tea fresher.

Fire Cider

Basic raw ingredients

150g fresh turmeric root
50g fresh ginger root
50 – 150g horseradish (the more, the stronger taste)
1 whole garlic bulb
1 large size onion or 2 small ones

Optional ingredients

Chili: 25 – 75g (depending on how spicy you want it to be)
Antiviral herbs: choose your favourites. I use rosemary, which I grow in my garden.
Spices: Add your personal favourites, such as anise seeds and cinnamon.

Brine

Approx. 1l apple cider vinegar

Accessories

1.5l glass bowl with lid
1.0l glass bottle with cap filter
Big bowl to mix the ingredients and filter the mixture
Small bowl to mix lemon with honey

Ingredients added after 1 month of storage

2 lemons

4 spoonful of acacia honey

Instructions

Wash all the ingredients. Cut the ingredients and chop or peel the herbs (e.g., rosemary). Mix the ingredients in a big bowl and empty them into the 1.5-l glass bowl. Add apple cider vinegar into the bowl until the ingredients are fully covered.

Close the glass with the lid and place it in a dark place. Let the ingredients soak for approximately a month. Shake the glass every now and then.

When the fire cider has matured, filter it.

Squeeze the lemons. Add acacia honey and dissolve the honey in the lemon juice by stirring it with a spoon. When it is completely dissolved, add it to the fire cider.

It is now ready to be poured into the bottle. Top up with water (optional). Store it in the fridge and shake it well before use.

Food waste, if any, can be composted or disposed of according to the regulations of the place where you live.

Usage

I add a spoonful to my nightcap (juice from half a lemon, water and fire cider). Alternatively, you can consume it directly from a spoon or shot glass at your preferred time of the day. If you get an infection, you can increase the intake up to three times a day.

Paleo Crispbread
Ingredients

50g chia seeds

50g flaxseeds

50g sunflower seeds
50g sesame seeds
50g pumpkin seeds
1egg
1.5dl tap water
1 tsp Himalayan salt

Instructions

Break the egg into a bowl. Add water into the bowl and whisk the egg. Add the remaining ingredients and mix them with a spoon. Let it rest for a quarter of an hour.

Fill the mixture on two baking sheets and distribute it evenly using a spoon. Divide the mixture into appropriate sizes. Bake at 140°C until they are crispy, which is approximately 40 minutes.